IBM
PERSONAL
SYSTEM/2

A BUSINESS PERSPECTIVE

JIM HOSKINS

D1091991

JOHN WILEY & SONS
New York • Chichester • Brisbane • Toronto • Singapore

Publisher: Stephen Kippur
Editor: Therese A. Zak
Managing Editor: Ruth Greif
Editing, Design & Production: G&H SOHO, Ltd.

Personal Computer AT is a registered trademark of the International Business Machines Corp.

Personal Computer XT is a trademark of the International Business Machines Corp.

Personal System/2 is a trademark of the International Business Machines Corp.

Micro Channel is a trademark of the International Business Machines Corp.

Proprinter is a trademark of the International Business Machines Corp.

Quietwriter is a registered trademark of the International Business Machines Corp.

Hayes is a registered trademark of Hayes Microcomputer Products, Inc.

Microsoft is a registered trademark of Microsoft Corporation.

All photographs courtesy of International Business Machines Corp.

> *This publication is designed to provide accurate and authoritative information in regard to the subject matter covered. It is sold with the understanding that the publisher is not engaged in rendering legal, accounting, or other professional service. If legal advice or other expert assistance is required, the services of a competent professional person should be sought. FROM A DECLARATION OF PRINCIPLES JOINTLY ADOPTED BY A COMMITTEE OF THE AMERICAN BAR ASSOCIATION AND A COMMITTEE OF PUBLISHERS.*

Library of Congress Cataloging-in-Publication Data

Hoskins, James W.
  IBM Personal System/2.

  1. IBM Personal System/2 (Computer system)
2. IBM Personal System/2 Model 50 (Computer)
3. IBM Personal System/2 Model 60 (Computer)
4. IBM Personal System/2 Model 80 (Computer)
5. Business—Data processing.   I. Title.
QA76.8.I25963H67   1987   004.165   87-13317
ISBN 0-471-63279-1

Printed in the United States of America
87 88 10 9 8 7 6 5 4 3 2

*To Monica, who saw to everything else
while I wrote . . .
and to my parents, for encouraging me
in everything I ever tried.*

Acknowledgments

Many "IBMers" assisted me in the preparation of this book. Some provided me with information concerning the products they were involved with. Others read the manuscript and provided helpful comments. To all those who assisted, I thank you. I would like to give special thanks to Doug Graybill, Vic Kruger, Gerry Merkel, Chuck Pecnik, Bill Rave, and Peter Schulz. Finally, hats off to the entire Personal System/2 development team and management with which I had the pleasure of working.

Foreword

On April 2, 1987, IBM made a worldwide announcement of the new line of systems called the IBM Personal System/2. Included in what was one of the most significant announcements ever by IBM were many hardware and software products from different IBM locations and divisions. For those of us on the development team in Boca Raton, Florida, responsible for the Models 50, 60, and 80 (and associated options), these three models were the heart of the announcement. The successful launch of these systems represents a team effort of not only this group but also IBMers around the world who contributed directly to the conception, development, and delivery of these exciting new products.

From the beginning of the project, approximately three years ago, the objective was clear (though the size of the task may not have been). It was already obvious that the success of the IBM PC family of products had moved these products from the enthusiast's workbench to being a main tool in all kinds of businesses, homes, and educational environments. For our large customers, it was also becoming clear that the PC was their "workstation of choice." This situation, coupled with the exciting applications that the computer industry was producing for the IBM PC family, provided the necessary road map. The demands of this evolving environment required quantum changes in function, reliability, ease of use, and perhaps, most importantly, required an architectural base to support the needs of the future. An entirely new line of systems became our objective, with the operative word being "system." This is the type of chore a development team relishes—starting from scratch with a "blank piece of paper." However, we knew that the most important customer requirement would be to protect his or her investment, which meant that these systems had to be *compatible*. The base of applications had to be preserved, which greatly increased the challenge of the development task.

In the beginning we trained ourselves not to say "PC" but to say "workstation." After studying today's environments and tomorrow's trends, we quickly had to broaden this to "business systems." The net result, we believe, is a line of systems that establishes new levels of standard function, is significantly easier to use and maintain, takes a quantum leap in reliability, and represents an architecture that not only has benefits for today but is also geared for the future. In addition, the systems are all compatible which, along with the new price/performance levels, makes these products outstanding "PCs" for today and a platform for tomorrow's inevitable growth.

Jim Hoskins was on the project team practically from the beginning. His assignments included being an engineer on the new memory card, a critical stint in the architecture group working on the overall system design and the IBM Micro Channel™, and being a development manager in the heart of the 50/60 team. These opportunities gave Jim particular insights into the capabilities and purpose of the new products. He expressed his desires early on to write this book, and the work necessarily started early in the project. As I watched the book evolve, it was clear that Jim's desire to explain and communicate in an understandable way was taking him outside his own areas of responsibility. He communicated with all parts of the organization and with other groups, including the essential operating system development team across the street. This wide-ranging experience makes his particular view of the products not only insightful but extremely useable.

I hope you enjoy this book and the IBM Personal System/2 as much as we enjoyed the opportunity to work on it.

Dennis Andrews
Systems Manager, Personal Systems
IBM Entry Systems Division

Contents

INTRODUCTION	1
WHAT THIS BOOK IS	1
WHAT THIS BOOK IS NOT	1
HOW TO USE THIS BOOK	2
A GLANCE BACKWARD AT THE PC FAMILY	3
CHAPTER 1. IBM PERSONAL SYSTEM/2: A NEW BEGINNING	5
MEET THE FAMILY	5
How Are Model 50/60/80 Computers Different from PCs?	9
Model 50 Specifics	10
Model 60 Specifics	12
Model 80 Specifics	15
Performance Overview	15
A CLOSER LOOK	17
The Microprocessors and Memory	18
Microprocessor/Memory and Performance	18
Advanced Microprocessor Capabilities	21
Disk Storage	22
Diskettes	22
Fixed Disks	24
Micro Channel Expansion Slots	25
Video Graphics Array	27
Standard Ports	30
The Enhanced Keyboard	31
Mechanical Packaging	32

CHAPTER 2. MODEL 50/60/80 OPTIONS AND PERIPHERALS   *34*

DISPLAYS   *34*

    Monochrome Display 8503   *35*
    Color Display 8512   *35*
    Color Display 8513   *37*
    Color Display 8514 and Adapter   *37*

PRINTERS   *39*

    4201 Proprinter II   *40*
    Quietwriter III   *42*

MEMORY EXPANSION OPTIONS   *43*

    Model 50/60 Memory Expansion   *45*
    Model 80 Memory Expansion   *47*

DISK STORAGE OPTIONS   *49*

    Second 1.44 MB Diskette Drive   *50*
    5.25-inch External Diskette Drive   *50*
    Second 44 MB Fixed Disk   *51*
    Second 70 MB Fixed Disk   *51*
    Second 115 MB Fixed Disk   *51*
    6157 Streaming Tape Drive   *52*
    Optical Disk Drives   *53*

COMMUNICATIONS OPTIONS   *54*

    Dual Async Adapter/A   *54*
    300/1200 Internal Modem/A   *55*
    IBM PC Network Adapters   *56*
    Token-Ring Network Adapter/A   *58*
    Multi-Protocol Adapter/A   *58*
    3270 Connection   *59*
    System 36/38 Workstation Emulation Adapter   *59*

OTHER OPTIONS   *60*

    Mouse   *60*
    Data Migration Facility   *61*
    80287 Math Co-processor   *61*
    80387 Math Co-processor   *62*

OPTION COMPATIBILITY MATRIX   *62*

CHAPTER 3. USING YOUR MODEL 50/60/80 COMPUTER   63

GETTING YOUR FEET WET   63

  Greetings from POST   64
  What If POST Finds an Error?   66
  Referring to the Reference Diskette   69
  Starting the Reference Diskette   70
  Strolling through the Main Menu   71

      Menu Option 1: Learn About the Computer   72
      Menu Option 2: Backup the Reference Diskette   74
      Menu Option 3: Set Configuration   77
      Menu Option 4: Set Features   83
      Menu Option 5: Copy an Option Diskette   89
      Menu Option 6: Move the Computer   90
      Menu Option 7: Test the Computer   91
      What Is the Disk Cache Program?   92

THE REAL SOFTWARE—A MODEL   92

  Application Programs   93
  Operating Systems   94
  BIOS   94
  How the Layers Work Together   95

SOFTWARE COMPATIBILITY—WILL PC PROGRAMS WORK?   97

  What Is Meant by "PC Compatibility"?   98
  What Affects "Compatibility"?   99
  Which Programs Are and Are Not Compatible?   101

SYSTEMS APPLICATION ARCHITECTURE—THE NEW STANDARD   102

CHAPTER 4. APPLICATION PROGRAMS   104

APPLICATION PROGRAM ALTERNATIVES   104

  Prewritten Application Programs   105

      Word Processing   105
      Spreadsheets   106
      Data Base Management   106
      Graphics   107
      Communications   108
      Variations on the Big Five   109

  Custom Application Programs   110

OPERATING SYSTEM DEPENDENCIES   111

CHAPTER 5. MODEL 50/60/80 OPERATING SYSTEMS   *113*

INTRODUCTION TO OPERATING SYSTEM CONCEPTS   *113*

What Is Multi-Application?   *114*
How Is Multi-Application Useful?   *114*
What Is Real Mode?   *116*
What Is Protected Mode?   *116*

REAL MODE OPERATING SYSTEMS   *117*

DOS   *117*
DOS Extended with TopView   *120*
DOS Extended with the 3270 Workstation Program   *121*

PROTECTED MODE OPERATING SYSTEMS   *123*

Operating System/2 (Standard Edition)   *123*
　　　Operating System/2's DOS Environment   *125*
　　　Operating System/2 Environment   *125*
Operating System/2 (Extended Edition)   *129*
　　　Communications Capabilities   *129*
　　　Data Base Capabilities   *130*
AIX   *130*

OPERATING SYSTEM SUMMARY CHART   *131*

CHAPTER 6. MODEL 50/60/80 COMMUNICATIONS   *132*

COMPUTER COMMUNICATIONS IN THE OFFICE—AN INTRODUCTION   *132*

TERMINAL EMULATION   *133*

Asynchronous Terminal Emulation   *134*
System/3X Workstation Emulation   *137*
System/370 Workstation Emulation   *138*
　　　3270 Display Terminal Emulation   *138*
　　　Control Unit Emulation   *139*

LOCAL AREA NETWORKS AND MODEL 50/60/80 COMPUTERS   *141*

Basic LAN Functions   *141*
　　　Data Sharing   *142*
　　　Program Sharing   *144*
　　　Equipment Sharing   *144*
　　　Electronic Messaging   *145*
Broadband IBM PC Network   *145*

Baseband IBM PC Network   *146*
IBM Token-Ring Network   *147*

GATEWAYS   *150*

CHAPTER 7. MODEL 50/60/80 COMPUTERS AND YOUR BUSINESS	*153*

CHOOSING THE SOFTWARE   *153*

CHOOSING MODEL 50/60/80 HARDWARE   *155*

Small Business Environment—Bob's Appliances   *156*
  Accounting/Inventory Workstation   *157*
  Secretarial Workstation   *158*
Medium Business Environment—Johnson and Thornbush   *159*
  PC Network Server   *159*
  General Purpose Workstation   *161*
Large Business Environment—Atole Enterprises   *162*
  Token-Ring Network Server/Gateway   *162*
  General Purpose Workstation   *165*
  Advanced Workstation   *165*

USER TRAINING   *166*

ERGONOMICS   *167*

Comfort for the Eyes   *168*
Workstation Comfort   *169*
What About Noise?   *170*

SECURITY   *170*

Loss Prevention   *170*
Theft Prevention   *171*

SERVICE   *171*

MIGRATING FROM PCs TO MODEL 50/60/80 COMPUTERS   *172*

Existing PC Hardware   *172*
Disk Logistics   *172*
  Exploiting Existing Communications   *173*
  Data Migration Facility   *173*
  5.25-inch Diskette Drive for Model 50/60/80 Computers   *174*
  3.5-inch Diskette Drives for PCs   *175*
  Backup Devices   *175*

APPENDIX A. PERFORMANCE TESTING   *177*

APPENDIX B. UNDER THE MODEL 50 COVERS   *193*

APPENDIX C. GUIDE TO OTHER PERSONAL
            SYSTEM/2 PUBLICATIONS   *195*

APPENDIX D. APPLICATION PROGRAM COMPATIBILITY GUIDE   *196*

INTRODUCTION   *197*

**IBM SOFTWARE COMPATIBLE WITH IBM PERSONAL SYSTEM/2
MODEL 30**   *197*

**INDEPENDENT PUBLISHERS' SOFTWARE ON IBM PERSONAL
SYSTEM/2 MODEL 30**   *204*

**IBM SOFTWARE COMPATIBLE WITH IBM PERSONAL SYSTEM/2
MODEL 50 AND MODEL 60 (8560–041)**   *207*

**INDEPENDENT PUBLISHERS' SOFTWARE ON IBM PERSONAL
SYSTEM/2 MODEL 50 AND MODEL 60 (8560–041)**   *213*

IBM SOFTWARE COMPATIBLE WITH IBM PC DOS VERSION 3.30   *216*

IBM SOFTWARE COMPATIBLE WITH IBM LOCAL AREA NETWORKS   *223*

**IBM SOFTWARE COMPATIBLE WITH PC LOCAL AREA NETWORK
PROGRAM 1.20**   *225*

**IBM SOFTWARE COMPATIBLE WITH IBM 3270 WORKSTATION
PROGRAM**   *228*

IBM OPERATING SYSTEM/2 APPLICATIONS   *229*

**INDEPENDENT PUBLISHERS' APPLICATIONS ON IBM OPERATING
SYSTEM/2**   *230*

IBM PC DOS APPLICATIONS ON IBM OPERATING SYSTEM/2   *231*

**INDEPENDENT PUBLISHERS' PC DOS APPLICATIONS ON IBM
OPERATING SYSTEM/2**   *233*

TRADEMARKS   *234*

APPENDIX E. PERIPHERAL COMPATIBILITY GUIDE   *236*

PRINTERS   *236*

PLOTTERS   *237*

SCANNERS   *237*

OTHER DEVICES   *237*

CABLES   *237*

INDEX   *238*

Introduction

WHAT THIS BOOK IS

This book is dedicated to members of a new family of small IBM computers, namely, IBM Personal System/2 (Models 50, 60, and 80). First, it *introduces* the new Personal System/2 products and compares the features of these new computers to those of earlier Personal Computers in a way understandable to the business user.

Second, the book guides you through a *"hands-on"* session with your Personal System/2 and the programs that come with each system. The different kinds of software necessary to do "real work" are also described to help you with software buying decisions.

Finally, *IBM Personal System/2: A Business Perspective* discusses some ways to *apply* the Personal System/2 to improve business operations. It is impossible to select and use the Personal System/2 products properly unless you understand how you can use these components to fill your business needs. The book presents specific Personal System/2 hardware and software configurations for typical environments and also discusses important computer automation planning issues.

WHAT THIS BOOK IS NOT

Many computer books try to be all things to all people. They start by explaining checkbook balancing and finish by covering the Space Shuttle's redundant flight computer complex. This book is not a general overview of computers. It is specific to Personal System/2 (a more than broad enough subject for a single book). This book is not a technical reference manual (IBM will sell you that), nor is it intended to teach computer programming. It provides instead a good description of the Personal System/2 computers and explains how to use them in the business environment.

Finally, this book will not treat you like an engineer. Businesspeople are typically short on time and patience as far as technical matters are concerned. While some technical discussions are necessary, I have tried to keep these discussions as light and concise as possible while still conveying necessary and useful information.

HOW TO USE THIS BOOK

Chapter 1 first introduces the entire Personal System/2 family and provides an overview of the Personal System/2 Model 50/60/80 computers. The latter part of the chapter, "A Closer Look," examines the elements (disk drives, microprocessor, etc.) that make up Model 50/60/80 computers. These elements are compared with those used in earlier PCs.

Chapter 2 surveys the many hardware options available for Model 50/60/80 computers, including displays, printers, disk expansion, and communications. It is provided primarily as a reference to help you select the proper options for your Model 50/60/80 computer.

Chapter 3 guides you through a "hands on" session with a Model 50/60/80 computer system. You will learn how to use the programs provided with every Model 50/60/80 computer. The latter part of the chapter, "The Real Software—a Model," describes the role of application programs, operating systems, and BIOS, the three types of programs necessary to do productive work with Model 50/60/80 computers.

Chapter 4 continues the discussion on application programs, describing the five primary types of application programs. It also addresses the question of "prewritten" vs. "custom" application programs.

Chapter 5 continues the discussion on operating systems. First, basic operating system concepts such as "multi-application" are defined in terms of their usefulness in the business environment. Then several operating system products designed for Model 50/60/80 computers are described (including the new OS/2) to help you determine which one best fits your needs.

Chapter 6 shows how specific Model 50/60/80 options and software products are used to participate in the computer communications environments commonly found in businesses.

Chapter 7 discusses issues related to the selection of Model 50/60/80 hardware and software. Small, medium, and large hypothetical businesses will be outfitted with the appropriate Model 50/60/80 computer systems. Then important topics such as user training, ergonomics, security, and maintenance are discussed.

To help you better understand the topics covered in this book, key terms and phrases are defined and highlighted when they are first introduced. These key terms are also listed in the index included in the back of this book. If while reading you forget the definition of a key term or phrase, the index will quickly point you to the page(s) where the term was discussed.

A GLANCE BACKWARD AT THE PC FAMILY

IBM entered the small computer business in August of 1981 when an informal leg of IBM (called an Independent Business Unit) in Boca Raton, Florida, announced the **IBM Personal Computer.** It was the low end of IBM's computer line and was designed primarily for the small to medium business market. It had an 8088 microprocessor, 16K of standard memory, 160K diskette drives, a text-only monochrome display, and a cassette port. How undemanding we were back in 1981! Today, just a few short years later, a personal computer with such characteristics could hardly satisfy a preschooler playing video games, let alone any serious business needs.

As time went on, IBM developed a family of Personal Computers and the Independent Business Unit became a full division, namely, Entry Systems Division (ESD). IBM published all of the PC's technical information, inviting third-party manufacturers to develop and market their own hardware and software for the PC— which they did. This practice of publishing technical details about a product is known as adopting an "open architecture policy." As more and more third-party hardware and software became available for the PC family of computers, their popularity grew, prompting even more third-party development activity. This self-fueling cycle was beneficial to IBM, third-party developers, and the end users. The success

Figure 1. IBM Personal Computer XT.

Figure 2. IBM Personal Computer AT.

of the open architecture policy has prompted IBM to continue publishing technical details about all subsequent Personal Computer systems, including the Personal System/2 family.

Today's Personal Computer family includes a wide range of products in terms of both function and price. Let's quickly look at the two core PC family members: the **Personal Computer XT**™ shown in Figure 1, and the **Personal Computer AT**® shown in Figure 2.

Personal Computer XT is based on the 8088 microprocessor used in the original PC. This was the first PC family member to support a fixed disk. The Personal Computer AT introduced the 80286 microprocessor to the PC family. It offered enhancements in the areas of performance, disk storage, and memory size.

Many of the other PC family members, such as the IBM 3270 PC, the IBM PC/370, and the IBM Portable PC, were developed directly from these core PC family members. All of these PC family members retained a high degree of software compatibility with preceding products, as do the new Personal System/2 computers.

IBM Personal System/2: A New Beginning

This chapter first provides an overview of the Personal System/2 family of computers and then focuses specifically on Models 50, 60, and 80. It covers the highlights of these models and finally moves in for a closer look at the details. The characteristics of the Model 50/60/80 computers are compared to members of the IBM Personal Computer (PC) family of products.

MEET THE FAMILY

The IBM Personal System/2™ is IBM's second generation of small computer systems. They offer enhanced performance and function while retaining a high degree of compatibility with programs written for the IBM Personal Computer. There are four computer systems that form the core of the Personal System/2 family: Model 30, Model 50, Model 60, and Model 80. Let's briefly look at each of these models.

The IBM Personal System/2 Model 30, as shown in Figure 3, is based on the 8086 microprocessor—a more powerful cousin of the 8088 used in the original IBM PC. The Model 30 is designed to sit on the user's desktop like earlier PCs. It features low cost, 720 KB (about 720 thousand byte capacity) diskette drives, graphics circuitry, and 640 KB of memory.

The IBM Personal System/2 Model 50 is shown in Figure 4. Model 50 features 1 MB (about 1 million bytes) of memory, 1.44 MB diskette drives, a 20 MB fixed disk, and advanced graphics circuitry. This desktop system is based on the 80286 microprocessor.

The Personal System/2 Model 60, shown in Figure 5, is also based on the 80286 microprocessor. This model, however, is designed to stand upright on the floor beside the user's desk. Among the standard features of Model 60 are 1 MB of memory, a 44 or 70 MB fixed disk, and seven expansion slots.

Figure 3. Personal System/2 Model 30.

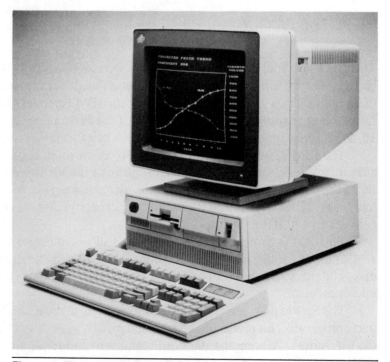

Figure 4. Personal System/2 Model 50.

Figure 5. Personal System/2 Model 60.

The IBM Personal System/2 Model 80, shown in Figure 6, is the most powerful Personal System/2. It is based on the powerful 80386 microprocessor. The Model 80 has many of the same features as Models 50 and 60 while offering the advanced performance and capabilities inherent in the 80386 and larger fixed disks.

While the IBM PC Convertible, shown in Figure 7, is not formally a Personal System/2 computer, it bears mentioning here because it is such a close "friend of the Personal System/2 family." The PC Convertible can exchange diskettes with Personal System/2 computers, allowing you to use the PC Convertible while away from the office and then easily transfer information back to your Personal System/2 computer upon your return. For this reason, the PC Convertible can be thought of as a fifth and portable member of the Personal System/2 family.

The Model 30 shares close architectural ties with the original IBM Personal Computer, allowing it to use programs and feature cards originally designed for the PC. The Model 30 is the least expensive member of the Personal System/2 family optimized to fill the needs of the education and small business environments.

While the Model 50/60/80 computers can also run programs originally written for the PC family, they share a more advanced architecture based on the 80286/386 microprocessors and the new Micro Channel. This advanced architec-

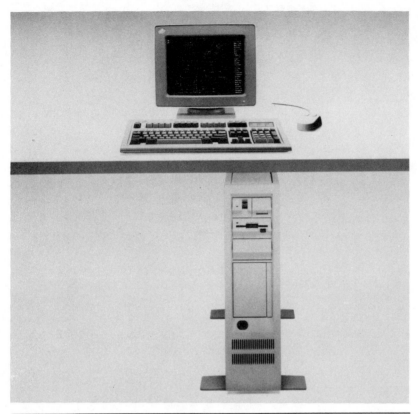

Figure 6. Personal System/2 Model 80.

Figure 7. IBM PC Convertible.

ture allows Model 50/60/80 computers to support a new family of improved feature cards and software. Model 50/60/80 computers fill a wide variety of business needs and will be the subject for the remainder of this book.

How Are Model 50/60/80 Computers Different from PCs?

What characteristics make Personal System/2 Model 50/60/80 computers different from IBM's PC family of computers? The answer lies in the integrated features, expansion capability, performance, and usability of the Personal System/2 family.

The 50/60/80 computers provide more **integrated** or "built-in" features in the base computer than did PCs. These include:

An Async Port used to attach external modems, printers, etc. This port operates at twice the speed of those in PCs.

A Parallel Port generally used to attach a printer.

A Pointing Device Port that supports the optional IBM Mouse.

Video Graphics Array that generates high resolution images on the computer display. Model 50/60/80 graphics circuitry provides higher quality images with more colors than the IBM Enhanced Graphics Adapter used by PCs.

Diskette drive controller that supports up to two 1.44 MB diskette drives.

Password security that discourages unauthorized use of Model 50/60/80 computers.

More memory than provided with PCs.

In addition to the many standard features, Model 50/60/80 computers also provide more **expansion capability** to support growing needs. Since the standard features discussed above are packaged on the System Board, all Model 50/60/80 expansion slots (three in Model 50 and seven in Model 60/80) are available for additional growth. To get a comparably configured IBM Personal Computer AT, for example, feature cards must be installed in five of the eight expansion slots:

1. Serial/Parallel Adapter
2. Second Serial Adapter (to support a Mouse)
3. Enhanced Graphics Adapter
4. Fixed Disk and Diskette Drive Adapter
5. Memory Expansion Adapter

Thus only three of the eight expansion slots in the Personal Computer AT would remain available for further growth. Further, the new **Micro Channel**™ expansion slots used in Model 50/60/80 computers support a new family of feature cards with enhancements in performance and function. Model 60/80 computers also provide for many times the fixed disk capacity than was possible with PCs.

The **performance** of a computer is the speed at which it can perform tasks. The higher the performance the better. Model 50/60/80 performance is from 40 percent to 150 percent higher than even the fastest Personal Computer AT. This performance advantage is afforded primarily by a combination of the faster microprocessors, memory, and disk systems used in Model 50/60/80 systems. We will look more closely at performance later in the chapter.

Although Model 50/60/80 computers offer more advanced capabilities, they are **easier to use** than PCs. First, the initial setup and installation of options can be done without any tools. This is because snaps and thumbscrews have replaced the bolts and screws used in PCs. Further, the user need never set any mechanical switches on feature cards or on the System Board as is necessary with PCs. In Model 50/60/80 computers, these mechanical switches have been replaced with electronic switches set by programs provided on the Model 50/60/80 Reference Diskette. Also provided on the Reference Diskette is a tutorial designed to acquaint the user with the system and an easy-to-use diagnostic program that assists the user in resolving problems if they arise. (Chapter 3 guides you, step by step, through the programs on the Reference Diskette.) The power switch has been moved to the front of the computer for easier access. Two indicator lights are provided near the power switch to indicate when the power is turned on and when the fixed disk is being accessed. Inserting and removing diskettes in Model 50/60/80 diskette drives is easier than it was in PCs. On Model 50/60/80 diskette drives, there are no mechanical doors to open and close. You simply push the diskette into the slot and it's in. To remove a diskette, you press the eject button and it's out. The display's improved image quality and tilt/swivel display stand make using Model 50/60/80 computers more comfortable. Finally, Model 50/60/80 computers occupy less desk space than PCs. This, in a sense, also makes these systems easier to use.

Model 50 Specifics

The Model 50 System Unit is shown in Figure 8. Like all Personal System/2 computers, Model 50 uses the "Pearl White" and "Graphite Gray" color scheme, similar to that of the PCs. This model of the Personal System/2 family is based on the 10 MHz 80286 microprocessor. The row of vents on the front of Model 50 allows an internal fan to draw air through the Model 50 System Unit to cool the internal components.

Smaller building blocks such as 3.5-inch diskette drives, 3.5-inch fixed disks, and surface mounted chips minimize the overall size of the the Model 50 while improving performance and function. This smaller size is important since Model 50 is designed to sit on a desktop where space is at a premium.

The Model 50 comes standard with one 1.44 MB diskette drive and a 20 MB fixed disk drive. Space is provided to accommodate an optional second 1.44 MB diskette drive. The System Board contains 1 MB of memory that is available for user programs and data.

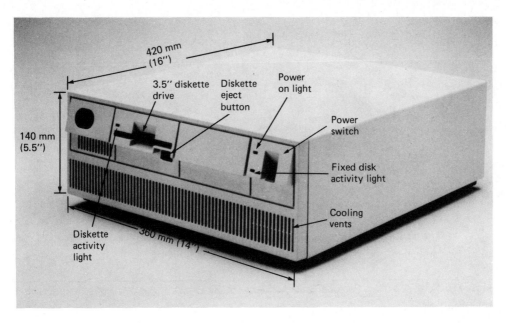

SYSTEM UNIT

Standard Equipment	Expansion
80286	(3) Micro Channel slots
1 MB memory	*2nd 1.44 MB diskette
128 KB ROM	*External 5.25" diskette
Clock/Calendar	80287 Math Co-processor
64 bytes CMOS	
(1) 1.44 MB diskette	
Parallel Port	
Async Port	
Pointing Device Port	
Video Graphics Array	
Enhanced Keyboard	
20 MB fixed disk	

*Options are mutually exclusive

Figure 8. Personal System/2 Model 50 specifics. Model 50 is designed to fit on the user's desktop.

The Model 50 has three Micro Channel expansion slots which can accommodate feature cards that augment both memory and function. We will cover some of these feature cards in Chapter 2.

Figure 9 shows a rear view of Model 50 and the various connectors for the ports. The key-lock secures the cover to the chassis, which discourages unauthorized tampering inside Model 50. The three cut-outs in Model 50's frame allow external cables to be connected to feature cards installed in the three Micro Channel expansion slots.

The Model 50 can accept an optional 80287 Math Co-processor. The 80287 augments the mathematical capabilities of the 80286 microprocessor and thus improves performance in numeric intensive applications.

A view of the elements inside the Model 50 is provided in Appendix B.

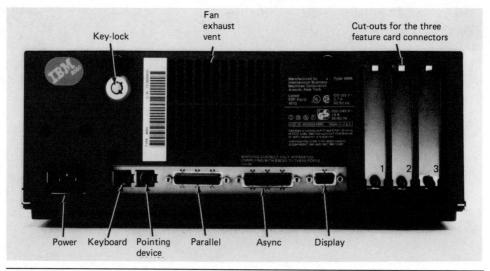

Figure 9.   Rear view of the Personal System/2 Model 50 System Unit. The connectors for the various ports are visible.

Model 60 Specifics

Model 60 is shown in Figure 10. Like the Model 50, Model 60 is based on a 10 MHz 80286 microprocessor. The Model 60, however, is significantly larger, allowing it to accommodate more fixed disk storage and feature cards than Model 50.

Model 60 is designed to stand on the floor beside a desk. This means that only the display and keyboard need occupy your desk space. The fold-out legs at the bottom of the System Unit provide support to prevent tipping. The height of Model 60 was kept to 597 mm (23.5 inches) to allow it to fit in the leg space under a standard height desk or table. The air vents visible on the side and front allow the internal fan to draw air through the System Unit for cooling. A key-lock secures the side panel to the chassis, which discourages unauthorized tampering inside Model 60.

Model 60 is available in two configurations differing only in the fixed disk storage provided. The 44 MB Model 60 comes standard with a 44 MB fixed disk drive and can be expanded with an optional second 44 MB fixed disk, yielding a total of 88 MB. The 70 MB Model 60 comes with a 70 MB fixed disk and can be expanded with an optional second 70 or 115 MB fixed disk, yielding a total of up to 185 MB. All Model 60 systems come standard with 1 MB of memory and a single 1.44 MB diskette drive. Seven Micro Channel expansion slots are also provided.

Figure 11 shows a rear view of Model 60 and the various connectors. The seven cut-outs in Model 60's frame allow external cables to be connected to feature cards. Model 60 can also accept an optional 80287 Math Co-processor.

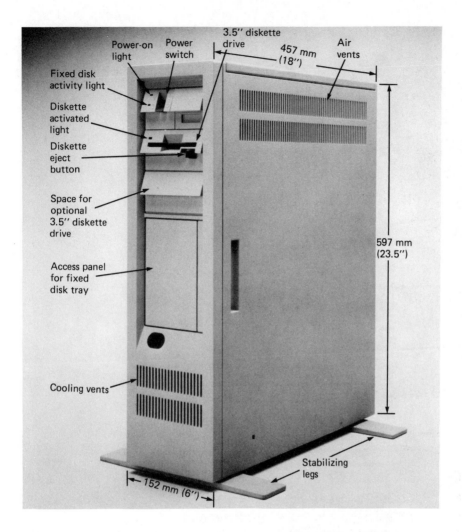

Model 60 System Unit

Standard Equipment	Expansion
80286	(7) Micro Channel slots
1 MB memory	*2nd 1.44 MB diskette drive
(1) 1.44 MB diskette	+2nd 44 MB fixed disk (44 MB Model 60 only)
Parallel Port	+2nd 70 MB fixed disk (70 MB Model 60 only)
Async Port	+115 MB fixed disk (70 MB Model 60 only)
Pointing Device Port	+Internal Optical Disk Drive
Video Graphics Array	*External 5.25" diskette
Enhanced Keyboard	80287 Math Co-processor
128 KB ROM	
Clock/Calendar	
2 KB CMOS	
44 MB fixed disk or	
70 MB fixed disk	

*Options are mutually exclusive
+Options are mutually exclusive

Figure 10. Personal System/2 Model 60 specifics. The Model 60 is designed to stand on the floor.

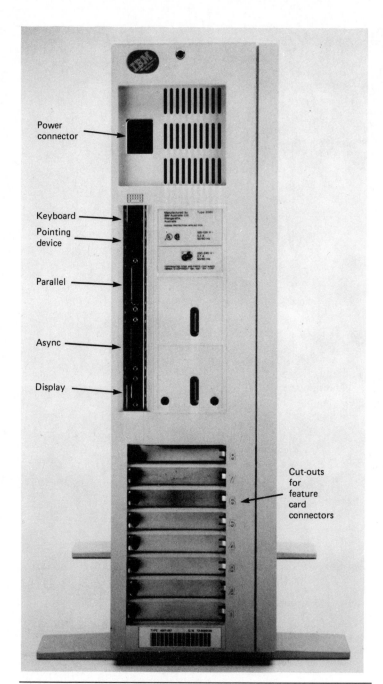

Figure 11. Rear view of the Personal System/2 Model 60 System Unit. (This is the same in the Personal System/2 Model 80 System Unit.)

Model 80 Specifics

Model 80 is shown in Figure 12. The Model 80 is based on the 80386 microprocessor, which, along with high speed memory and faster fixed disks, gives it a clear performance advantage over Model 50/60 systems. Model 80 uses the same mechanical structure as Model 60 and therefore also stands on the floor.

Model 80 comes standard with a 1.44 MB diskette drive and three different fixed disk configurations. The 44 MB Model 80 has a 44 MB fixed disk drive and 1 MB of memory, while the 70 MB Model 80 comes with a 70 MB fixed disk and 2 MB of memory. A third configuration, the 115 MB Model 80, comes with a 115 MB fixed disk and 2 MB of memory. The 20 MHz 80386 microprocessor and faster memory used in this third configuration result in higher performance than the 16 MHz 80386 and memory used in the other two Model 80 configurations. All Model 80 configurations can accommodate a second fixed disk drive.

The rear view of Model 80 is identical to that of the Model 60 shown in Figure 11. As with Model 60, Model 80 provides seven Micro Channel expansion slots. Model 80 can support an optional 80387 Math Co-processor. This is the higher performance cousin of the 80287 used in Models 50 and 60.

Performance Overview

One important aspect of a computer system is the speed at which the computer can perform tasks. This speed is known as the **performance** of the computer. The higher the performance, the less time the user spends waiting for the computer to complete a given task.

Many things, such as the microprocessor, memory, fixed disks, and programs, affect the performance of a personal computer. In order to determine the overall performance of a computer system, **benchmark testing** can be done. This testing involves running various computer programs and measuring the time it takes for the computer to perform the program tasks. Through benchmark testing, the performance of selected computer systems can be compared.

An independent test lab has performed benchmark testing to compare the performance of the various Personal System/2 models with each other and with PC family members. This testing consisted of running many popular application programs and measuring how long it took to perform various tasks.

The graph in Figure 13 shows the overall results of this benchmark testing based on the average of all application program types in the test. The IBM PC/XT was selected as the baseline and assigned an index of 1.0. The performance of all other computers in the test is expressed in relation to the PC/XT. The longer the bar in that graph, the higher the performance of the computer. The average performance of Model 50 and the 44 MB Model 60 was 4.3 and 4.5, which means that on the average they ran over four times faster than a PC/XT using the same programs. Further, the Model 50 and Model 60 outperformed the fastest Personal Computer AT model by over 40 percent. The performance advantage of the Model 60 over the Model 50 can be attributed to the faster fixed disks used in Model 60.

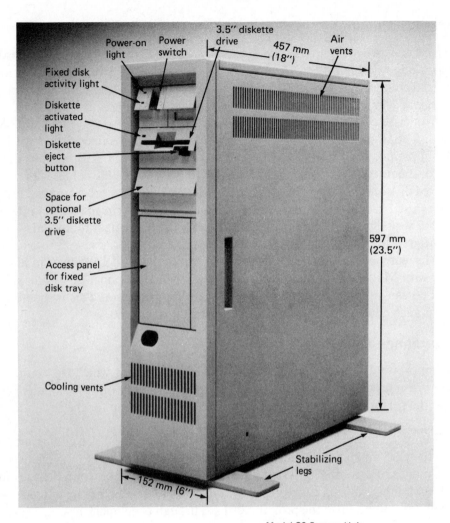

Model 80 System Unit

Standard Equipment	Expansion
80386	(4) 16-bit Micro Channel slots
1 MB memory (44 MB Model 80)	(3) 16/32-bit Micro Channel slots
2 MB memory	*2nd 1.44 MB diskette drive
(70 or 115 MB Model 80)	+2nd 44 MB fixed disk (44 MB Model 80 only)
(1) 1.44 MB diskette	+2nd 70 MB fixed disk
Parallel Port	(70 or 115 MB Model 80)
Async Port	+2nd 115 MB fixed disk
Pointing Device Port	(70 or 115 MB Model 80)
Video Graphics Array	+Internal Optical Disk Drive
Enhanced Keyboard	80387 Math Co-processor
128 KB ROM	*External 5.25″ diskette drive
Clock/Calendar	80386 System Board Memory Expansion
2 KB CMOS	Kit (44 MB or 115 MB Model 80)
44 MB fixed disk (44 MB Model 80)	
70 MB fixed disk (70 MB Model 80)	
115 MB fixed disk (115 MB Model 80)	

*Options are mutually exclusive
+Options are mutually exclusive

Figure 12. Personal System/2 Model 80 specifics.

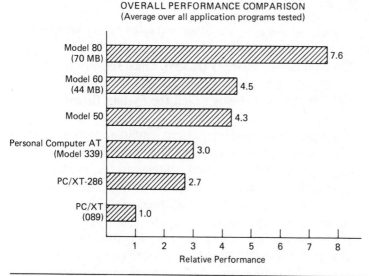

OVERALL PERFORMANCE COMPARISON
(Average over all application programs tested)

Figure 13. Overall performance comparison measured by executing popular application programs.

The 70 MB Model 80 computers outperformed the Personal Computer AT by over 150 percent and beat the Model 60 by over 65 percent. The improved performance of the Model 80 can be attributed to the faster 80386 microprocessor, memory, and fixed disk used in this computer. At the time of this writing, no performance information was available on the 115 MB Model 80. The 115 MB Model 80 will be significantly faster than the 70 MB Model 80 due to its faster microprocessor and memory. More detail on this performance testing is provided in Appendix A.

A CLOSER LOOK

There are many elements that together provide the functions and performance of Personal System/2 Model 50/60/80 computers. The remainder of this chapter will provide a closer look at the following elements of the Personal System/2 Model 50/60/80 systems:

- □ Microprocessor and memory
- □ Disk storage
- □ Graphics
- □ Standard ports
- □ Micro Channel expansion slots
- □ Keyboard
- □ Mechanical design

The Microprocessors and Memory

While there are many electronic circuits in Model 50/60/80 systems, two key elements contribute the most to their capabilities and performance. These are the **microprocessor** and the **Random Access Memory (RAM),** called simply the memory. The microprocessor and memory, along with other circuits, reside on a large circuit board inside the Model 50/60/80 systems called the **System Board** (see Appendix B).

The microprocessor is typically the most important item in a computer system because it is the control center for information flow inside the computer. It is a single computer chip containing thousands of microscopic circuits that work together to execute computer programs. The microprocessor does the data manipulation or "thinking" necessary to perform tasks for the user. The speed of the microprocessor has a significant effect on the performance of the computer. The internal structure or architecture of the microprocessor also determines the inherent capabilities of the personal computer in which it is used. The Model 50 and 60 systems both use the **80286** microprocessor. The Model 80 uses the **80386** microprocessor.

The memory is also a very important part of a computer. **Memory** is the set of electronic chips that provide a "workspace" for the microprocessor. The memory holds the information being used by the microprocessor. This memory is called **random access** because it can store and retrieve any piece of information independent of the sequential order in which it was originally stored.

At this point it is prudent to mention two other types of memory in all Model 50/60/80 computers: **Read Only Memory (ROM)** and **Complementary Metal Oxide Semiconductor (CMOS) memory.** Each Model 50/60/80 computer contains 128 KB of ROM which permanently stores some special housekeeping programs used to manage the internal operation of the computer. The memory is called ROM because information cannot be altered or written to like RAM. The information ⸂stored in ROM is preserved even when the computer is turned off. Programs stored in ROM will be more closely examined in Chapter 3.

CMOS memory gets its name from the transistor technology used to build the memory. The information in CMOS memory, unlike the information in ROM, can be altered at any time. The low power consumption inherent in CMOS technology allows the internal battery to preserve the information stored in CMOS memory even when the computer is turned off. The CMOS memory is used to store system configuration and diagnostic information. Model 50 has 64 bytes of CMOS memory while Models 60 and 80 have an additional 2 K bytes of CMOS memory since they have more feature cards and thus more configuration information. The CMOS memory chip also has circuitry that automatically keeps track of the current time of day and date. This time and date is used to keep track of when disk files were created or last modified.

Microprocessor/Memory and Performance

The speed of the microprocessor and the memory used in a computer typically have the largest effect on the performance of the computer system. The **system clock** is an electrical signal that steps the microprocessor through the instructions of a program. It is the time reference of the microprocessor and sets the pace for all microprocessor activity. The speed at which the system clock runs is called the **system clock rate** and is measured in millions of clock steps per second or **Megahertz (MHz).** The 80286 in the fastest Personal Computer AT runs at 8 MHz (8 million clock steps per second). The 80286 in Models 50 and 60 runs at 10 MHz, and the 80386 in Model 80 runs at 16 MHz or 20 MHz depending on the particular configuration chosen.

While a faster clock directly increases system performance, there is more to the performance story than the clock rate. Since the microprocessor spends a great deal of time moving information in and out of memory, the speed of the memory also significantly affects system performance. Why is so much time spent moving information between the microprocessor and the memory? There are two major reasons: first, a program being executed by the microprocessor resides in the memory. Therefore, the microprocessor must retrieve every instruction it executes from the memory. Second, the memory holds most of the data to be acted upon by the microprocessor. When the microprocessor sends or receives information to or from the memory, the microprocessor is said to be performing a **memory cycle.**

If the memory cannot keep pace with the microprocessor, the memory will delay the microprocessor in midstride until the memory has time to comply with the request. The memory causes this delay by requesting the microprocessor to perform one or more **wait states.** A wait state is a period of time during which the microprocessor simply does nothing, i.e., it waits. The length of this wait state is related to the clock rate in that one wait state equals one step of the clock. The higher the clock rate, the shorter the wait states. The slower the memory, the more wait states the memory forces on the microprocessor. Thus, the memory basically "throttles" the rate at which the microprocessor can move information and thus directly affects performance. The memory used in Model 50, Model 60, and the 44 or 70 MB Model 80 will cause one wait state for every memory cycle, as does the Personal Computer AT. However, since the Model 50/60/80's clock rate is higher than that of the Personal Computer AT, the Model 50/60/80 wait states are shorter, thus contributing to their higher performance.

The memory in the 115 MB Model 80 has a **paged memory system** to speed up its memory beyond the other Model 80s. With the paged memory approach, memory cycles within the same 512 byte page are done with no wait states. By nature, most computer programs will stay within a page for many memory cycles. When a program does change pages, the memory will insert two wait states. In typical applications, paging results in faster overall memory operation.

There is another aspect of microprocessor performance that gives the 80386 used in Model 80 an advantage over the 80286 used in Model 50/60 computers. The 80386 can move twice as much information in a single memory cycle as can the 80286. The smallest piece of information a computer can use is called a **bit.** These bits are grouped into **bytes (8 bits), words (16 bits),** and **double words (32 bits)** to form the computer's representation of numbers, letters of the alphabet, and instructions in a program. Figure 14 compares the number of bits that can be moved in a single memory cycle by the two microprocessors of interest. The 80386 can move 32 bits (a double word) in a single memory cycle, as opposed to the 16 bits (a word) moved by a single 80286 memory cycle. Thus, the "pipe" through which data flows or **data bus** of the 80386 is twice as wide as that of the 80286. As with a garden hose, the wider the "pipe" the more that can flow through at once. Since a large part of the activity performed by a computer involves moving these bits of information from one place to another, this wider data bus offers a key performance advantage.

DATA MOVEMENT CAPABILITY COMPARISON

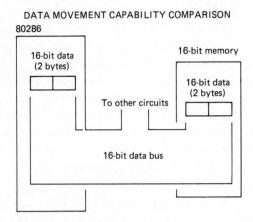

(a) Personal System/2 Models 50 and 60 (Personal Computer AT, XT-286)

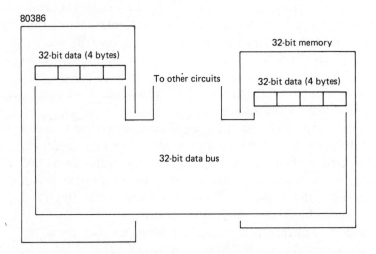

(b) Personal System/2 Model 80

Figure 14. Data handling comparison. (a) The 80286 microprocessor moves up to 16 bits (one word) of data for every transfer to or from memory. (b) The 80386 microprocessor can move up to 32 bits (two words) of data in transfers to or from memory. This wider data bus of the 80386 provides better performance.

Advanced Microprocessor Capabilities

Aside from the performance issues discussed above, the 80286 and 80386 have some fundamental and far-reaching capabilities worth discussing. Both microprocessors have the ability to operate in either **Real Mode** or **Protected Mode.** While operating in Real Mode, the 80286 and 80386 act just like a high speed version of the 8088 microprocessor used in the original IBM PC. This allows Model 50/60/80 computers (as well as the Personal Computer AT and XT-286) to execute programs originally written for the IBM PC. When operating in Protected Mode, the 80286 and 80386 forfeit this ability to execute programs written for the IBM PC. What Protected Mode gives you in return are three basic enhancements available only during Protected Mode operation: extended memory support, full multi-application support, and virtual memory support.

Extended memory support refers to the microprocessor's ability to directly address memory above the 1 MB limit inherent in the 8088 microprocessor. In Protected Mode, the 80286 and 80386 can support up to 16 MB (over 16 million alphanumeric characters) and 4 GB (over 4 billion alphanumeric characters) of memory respectively. 16 MB is enough memory to store over 8,000 pages of single-spaced computer output. With 4 gigabytes, you could store over 1.3 million pages of computer output, or a stack over 70 stories high.

The extended memory area gives relief to problems users have experienced when attempting to use a large program and/or large amounts of data. Extended memory is especially useful when used with the multi-application support features of the 80286 and 80386 to run multiple programs at the same time.

Protected Mode's **multi-application support** is in the form of a "protection mechanism" that prevents one program from interfering with another. This allows a user to execute multiple programs simultaneously. Protected Mode was named for this protection mechanism.

Protected Mode's **virtual memory support** allows for the efficient swapping of information (programs and data) between a fixed disk and the memory such that it appears that the computer system has more memory than it actually does. Dormant portions of programs are temporarily stored on disk rather than in memory and swapped back into memory when needed. Virtual memory support allows the maximum size program or combination of programs to be limited only by the amount of disk space rather than by the amount of memory. The 80286's support of virtual memory allows for up to 1 gigabyte (space for over 1 billion alphanumeric characters) of virtual memory space, or enough storage to hold over 500,000 pages of double-spaced computer output. The 80386's support of virtual memory allows the Model 80 system to act as if it had nearly 64 terabytes (over 70 trillion alphanumeric characters). This is enough memory to store over 16 billion pages of computer output, or a stack over two thousand miles high!

Beyond the features discussed so far, the 80386 has some unique additional capabilities that help make the Personal System/2 Model 80 the most powerful Personal System/2 computer system. These are Paging and Virtual 86 Mode.

Paging is a mechanism inside the 80386 that allows the memory to be treated as if it were actually many small 4 KB chunks. Treating the memory as a series of these small chunks, called **pages,** allows operating systems to, among other things, implement highly efficient virtual memory schemes. This is not related to the paged memory system discussed earlier.

Virtual 86 Mode is a third operating mode of the 80386 that can combine Real Mode's ability to execute PC programs unchanged with the multi-application capabilities of Protected Mode. It is called Virtual 86 Mode because it allows the 80386 to run programs written for the 8086 microprocessor (a software compatible cousin to the 8088 used in the original IBM PC).

In order to take advantage of extended memory, multi-application, virtual memory, paging, and Virtual 86 Mode, there must be support for these features in the **operating system.** This is the program that manages the computer system's internal environment. Chapter 5 of this book covers some new operating systems that allow the user to exploit advanced 80286/80386 capabilities.

Disk Storage

Disk storage, commonly used in personal computers, provides a relatively inexpensive way to store computer data and programs. The information stored on disk can be easily modified or kept unchanged over long periods of time as an archive. The information remains intact whether the computer is turned on or off. Thus, disk storage is said to be **nonvolatile.** The Model 50/60/80 systems use two types of disk storage: **diskettes** and **fixed disks.**

Diskettes

Diskettes are a portable magnetic storage media that can be used to record and later retrieve computer information via a **diskette drive.** All Model 50/60/80 systems use 3.5-inch diskettes as opposed to the 5.25-inch diskettes used by most earlier PCs. These diskette types are compared in Figure 15. The outer case of the 5.25-inch diskettes is flexible and doesn't completely cover the sensitive magnetic material actually containing the information. The 3.5-inch diskette has a rigid outer case that completely encloses the magnetic material. A sliding metal cover, which protects the magnetic material, is retracted only while the diskette is inside the diskette drive. For these reasons, the 3.5-inch diskettes are less susceptible to damage that may result during normal handling. Further, the new 3.5-inch diskettes are small enough to fit conveniently into a shirt pocket or purse. The write protect switch (not visible) in the lower left corner on the back of the diskette allows you to prevent the accidental overwriting of information. When the switch is positioned so that the square hole in the lower left corner is open, the diskette is write protected. When the switch is blocking the square hole, information can be written to the diskette. Some diskettes, such as the Reference Diskette, will not have this switch and are therefore permanently write protected.

One of the primary functions of the diskette is to provide portable disk storage allowing for the transfer of programs and data between computers. Model 50/60/80

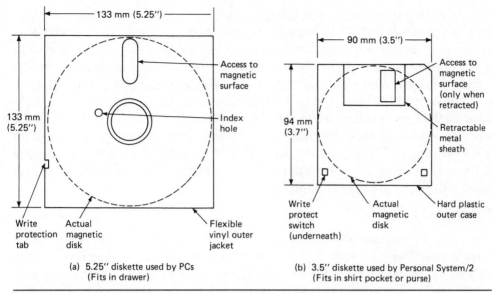

(a) 5.25" diskette used by PCs
(Fits in drawer)

(b) 3.5" diskette used by Personal System/2
(Fits in shirt pocket or purse)

Figure 15. The 5.25-inch diskettes used by most PCs and Personal System/2's 3.5-inch diskettes.

computers can use one of two different density 3.5-inch diskettes: 720 KB and 1.44 MB. The 720 KB diskettes are fully interchangeable with those used in the Personal System/2 Model 30 and the IBM PC Convertible. This allows the user, for example, to use the PC Convertible during a trip and then use the information stored on the PC Convertible diskettes in his Model 50/60/80 when he returns to the office.

The 1.44 MB diskettes, while physically smaller, can hold about 17 percent more than the high density diskettes used by the Personal Computer AT and four times as much as the diskettes used in the IBM PC and PC/XT (see Figure 16).

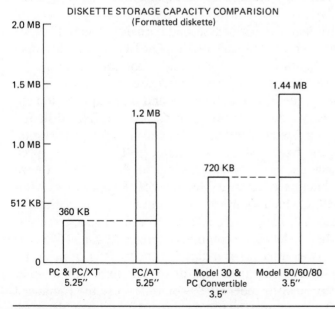

Figure 16. Storage capacity comparison of various diskettes.

The 1.44 MB diskettes can be exchanged between any Model 50/60/80 computers and have the letters "HD" for High Density in the upper right corner. The HD diskettes are not designed to be formatted to the lower 720 KB density. Likewise, the low density diskettes (720 KB) are not designed to be formatted to the higher 1.44 MB density. Violating these rules may result in loss of information stored on the diskette.

In Model 50/60/80 systems, the diskette drive controller electronics are packaged on the System Board, leaving the Micro Channel expansion slot available for other uses. In most PCs, the diskette drive controller electronics are packaged on a feature card and occupy an expansion slot. With the external 5.25-inch diskette drive and associated adapter, Model 50/60/80 computers can also use the 5.25-inch diskettes used by PCs (see Chapter 2).

Fixed Disks

The other kind of disk storage standard on all Model 50/60/80 systems is called a **fixed disk.** These are high-capacity magnetic storage devices commonly used in PCs as well as large computer systems. They consist of a drive mechanism with permanently installed metallic disks coated with a magnetic material. The drives are installed inside the Model 50/60/80 System Units. An **activity light** is provided on all models and is illuminated to let the user know when a fixed disk is being accessed. The circuitry that controls these fixed disks is packaged on a feature card, called the **fixed disk adapter,** which is installed in a special socket on the System Board.

The Model 50/60/80 systems are available with several different fixed disk configurations. The Model 50 comes standard with a 20 MB fixed disk drive and the necessary fixed disk adapter. Model 60 comes standard with either a 44 or 70 MB fixed disk and Model 80 comes with either a 44, 70, or 115 MB fixed disk. All Models 60 and 80 systems' fixed disk storage can be expanded by installing a second fixed disk drive in the System Unit. The provided fixed disk adapter can support both the standard fixed disk and an optional second fixed disk. Figure 17 shows the fixed disk configurations supported by each model. The PC/XT and Personal Computer AT fixed disk configurations are also included for comparison.

Fixed disk performance is important to the performance of a computer in most applications. This is especially true in virtual memory and multi-application environments where there is heavy transfer of information between fixed disk and memory. The performance of a fixed disk refers to the rate at which information can be transferred between the fixed disk and the memory. This transfer speed depends on many things, such as the way information is organized on the disk, known as the **interleave factor.** The interleave factor on Model 50/60/80 fixed disks is improved over that of earlier PCs, which significantly improves the overall transfer rate up to threefold. The fixed disk adapter also affects the transfer speed of disks. The Model 50 and the 44 MB Model 60/80 computers come with an **ST506** type of fixed disk adapter. ST506 is an interface standard for the transfer of information between a fixed disk adapter and a fixed disk drive. The fixed disk adapter provided with the 70 MB versions of Model 60/80 computers use the **Enhanced Small Device Interface (ESDI)** standard. The ESDI standard is more sophisticated than the ST506 standard and provides faster information transfer between the fixed

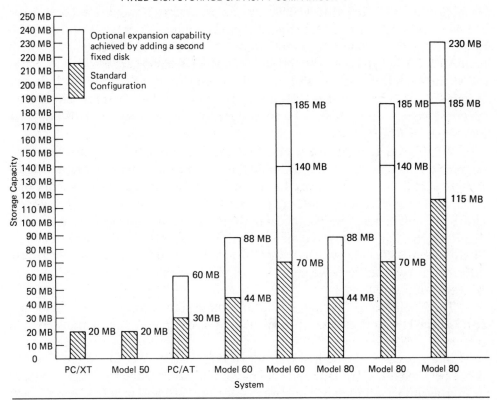

Figure 17. Fixed disk storage capacity comparison of Model 50/60/80 systems and selected PCs.

disk and adapter. Both the ESDI and ST506 fixed disk adapters use the high speed **Direct Memory Access (DMA)** capability of the Micro Channel expansion slots to further speed up performance.

One other feature of Model 50/60/80 computers significantly increases the performance of their fixed disks. The **IBM Disk Cache** program is provided on the Reference Diskette that comes with every Model 50/60/80 computer. The Disk Cache program reserves an area of memory that it will use to temporarily store information retrieved off the disk. Later, if that information is needed (as it usually is), the delay associated with finding and transferring the information on the fixed disk is eliminated. That is, information you would normally read off the fixed disk is already in memory and ready for use. To enjoy the performance improvement afforded by the Disk Cache program, you must install it on your fixed disk. Instructions for doing this are provided with your Model 50/60/80 computer. Refer to Appendix A for more information on the IBM Disk Cache.

Micro Channel Expansion Slots

Part of the reason for the popularity of the original IBM PC was that the expansion slots allowed for functional growth and customization through the addition of optional feature cards.

The Model 50/60/80 systems also contain expansion slots that allow users to install feature cards. The Model 50/60/80 expansion slots, however, have been completely redesigned to provide enhanced expansion capabilities never possessed by earlier PCs and an architecture to support the future growth of the Personal System/2 family. These new expansion slots are know as **Micro Channel** expansion slots. Since the Micro Channel expansion slots are a new design, none of the PC's or Personal System/2 Model 30's feature cards will work (or fit, for that matter) in any Model 50/60/80 system. In Chapter 2 we cover some of the new feature cards designed for use in the Micro Channel.

What is different about the Micro Channel? For one thing, information can be transferred between feature cards and the microprocessor at faster rates. Model 50/60 Micro Channel slots have a 16-bit data bus as do those of the Personal Computer AT, but Model 50/60 slots are operated 25 percent faster. Model 80 systems have some 16-bit slots just like those in Model 50 and 60 systems as well as some 32-bit Micro Channel slots to match the width of the 80386 data bus. Since these Micro Channel slots are twice as wide as the 16-bit Micro Channel slots, they move information twice as fast (two and a half times faster than the Personal Computer AT expansion slots).

The 32-bit Micro Channel slots also contain some extra pins needed to support **matched memory** cycles, which are used to speed up information transfers even further.

In many cases, the desired transfer of information over the Micro Channel is not between a feature card and the microprocessor. Quite often it is necessary to transfer information directly between a feature card and memory. An efficient way of performing information transfers directly between a feature card and memory is through **Direct Memory Access (DMA) channels.** An IBM designed DMA chip on the Model 50/60/80 systems can perform an information transfer directly between memory and the feature card, freeing the microprocessor for other activity. While this DMA capability was also provided in PCs, the Model 50/60/80's DMA is up to one and a half times faster than that of the Personal Computer AT. Faster DMA again means better performance.

Aside from performance enhancement, there are other improvements with the Micro Channel Architecture. The Micro Channel **interrupt signals** are different from those of PCs. Interrupt signals are used by feature cards to get the microprocessor's attention when they require service. The interrupt structure used in the Micro Channel slots allows each interrupt signal to be shared among several feature cards. This sharing allows more feature cards to operate simultaneously without interfering with one another. In PCs, most interrupt signals could support only a single feature card each. The Micro Channel has also introduced some new features not found in PC expansion slots: multi-device arbitration, Programmable Option Select (POS), audio signal, and the Auxiliary Video Connector.

The **multi-device arbitration** mechanism is used to support the DMA function and also allows high function feature cards, called **masters,** to temporarily take complete control of the system and transfer information without the assistance of the microprocessor or the DMA chip. Through this new arbitration mechanism, the Micro Channel architecture allows up to 15 masters or DMA feature cards to efficiently share control of the system with the microprocessor. Although Model 50/60/80 computers don't have 15 Micro Channel slots, this shows the kind of growth built into the Micro Channel architecture.

The new **Programmable Option Select (POS)** mechanism replaces all mechanical switches on the System Board and feature cards with electronic switches that can be set by computer programs. Before POS, users had to set mechanical switches manually to establish parameters of their operating environment. These switches cause confusion and frustration. With POS, the user need not set any mechanical switches. The user need only install the feature cards and turn the power on. The provided setup program will then assist the user, via a series of menus, and set the appropriate electronic switches. These switch settings are then stored in the battery-backed CMOS memory area that preserves the information even when the power is turned off. From then on, when the user turns the power on, the electronic switches are automatically set with no user intervention. The same POS function provides a mechanism to isolate any one of the Micro Channel slots and determine if the slot is occupied or empty. This capability aids in testing the health of the system and in problem determination.

The **audio signal** in all Micro Channel slots gives feature cards access to the speaker provided in all System Units. This means that feature cards can produce sounds (e.g., telephone call progress tones, music, and voice messages).

Finally, the 20-pin **Auxiliary Video Connector** provides a feature card with access to key electrical signals associated with the graphics circuitry. This allows feature cards to either monitor this video information or take over these signals and drive the display directly over the 15-pin display connector on the back of Model 50/60/80 computers. Thus, a graphics feature card can coexist and extend the standard Model 50/60/80 graphics circuitry without having to duplicate its function to preserve software compatibility. The end result is that higher function graphics feature cards will cost less. The IBM Personal System/2 Display Adapter 8514/A is an example of such a feature card. An Auxiliary Video Connector is provided in one Micro Channel slot in each Model 50/60/80 system. The Micro Channel slots can be seen in Appendix B. As part of the open architecture policy, IBM has published the information necessary to allow others to design feature cards for the Micro Channel.

Video Graphics Array

Images presented on a computer's display are used to present information to the user. The quality of these images can directly affect the user's productivity and enjoyment during a work session. There are two hardware elements that work together to generate computer images: the display and the Video Graphics Array. The **display** is the device that resembles a small television set and actually transforms the electronic signals from the computer system into light images discernible by the human eye. The displays used by Model 50/60/80 systems are **analog displays** as opposed to the **digital displays** commonly used by PCs. Digital displays are inherently limited in the number of colors and shades of gray that can be simultaneously displayed, while analog monitors are free from these limitations. We will examine the displays supported by the Model 50/60/80 systems in Chapter 2.

The heart of the Model 50/60/80 system's graphics circuitry is the **Video Graphics Array (VGA).** This IBM-designed chip works with other support circuitry to generate images on the computer display. The VGA is provided as standard equipment and packaged on the Model 50/60/80 System Boards. This is a departure from the approach taken in PCs where graphics circuitry was packaged on an optional feature card and installed in an expansion slot. Since Model 50/60/80 systems have this circuitry on the System Board, the user need not occupy a Micro Channel expansion slot for this function. Further, since every Model 50/60/80 system has this advanced graphics capability, it is likely to become broadly accepted within the industry.

The images generated by the VGA are made up of patterns of many individual dots on the display, called **Picture Elements (PELs),** that blend together to form the desired image. The PEL patterns and colors that appear on the screen are determined by the patterns of bits and bytes written to the **graphics memory.** This special purpose memory, controlled by the VGA, is used only to store information that is to be translated directly into images on the display.

Two basic types of computer images can be generated through this PEL pattern technique. The first type of images are called **alphanumeric images.** These are generated by selecting from predetermined libraries of characters called **character sets.** These character sets contain upper- and lowercase letters, numbers, punctuation marks, and many other symbols such as " >", "/", and "@". The alphanumeric technique is depicted in Figure 18. Three different character sets (256 characters each) are provided in the Model 50/60/80 systems' ROM. Two are identical to the character sets provided by the PC's Monochrome Display/Printer Adapter, Color Graphics Adapter, and Enhanced Graphics Adapters. The third is a new character

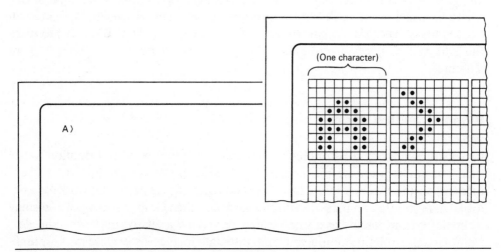

Figure 18. Mechanics of an alphanumeric image.

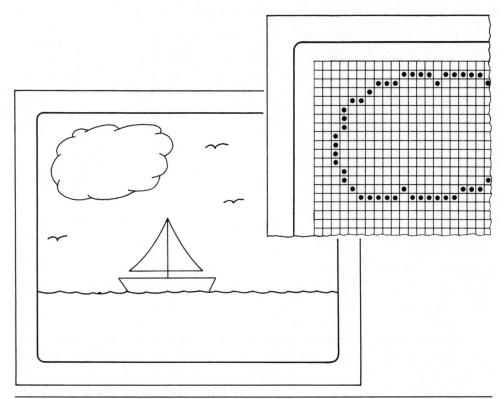

Figure 19. Mechanics of an APA image.

set providing a slightly different character appearance. Five more "custom" character sets can be loaded into graphics memory by a program.

The second type of image that VGA can generate is called an **All-Points-Addressable (APA) image.** With APA images, there is no predetermined library of characters. Each individual PEL on the display screen can be independently turned on or off by writing the appropriate bit patterns to the graphics memory. By changing this bit pattern, the color of any PEL can also be changed. This technique is depicted in Figure 19. It can be used to generate complex "television type" images. Since APA images can be more complex than alphanumeric images, the former require more graphics memory.

Figure 20 compares the capabilities of the VGA to those of some earlier graphics feature cards available for PCs in terms of **maximum colors** and **maximum resolution.** The total number of colors that can be displayed at any one time is important for making information displayed on a computer screen as clear as possible, as well as making the image more pleasant. The resolution of a display refers to the level of detail that can be displayed on a computer screen. The higher the density of the PELs, the higher the resolution, and the more detailed and clear an image will be. In other words, higher resolution images make using a computer easier on the eyes.

The table in Figure 20 shows that the VGA provides the highest resolution alphanumeric modes while maintaining 16 colors (or shades of gray on a

COMPARISON OF GRAPHICS CAPABILITY

	Monochrome/ Printer Adapter (used by PCs)	Color Graphics Adapter (used by PCs)	Enhanced Graphics Controller (used by PCs)	Video Graphics Array (used by Model 50/60/80)
Graphics Memory Size	4 KB	16 KB	*256 KB	256 KB
Best Alphanumeric Modes Maximum resolution	720 × 350	640 × 200	640 × 350	720 × 400
Maximum colors	2 (black & white)	16	16	16
Best APA Modes Maximum resolution	Not supported	640 × 200 (2 colors)	640 × 350	640 × 480 (16 colors)
Maximum colors	Not supported	4 (320 × 200)	16	256 (320 × 200)

Maximum resolution and maximum colors are supported simultaneously unless otherwise indicated.

*EGC comes standard with 64 KB and can be expanded to 256 KB through graphics memory expansion options.

Figure 20. Capability comparison of PC graphics feature cards and Model 50/60/80's standard graphics circuitry.

monochrome display). This means the Model 50/60/80 computers generate text that is easier to read. This is important in word processing and spreadsheet applications.

By taking advantage of the 256 KB of graphics memory standard with the VGA, high-resolution/multiple-color images can also be produced in the APA mode. In the highest resolution APA mode, the VGA controls 640 × 480 individual PELs with up to 16 colors in the image. Another APA mode supported by the VGA allows a single image to contain up to 256 colors with a resolution of 320 × 200 PELs. These 256 colors can be selected from a predefined color library of over 256,000 colors called the **palette.** Again, these APA modes are superior to those provided by the other PC graphics adapters. This means that Model 50/60/80 computers can display more information and are easier on the eyes in applications such as business graphics. These alphanumeric and APA modes are superior to the modes available with earlier PC graphics adapters. In order to gain the full benefits of the new VGA modes, the program being used must be written to take advantage of them. This means that application programs originally written for the PC will not employ all of the VGA functions. However, because the VGA also maintains compatibility with prior graphics feature cards, existing programs will function properly.

Standard Ports

In addition to the VGA circuitry just discussed, the Model 50/60/80 systems have four **ports** that come as standard equipment. Ports provide a means of attaching external devices such as a printer, mouse, or keyboard to the computer. The ports provided with all Model 50/60/80 computers include an Async Port, a Parallel Port, a Keyboard Port, and a Pointing Device Port. The electronic signals are brought from the system resident circuits to their respective connectors, which are cabled to the appropriate device. In the past, these ports were usually packaged on feature cards and purchased separately.

The **Async Port** is accessible through a 25-pin D-shell connector. This port transfers information (one bit at a time) using the asynchronous communications protocol at a rate of up to 19.2 KB (19,200 bits per second). This is twice as fast as the Async Ports on PCs. This port can be used to connect many varying devices to Model 50/60/80 systems such as printers, plotters, external modems, and auxiliary terminals. This port can also be used to transfer information between computer systems.

The **Parallel Port** is accessible via the 25-pin D-shell connector. It is called a "Parallel" Port because it transfers information one byte at a time, or eight bits in "parallel." This port is a functional extension of a widely used industry standard often used to communicate with a printer. A new feature of this Parallel Port allows information to be transferred between computer systems using the Data Migration facility discussed in Chapter 2.

The **Keyboard and Pointing Device Ports** provide for the attachment of the standard IBM Enhanced Keyboard and the optional IBM Mouse, discussed further in Chapter 2.

The Enhanced Keyboard

Model 50/60/80 systems use the IBM PC Enhanced Keyboard shown in Figure 21. This keyboard has the same layout as the Enhanced Keyboard used by the Personal Computer AT. This layout is being used across many different IBM computer products, which means that once the user becomes familiar with this layout, he or she will not have to adapt to different keyboard layouts when using other IBM com-

Figure 21. The IBM Enhanced Keyboard supported by Model 50/60/80 systems as well as PCs.

puter equipment. This same keyboard is available in different languages to fill the needs of many different users around the world.

The keyboard cable plugs into the Keyboard Port provided on the Model 50/60/80 systems. Small retractable legs on the bottom of the keyboard can be extended to change the angle of the keyboard, if desired. While earlier PC keyboards will not work with Model 50/60/80 systems, the Enhanced Keyboard is now standard with PCs.

Mechanical Packaging

The overall physical size of the Model 50/60/80 systems has been kept to a minimum. Several things contributed to the compactness of the design. I have already mentioned that the diskette drives used by these models are smaller than those used by PCs. Also the feature cards used in Micro Channel slots are significantly smaller than those used in PCs. Figure 22 compares the size of Model 50/60/80 feature

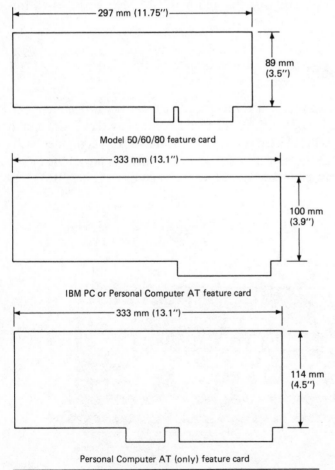

297 mm (11.75")

89 mm (3.5")

Model 50/60/80 feature card

333 mm (13.1")

100 mm (3.9")

IBM PC or Personal Computer AT feature card

333 mm (13.1")

114 mm (4.5")

Personal Computer AT (only) feature card

Figure 22. Comparison of IBM PC, Personal Computer AT, and Model 50/60/80 feature card sizes.

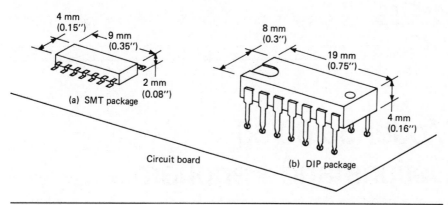

Figure 23. Comparison of SMT and DIP electronic package types. (a) SMT electronic chip package widely used in Model 50/60/80 systems. (b) Corresponding electronic DIP package style used in PCs.

cards with that of PCs. The use of **Very Large Scale Integration (VLSI)** and **Surface Mount Technology (SMT)** also reduced the overall size of the systems. VLSI is an electronic fabrication technology that allows literally thousands of electronic circuits to be packaged on a single electronic chip. Model 50/60/80 systems made extensive use of this technology. Since VLSI allows more circuits to fit on a single chip, there are fewer interconnections between chips. For this reason, VLSI provides the additional benefit of increased reliability.

SMT is an industry standard mechanical package type that houses electronic circuits and allows them to be mounted on the surface of the circuit board. SMT packages are smaller than the standard Dual-In-line-Package (DIP) used in most earlier PCs. Figure 23 compares the package size of a typical SMT package to a more traditional DIP package.

Aside from compactness, the mechanical design of the Model 50/60/80 systems is such that no tools are required to install options or set up the systems. Where normal screws are used in PCs, snaps and thumbscrews are used on Model 50/60/80 systems. The Model 50/60/80 computers are also quieter than PCs.

2

Model 50/60/80 Options and Peripherals

Model 50/60/80 systems are likely to be found in many diverse environments, ranging from a corporate president's desk to a physics laboratory bench. The activities performed by people in these environments vary widely and so do their computing needs. Model 50/60/80 computers can be customized to many environments by selecting the appropriate optional equipment. This optional equipment includes **feature cards** and **peripherals.** Feature cards are circuit boards containing electronics that provide additional functions to Model 50/60/80 computers. They can be installed in one of the Micro Channel expansion slots provided on all Model 50/60/80 System Boards. Peripherals are external devices that attach to Model 50/60/80 computers usually via a cable and perform functions under the computer's control. There are also other optional devices such as disk drives and Math Co-processors that are available to expand Model 50/60/80 computers. This chapter covers:

- ▢ Displays
- ▢ Printers
- ▢ Memory Expansion
- ▢ Disk storage expansion
- ▢ Communications
- ▢ Other options

This chapter does not provide comprehensive coverage of all optional equipment that can be used with Model 50/60/80 computers. It does, however, introduce the reader to many devices that are representative of those most commonly used in the business environment.

DISPLAYS

A computer's display is the TV-like device that converts the computer's electrical signals into light images that convey information to the user. The electrical signals that drive the display are generated by the graphics circuitry provided as standard equipment on all Model 50/60/80 computers.

Some type of display device is required to allow the user to interact with Model 50/60/80. The user can choose from the following display alternatives:

- ▫ IBM Personal System/2 Monochrome Display 8503
- ▫ IBM Personal System/2 Color Display 8512
- ▫ IBM Personal System/2 Color Display 8513
- ▫ IBM Personal System/2 Color Display 8514 and adapter

All four displays can be driven by the Video Graphics Array (VGA) provided on all Model 50/60/80 System Boards. The Color Display 8514, however, is really designed to support the advanced graphics capability of the IBM Personal System/2 Display Adapter 8514/A, which provides graphics capability beyond the standard VGA.

All of these displays are **analog** displays, as opposed to the **digital** displays commonly used by PCs. These terms refer to the type of electrical signals that the graphics circuitry must provide to drive the display. The digital displays commonly used with PCs are inherently limited to 16 or 64 colors per image by the digital nature of the signals that determine the image colors. The analog nature of the displays used with Model 50/60/80 computers allows for virtually any number of colors in a single image. The VGA can generate images with up to 256 colors on these analog displays. Having more colors means images can convey more information more clearly on a given computer screen. Let's look at the four Model 50/60/80 displays.

Monochrome Display 8503

The IBM Personal System/2 Monochrome Display 8503 has a 12-inch screen and provides a white on black image. This display is shown in Figure 24. The display does not provide full color images, but rather images consisting of different brightness levels or **shades of gray.** This allows the display to present images similar to those of a black-and-white television set.

The Monochrome Display 8503 has an independent on/off switch along with controls for contrast and brightness. These controls are located on the side of the display to minimize its overall width. The standard tilt/swivel stand allows the user to adjust the viewing angle.

Color Display 8512

The IBM Personal System/2 Color Display 8512 is shown in Figure 25. This low-cost display provides a full color image on a 14-inch screen. These images are generated by selectively illuminating the appropriate areas of the phosphor deposited

```
┌
│  Screen size:        12 inches (diagonally measured)
│  Type:               White-on-black (up to 64 gray shades)
│  Tilt/swivel stand:  Standard
└
```

Figure 24. Monochrome Display 8503. This display provides a white on black image.

```
┌
│  Screen size:        14 inches (diagonally measured)
│  Type:               Full-color
│  Phosphor pitch:     0.41 mm
│  Tilt/swivel stand:  Optional
└
```

Figure 25. Color Display 8512. This low-cost display provides a full color image.

```
┌                                                              ┐
  Screen size:        12 inches (diagonally measured)
  Type:               Full-color
  Phosphor pitch:     0.28 mm
  Tilt/swivel stand:  Standard
└                                                              ┘
```

Figure 26. Color Display 8513. This display provides a full color image
of better quality than the Color Display 8512.

on the glass screen. The closer these phosphor deposits are spaced, the more finely
detailed the image. This spacing, called the **phosphor pitch,** is one way color displays
are compared. The 8512 has a pitch of 0.41 mm, which provides good image quality for the price. The display has an independent on/off switch along with controls
for contrast and brightness. The tilt/swivel stand for this display is a separately purchased option.

Color Display 8513

The IBM Personal System/2 Color Display 8513 provides a full color image on a
12-inch screen. This display is shown in Figure 26. The phosphor spacing or pitch
of this display is 0.28 mm as opposed to 0.41 mm on the Color Display 8512. The
smaller screen size and tighter pitch of the 8513 result in a sharper image than provided by the 8512 while occupying less desk space. This is important in high display
content applications such as business graphics, or when the user will view the screen
for several hours at a time. The display also has an independent on/off switch along
with controls for contrast and brightness. The tilt/swivel stand is standard with this
display.

Color Display 8514 and Adapter

The IBM Personal System/2 Color Display 8514, shown in Figure 27, is the highest
function display of those covered in this chapter. It provides a full color image on

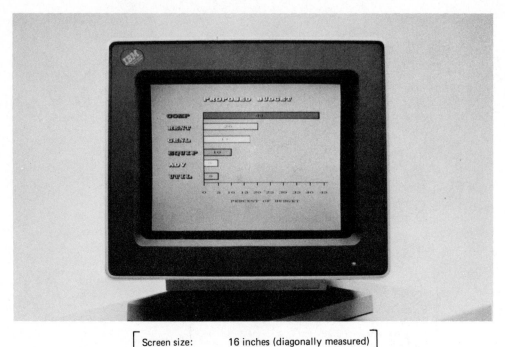

> Screen size: 16 inches (diagonally measured)
> Type: Full-color
> Phosphor pitch: 0.31 mm
> Tilt/swivel stand: Standard

Figure 27. Color Display 8514 and Display Adapter 8514/A. This display and adapter give Model 50/60/80 systems advanced graphics capabilities beyond those provided by the VGA.

a large 16-inch screen. While this display can be used with the VGA, which is standard on the Model 50/60/80 computers, it is really designed to work with the more advanced video capability of the IBM Personal System/2 Display Adapter 8514/A. This adapter may be installed in a Model 50/60/80 Micro Channel expansion slot to add to the APA graphics capabilities of the VGA. The adapter comes with 512 KB video memory standard and can generate an image of 1024 × 768 PELs with 16 colors. By adding the IBM Personal System/2 8514 Memory Expansion Kit, the adapter can generate an image of 1024 × 768 PELs with 256 colors. Figure 28 compares the capabilities of Display Adapter 8514/A with those of the VGA and the IBM PC Professional Graphics Controller (PGC) and Display used with PCs. The 8514 display and adapter provide higher-resolution 256-color images than either the VGA or the PGC. This means that a given image can contain more information on a single screen. Applications such as advanced business graphics, desktop publishing, and Computer Aided Design (CAD) benefit from this higher image content capability.

Since the Display Adapter 8514/A uses the Auxiliary Video Connector (discussed in Chapter 1), the user can still employ the full capabilities of the VGA when the 8514 adapter is installed. This means that you can have two independent displays attached to Model 50/60/80 computers: one controlled by the VGA and one providing 1024 × 768 images on the Color Display 8514. This dual display capability

ADVANCED VIDEO CAPABILITY COMPARISON

	Video Graphics Array (VGA) (Model 50/60/80 only)	Professional Graphics Display and Controller (PCs only)	Color Display 8514 and Adapter/A (Model 50/60/80 only)
Graphics Memory Size	256 Kbytes	320 Kbytes	*1024 Kbytes
Best Alphanumeric Modes Maximum resolution	720 × 400	640 × 400	(same as VGA function)
Maximum colors	16	16	
Best APA Modes Maximum resolution	640 × 480 (16 colors)	640 × 480	1024 × 768
Maximum colors	256 (320 × 200)	256	256

Maximum resolution and maximum colors are supported simultaneously unless otherwise indicated.

*Display Adapter 8514/A comes with 512 KB and can be expanded to 1024 KB (1 MB).

Figure 28. Comparison of Color Display 8514 and adapter with VGA and the Professional Graphics Controller used with PCs.

can be very handy in graphics applications where one screen provides menu choices and the other displays the image being constructed. Use of the Auxiliary Video Connector also eliminates the need to duplicate the VGA function on the 8514 adapter, thus reducing the cost of the adapter. Traditionally, advanced graphics cards for PCs had to duplicate the function of earlier graphics cards to maintain software compatibility. The Display Adapter 8514 can also be used with all of the displays discussed above, but only the VGA level of graphics is supported in those configurations.

Software is available to allow the 8514 Display and adapter to support programs originally written for the Graphics Development Toolkit 1.10. A new Adapter Interface program provides a way for the programmer to efficiently control the hardware elements of the adapter. The adapter also provides advanced graphics functions such as mixed text/graphics and hardware assisted "BITBLT" (the ability to change graphic images quickly).

PRINTERS

Printers are electro-mechanical devices that print Model 50/60/80's electronically encoded information onto paper. There are many printers that work with Model 50/60/80 and exhaustive coverage of these printers is beyond the scope of this book. We will limit our discussion here to two representative printers that fit the needs of many business environments:

□ Proprinter™ II (4201)

□ IBM Quietwriter® III (5202)

A list of other printers tested with Model 50/60/80 as of this writing is provided in Appendix E. Further, since the Model 50/60/80's Serial and Parallel Ports are compatible with those of PCs, many other printers not listed may also work with Model 50/60/80.

4201 Proprinter II

The IBM Proprinter II (4201) is shown in Figure 29. This printer can produce draft quality documents at speeds from 200 to 240 characters per second (cps) depending on the character spacing, or **character pitch**, selected. When operating in "near letter quality" mode, the clarity of the document produced is improved at the cost of reduced printing speed. Some sample documents printed on the Proprinter II are shown in Figure 30.

The Proprinter II is based on the **dot-matrix** printing technique. With this technique the image is created by causing a series of small pins contained in the print head to hit a ribbon that in turn strikes the paper. By selecting the proper

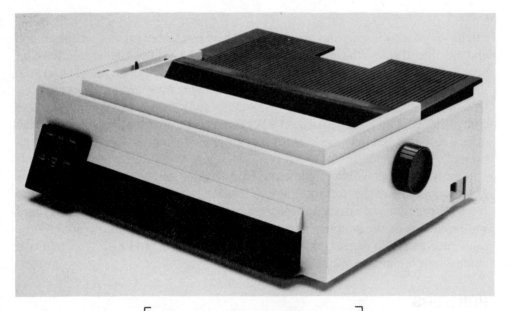

Type:	Near letter quality
Technology:	9-wire dot matrix
Printing speed: (pitch of 10)	200 cps (Draft mode) 100 cps (Emphasized mode) 40 cps (near letter quality)
APA resolution:	Up to 144 × 144 PELs per square inch
Print line:	203 mm (8")
Interface:	Parallel or Async Port
Print buffer:	4 K standard

Figure 29. The Proprinter II. This printer is based on a dot matrix technique and provides draft and near letter quality output.

(a) Data processing quality

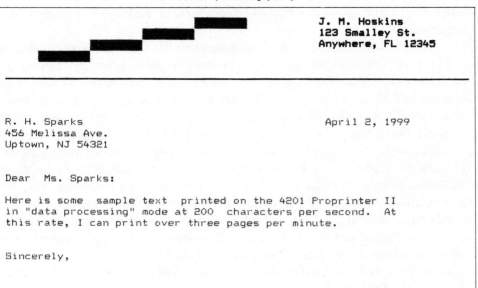

```
                                        J. M. Hoskins
                                        123 Smalley St.
                                        Anywhere, FL 12345



R. H. Sparks                               April 2, 1999
456 Melissa Ave.
Uptown, NJ 54321


Dear  Ms. Sparks:

Here is some  sample text  printed on the 4201 Proprinter II
in "data processing" mode at 200  characters per second.  At
this rate, I can print over three pages per minute.

Sincerely,



J. M. Hoskins
```

(b) Near letter quality

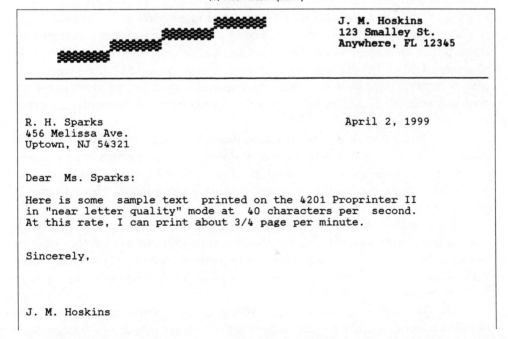

```
                                        J. M. Hoskins
                                        123 Smalley St.
                                        Anywhere, FL 12345



R. H. Sparks                               April 2, 1999
456 Melissa Ave.
Uptown, NJ 54321


Dear  Ms. Sparks:

Here is some  sample text  printed on the 4201 Proprinter II
in "near letter quality" mode at  40 characters per  second.
At this rate, I can print about 3/4 page per minute.

Sincerely,



J. M. Hoskins
```

Figure 30. Sample print produced by the Proprinter II. (a) Draft quality output at 200 cps. (b) Near letter quality output at 40 cps. (*Note:* Although these letters have been reduced from their original size, you can still see the difference in quality.)

pins, a fine dot pattern is generated. As with the dot pattern illuminated on a computer's display, the human eye naturally blends these printed dots to form the desired image.

The Proprinter II can operate in **Alphanumeric Mode** or **All Points Addressable (APA)** Mode. These two modes refer to the method used to generate the image and are just like those discussed in Chapter 1. In Alphanumeric Mode, the printer can generate any alphanumeric character and a number of special symbols from a predefined library called the character set. In APA Mode, complex images can be generated by allowing virtually any combination of dots to be generated.

Proprinter II is compatible with earlier PC printers and comes standard with two different type styles or **fonts.** A third font can be loaded into the printer by a computer program providing for additional type styles. The Proprinter II can also provide **proportional spacing** in which the distance between characters is adjusted based on the character width to provide an overall uniform appearance. The font, spacing, and speed can be selected from the printer's operator panel or by a program. The printer comes standard with the ability to handle either continuous forms or single precut sheets. A 4 KB buffer holds information waiting to be printed, freeing the computer for other tasks.

Quietwriter III

The IBM Quietwriter III (5202), shown in Figure 31, provides three different print quality modes of operation: draft mode, quality mode, and enhanced mode. Draft mode produces the near letter quality print at a rate of 160 to 274 characters per second depending on the character pitch being printed. Quality mode produces letter quality print at rates of 100 to 171 characters per second. Enhanced mode prints at a rate of 80 to 136 characters per second. Enhanced mode is used when high quality printing must be maintained under special conditions, e.g., high humidity, textured paper, etc. Some sample documents printed on the Quietwriter III are shown in Figure 32.

The Quietwriter III uses the **resistive ribbon** technique of producing a printed image. Unlike the impact technique used in dot matrix printing, this technique uses electric current to actually melt selected portions of the ribbon onto the paper. This makes for high quality and very quiet printing (45 DBA), which is where the printer got its name.

The Quietwriter III comes standard with four different fonts. Proportional spacing is available with the addition of an optional font cartridge. A total of eight fonts can be active. Also, a special download cartridge can be installed and loaded with still other fonts. Fonts can be selected by programs or by the operator through the switches on the front of the printer.

The Quietwriter III also supports APA graphics commands compatible with the IBM Proprinter and provides some enhanced capabilities as well. Images with a resolution of up to 240 PELs per inch horizontally and 240 PEL lines per inch vertically can be generated.

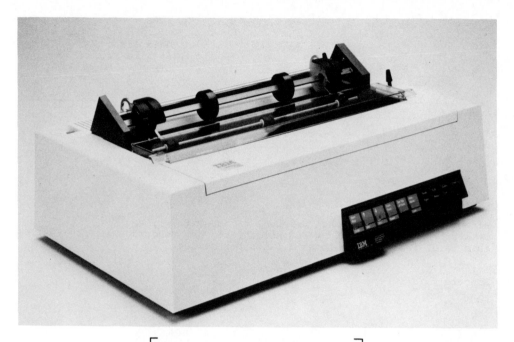

$$
\begin{array}{ll}
\text{Type:} & \text{Letter quality} \\
\text{Technology:} & \text{Resistive ribbon} \\
\text{Printing speed:} & \text{160 cps (Draft mode)} \\
\text{(pitch of 10)} & \text{100 cps (Quality mode)} \\
& \text{80 cps (Enhanced mode)} \\
\text{APA resolution:} & \text{Up to 240} \times \text{240 PELs per} \\
& \text{square inch} \\
\text{Print line:} & \text{335 mm (13.2'')} \\
\text{Interface:} & \text{Parallel Port only} \\
\text{Print buffer:} & \text{16 K standard}
\end{array}
$$

Figure 31. The Quietwriter III. This printer can produce either draft quality documents or letter quality documents with very little noise.

With the standard configuration, individual cut sheets are manually loaded into the printer. With optional equipment, cut sheets, continuous forms, and envelopes can be automatically fed. The resistive ribbon technology used by this printer also allows it to print directly on some transparencies used for overhead projection. The standard 16 KB print buffer holds information waiting to be printed, thereby freeing the computer for other tasks.

MEMORY EXPANSION OPTIONS

Nothing seems to grow faster than the computer user's appetite for memory. There are several different options that allow the user to expand the memory in Model 50/60/80 computers. However, since Model 50/60's memory is 16 bits wide and Model 80's memory is 32 bits wide, memory expansion options are not interchangeable between Model 50/60 and Model 80 computers.

(a) Draft mode

                                              Eddie Ilano
                                              456 Rita St.
                                              Anywhere, FL 12345

Teresa Almario   April 2, 1999
456 Timothy Ave.
Chicago, IL 54321

Dear Ms. Almario:

Here is some sample text printed on the Quietwriter III
printer in "draft" mode at 160 characters per second. At
this rate, I can print almost 3 pages per minute.

Sincerely,

Eddie Ilano

(b) Quality mode

                                              Eddie Ilano
                                              456 Rita St.
                                              Anywhere, FL 12345

Teresa Almario   April 2, 1999
456 Timothy Ave.
Chicago, IL 54321

Dear Ms. Almario:

Here is some sample text printed on the Quietwriter III
printer in "quality" mode at 80 characters per second. At
this rate, I can print over one page per minute.

Sincerely,

Eddie Ilano

Figure 32. Sample print produced by the Quietwriter III. (a) Draft quality at 160 cps. (b) Letter quality at 80 cps. (Note: Although these letters have been reduced from their original size, you can still see the difference in quality.)

Model 50/60 Memory Expansion

There are two feature cards that can be installed to expand Model 50/60 memory beyond the 1 MB provided as standard on the System Board: the IBM Personal System/2 80286 Memory Expansion Option and the IBM Personal System/2 80286 Expanded Memory Adapter/A.

The IBM Personal System/2 80286 Memory Expansion Option, shown in Figure 33, allows the user to expand Model 50/60's memory beyond the 1 MB provided on the System Board. The memory components used on the 80286 Memory Expansion option are called **Single In-line Packages (SIPs).** These SIPs are themselves little circuit boards containing memory chips that are installed directly on the 80286 Memory Expansion Option. Each SIP contains 256 KB of memory. Two SIPs come pre-installed on the 80286 Memory Expansion Option to provide 512 KB. Pairs of additional SIPs can be purchased (i.e., the IBM Personal System/2 80286 Memory Expansion Kit) and installed in the empty sockets provided on the 80286 Memory Expansion Option, yielding 1.0 MB, 1.5 MB, or 2.0 MB of memory expansion. In turn, multiple 80286 Memory Expansion Options can be installed in Model 50/60 expansion slots to provide a system with a very large memory.

A new feature of the 80286 Memory Expansion Option is the ability to perform **Dynamic Memory Relocation.** This allows any 16 KB sections of adapter memory to reside at any memory address. One use for Dynamic Memory Relocation is to disable and bypass any bad sections of memory. In PCs, a memory failure would require the computer to be serviced before operation could continue. If some portion of the memory on the 80286 Memory Expansion Option fails, the user can disable the bad section of memory, reshuffle the remaining good memory as necessary, and then restart operation with the remaining good memory. While the

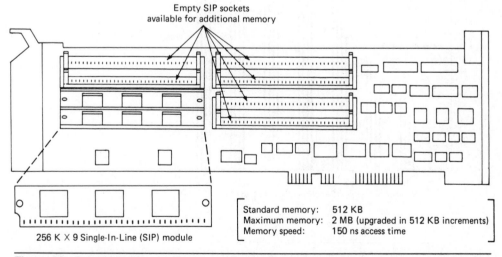

Figure 33. The 80286 Memory Expansion Option. This feature card can be installed in Model 50 or Model 60 computers to expand the system's memory. The feature card comes with 512 KB installed. By using additional memory SIPs, it can be expanded in 512 KB increments up to 2 MB.

memory must be serviced eventually, the user can still use his or her computer until the service can be arranged. This results in higher system availability to the user.

Alternatively, the 80286 Expanded Memory Adapter/A can be installed into a Model 50/60 expansion slot to provide an additional 2 MB of memory. This memory expansion adapter is specially designed to work with the IBM 3270 Workstation program, discussed in Chapter 5, to provide support for **bank switching.** Bank switching provides one way to break through the 640 KB memory barrier that has been with us since the original IBM PC. This 80286 Expanded Memory Adapter/A can be used as a standard 80286 Memory Expansion Option with other operating systems.

Figure 34 shows the possible memory sizes achievable by the addition of either memory expansion card. Model 50 computers support up to three memory expan-

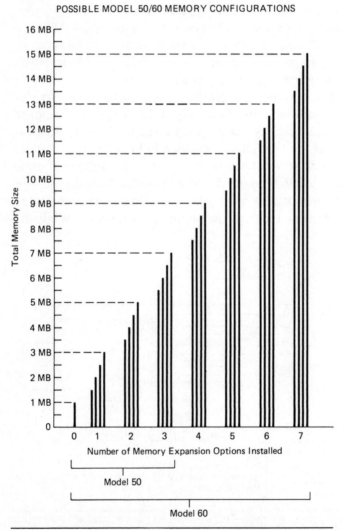

POSSIBLE MODEL 50/60 MEMORY CONFIGURATIONS

Figure 34. Model 50/60 Memory Expansion capability. This table shows the possible memory sizes Model 50 or Model 60 can provide through the installation of memory expansion cards.

sion cards providing up to 7 MB of total system memory. Model 60 can contain up to seven memory expansion cards yielding up to 15 MB of total memory.

Model 80 Memory Expansion

There are two methods of expanding Model 80 memory beyond that provided as standard: the IBM Personal System/2 80386 System Board Memory Expansion Kit or the IBM Personal System/2 80386 Memory Expansion Option.

The System Board Memory Expansion Kit for the 44 MB Model 80 is a circuit board containing 1 MB of memory. It can be installed in the second memory socket provided on the 44 MB Model 80 System Board, shown in Figure 35. This allows the 44 MB Model 80 System Board to contain a total of 2 MB without consuming any of the seven Micro Channel expansion slots. The 70 MB Model 80 comes with this kit pre-installed providing 2 MB of memory as standard. There is also an 80386 System Board Memory Expansion Kit for the 115 MB Model 80. This

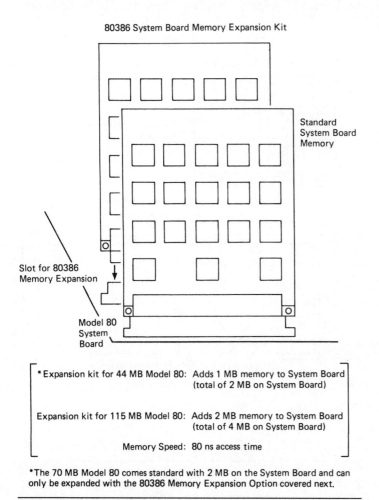

Figure 35. 80386 System Board Memory Expansion Kit.

kit is a circuit board containing 2 MB of memory and can be installed in the second memory socket provided on the 115 MB Model 80 System Board. This kit brings the total memory on the 115 MB Model 80 System Board to 4 MB.

The 80386 Memory Expansion Option is the second way Model 80 memory can be expanded (see Figure 36). It is a standard sized feature card designed to be installed in any of the three 32-bit expansion slots on the Model 80 System Boards. The actual memory components used on this adapter are small circuit boards called daughter cards. Each contains 2 MB of memory. The 80386 Memory Expansion Option comes standard with one daughter card pre-installed. The user can purchase and install additional daughter cards (i.e., 80386 Memory Expansion Kits). These increase the memory on a single 80386 Memory Expansion Option to 6 MB in 2 MB increments. In turn, multiple 80386 Memory Expansion Options can be installed in Model 80 expansion slots to provide a system with a very large memory. Figure 37 shows the possible memory sizes achievable by the addition of the 80386 System Board Memory Expansion Kit and 80386 Memory Expansion Options. Model 80 can contain up to 16 MB of memory. Advanced features of the 80386 used in Model 80 remove the need for special hardware features like those to support bank switching.

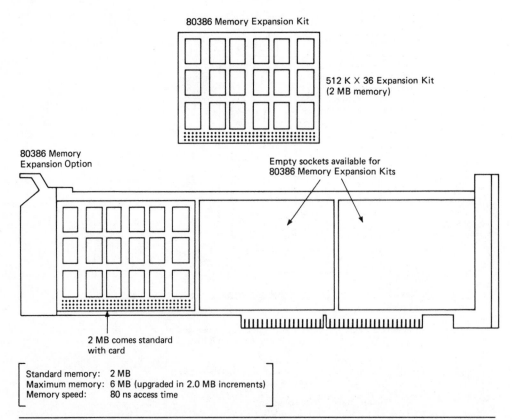

Figure 36. 80386 Memory Expansion Option. This feature card is installed in any of the three 32-bit Micro Channel expansion slots provided on any Model 80 System Board to expand system memory. This card comes with 2 MB installed and can be expanded to contain 6 MB.

POSSIBLE MODEL 80 MEMORY CONFIGURATIONS

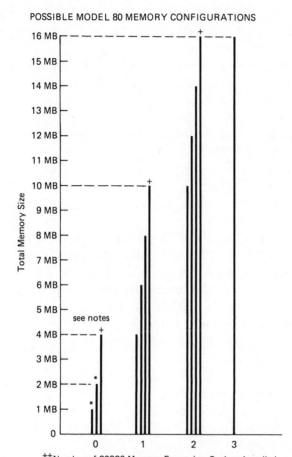

$^{++}$Number of 80386 Memory Expansion Options Installed

*The 44 MB Model 80 comes standard with 1 MB of memory on the System Board. Through its 80386 System Board Memory Expansion Kit, the System Board memory can be increased to 2 MB. The 70 MB Model 80 comes standard with 2 MB of memory on the System Board.

$^{+}$The 115 MB Model 80 comes standard with 2 MB of memory on the System Board. Through its 80386 System Board Memory Expansion Kit, the System Board memory can be increased to 4 MB.

$^{++}$Any Model 80 can accept up to three 80386 Memory Expansion Options

Figure 37. Model 80 Memory Expansion capability. This table shows the possible memory sizes Model 80 can provide through the installation of the 80386 System Board Memory Expansion Kit and the 80386 Memory Expansion Option(s).

DISK STORAGE OPTIONS

All Model 50/60/80 systems come standard with a single 1.44 MB diskette drive and a single fixed disk of varying sizes. There are several options that allow the user to expand the disk storage of Model 50/60/80 computers:

- Second 1.44 MB Diskette Drive
- 5.25-inch External Diskette Drive/adapter

- Second 44 MB Fixed Disk
- Second 70 MB Fixed Disk or second 115 MB Fixed Disk
- Second 115 MB Fixed Disk
- 6157 Streaming Tape Drive
- Optical Disk Drives

While the 6157 Streaming Tape Drive is not really a disk option, it is related closely to disks, which is why it will be discussed here.

Second 1.44 MB Diskette Drive

All Model 50/60/80 systems can support the IBM Personal System/2 1.44 MB Diskette Drive option. This drive is identical to the 3.5-inch diskette drive that comes standard with Model 50/60/80 computers. It is installed in the 3.5-inch cavity shown on the front of the System Units, providing a dual diskette drive system. The drive can read or write either 1.44 MB diskettes or the 720 KB diskettes used by some PCs (e.g., PC Convertible) and the Personal System/2 Model 30. The diskette drive control circuitry on the Model 50/60/80 System Boards fully supports this option.

5.25-inch External Diskette Drive

Most earlier PCs used 5.25-inch diskettes. Since Model 50/60/80 computers use 3.5-inch diskette drives, users must be given a way to migrate PC programs and data to Model 50/60/80 computers. The IBM Personal System/2 5.25-inch External Diskette Drive option provides one method for this migration (other methods will be covered in Chapter 7.) When installed, the external drive becomes the "B" drive in the system and is accessible through the same BIOS and DOS functions as any other diskette drive. This option provides the user with an easy way to copy PC programs and data from 5.25-inch diskettes to Model 50/60/80 3.5-inch diskettes or fixed disks and visa versa. Alternately, it allows programs and data on 5.25-inch diskettes to be used directly on Model 50/60/80 computers if the program can be used from drive "B." The external drive is compatible with PC diskette densities from 160 KB to 360 KB. The Personal Computer AT's 1.2 MB diskettes are not supported by this option.

Figure 38 shows the 5.25-inch External Diskette Drive for Model 50/60/80 computers. The drive itself sits on a desk or tabletop near the Model 50/60/80 computer. A built-in power supply provides the power to the drive. The IBM Personal System/2 5.25-inch External Diskette Drive Adapter is installed in one of the Model 50/60/80 Micro Channel expansion slots. An external cable, permanently attached to the drive, attaches to the adapter's 37-pin D-shell connector. The Drive Connector assembly is installed in the System Unit cavity. This makes the External 5.25-inch Diskette Drive option mutually exclusive with the second 1.44 MB Diskette Drive option.

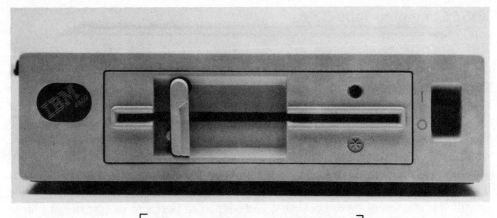

> Diskette type: 5.25" (from 160 to 360 KB)
> Configuration: Becomes "B" drive

Figure 38. The External 5.25-inch Diskette Drive and associated adapter give Model 50/60/80 computers the ability to read and write the 5.25-inch diskettes used by PCs. This option is mutually exclusive with the second 1.44 MB Diskette Drive option.

Second 44 MB Fixed Disk

The 44 MB Models 60 and 80 come standard with a 44 MB fixed disk drive and its adapter. To expand disk storage, the IBM Personal System/2 44 MB Fixed Disk Drive can be installed bringing the total fixed disk storage to 88 MB. This second 44 MB fixed disk is installed inside the System Unit in front of the standard fixed disk. The standard ST506 Fixed Disk Adapter provided with 44 MB Model 60 and the 44 MB Model 80 supports this second 44 MB fixed disk option, thus no additional Micro Channel expansion slots are used.

Second 70 MB Fixed Disk

The 70 MB Model 60, 70 MB Model 80, and 115 MB Model 80 can all accept the IBM Personal System/2 70 MB Fixed Disk Drive. This fixed disk option brings Model 60 up to 140 MB of total fixed disk storage while bringing the Model 80 to either 140 MB or 185 MB, depending on the size of the first fixed disk. The ESDI Fixed Disk Adapter provided as standard equipment with these models fully supports a second 70 MB fixed disk or the 115 MB fixed disk.

Second 115 MB Fixed Disk

The IBM Personal System/2 115 MB Fixed Disk Drive can be installed as the second fixed disk in the 70 MB Model 60, the 70 MB Model 80, or the 115 MB Model 80. This fixed disk option brings Model 80 to either 185 MB or 230 MB depending on the size of the first fixed disk.

6157 Streaming Tape Drive

Various Model 50/60/80 systems can contain anywhere from 20 to 230 MB of information on fixed disks. This information probably has significant value to the user (otherwise why keep it in the first place?). To insure that a fixed disk failure or human error of some kind does not cause all of that information to be lost, some sort of regular backup strategy is recommended, as we will see in Chapter 7. The IBM 6157 Streaming Tape Drive provides one means of backing up fixed disks (see Figure 39). This tape drive provides an efficient and cost effective way to back up any or all of the information contained on Model 50/60/80's fixed disks to 1/4-inch tape cartridges. A single tape can contain up to 55 MB of information. The drive is called a **streaming** drive because it is designed to perform its transfers as large continuous blocks of information, or as a "stream" of data. Information can be written to the tape at a maximum rate of 5 MB/minute. The SY-TOS Utility program allows the user to back individual files, fixed disk partitions, or the entire fixed disk. In the event that the information on the fixed disk is lost, the information can be restored from the tape cartridge with this utility program. Aside from data backup, the tape backup device can also be used to transfer information between the fixed disks of computers (e.g., from Personal Computer AT to Model 50/60/80). We will discuss this further in Chapter 7.

The separately purchased IBM 6157 Tape Attachment Feature is needed to allow the tape drive to be used with Model 50/60/80 computers. This adapter uses the efficient DMA technique (see Chapter 1) to efficiently move information inside the Model 50/60/80 computers. The adapter also employs error detection to insure error-free information transfer between the adapter and the tape drive. A cable attaches the tape drive to the 37-pin D-shell connector on the adapter.

Figure 39.   6157 Streaming Tape Drive. This device can be used to back up information stored on Model 50/60/80 fixed disks.

Optical Disk Drives

There are two optical disk drives that can be used with Model 50/60/80 computers: the IBM Internal Optical Disk Drive and the IBM 3363 Optical Disk Storage Unit, shown in Figure 40. Optical disks are useful in applications requiring extremely large amounts of disk storage. They use a 200 MB removable disk cartridge that provides enough storage to hold over 4,000 sheets of computer output, or a stack over 30 feet high. Once information is written to the optical disk cartridge, it cannot be erased but can be read as many times as necessary.

Optical disks, with the provided "File Systems Driver" program, can be used for backing up fixed disks, thus providing an alternative to the 6157 Streaming Tape Drive. Optical disks have many other potential uses. Program libraries or prerecorded documents (e.g., financial reports, manuals, etc.) can be distributed on optical disks. Further, optical disks can be used for storing electronic images of documents, digitally encoded voice data, and large data bases. The software provided works with the Disk Operating System (DOS), allowing most PC application programs to access information on an optical disk as if it were a normal disk drive. Further, the software provides extensions to DOS allowing for such things as maintaining multiple versions of the same data (reflecting a history of the changes) and maintaining data files greater than 32 MB each. The multiple-version and nonerasable features are useful in maintaining audit trails in accounting applications, for example.

The Internal Optical Disk Drive is supported by Model 60 and Model 80. It is installed inside the System Unit in the space provided for a second fixed disk.

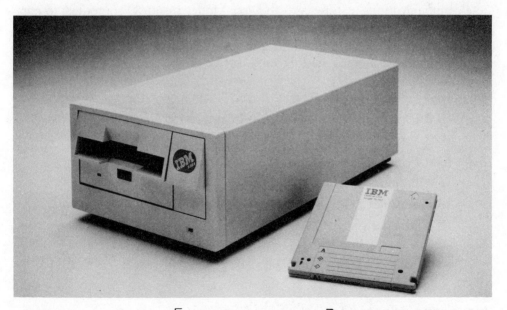

$$\left[\text{Cartridge Capacity: } 200 \text{ Mbytes}\right]$$

Figure 40. 3363 Optical Disk Storage Unit. This option allows any Model 50/60/80 computer to use optical disks.

Model 50 does not support the Internal Optical Disk Drive due to mechanical limitations and power supply constraints. The 3363 Optical Disk Storage Unit can be used with any Model 50/60/80 computer. The drive itself sits on the desk or tabletop near the computer. An Optical Disk Adapter card is provided with either optical disk system and must be installed in a Micro Channel expansion slot.

If 200 MB of optical disk storage is still not enough, up to four Optical Disk Adapters can be installed in a single computer, allowing for the attachment of eight Optical Disk Drives (two per adapter). This means up to 16,000 MB of information can be stored on one computer! This is enough disk space to store about half a million pages of computer output—a stack over 25 stories high.

The Optical Disk Systems stores information on the disk by actually melting portions of the reflective surface of the disk with a laser beam. The information is read back by the same laser beam (at a lower power). Once the surface is burnt, it can be read as often as needed. However, since this surface cannot be "unburned," no other information can be written to that particular portion of the optical disk. Optical disks of this type are called Write-Once-Read-Many or WORM optical disk systems.

COMMUNICATIONS OPTIONS

Today's businesses are placing an increasing emphasis on computer communications. This section provides an overview of some communications feature cards available for Model 50/60/80 systems. Chapter 6 is devoted to showing how to use these communications feature cards to allow Model 50/60/80 computers to participate in various communication configurations. If your interest is in communications environments rather than the feature cards themselves, skip to Chapter 6.

This section examines the following feature cards:

- □ IBM Personal System/2 Dual Async Adapter/A
- □ IBM Personal System/2 300/1200 Internal Modem/A
- □ IBM Personal Computer Network Adapters
- □ IBM Personal System/2 Token-Ring Network Adapter/A
- □ IBM Personal System/2 Multi-protocol Adapter/A
- □ IBM Personal System/2 3270 Connection
- □ IBM Personal System/2 System 36/38 Workstation Emulation Adapter

All of these feature cards are designed to work in any Model 50/60/80 system.

Dual Async Adapter/A

The IBM Personal System/2 Dual Async Adapter/A adds two independent Async Communication Ports functionally identical to the Async Port that comes stand-

ASYNCHRONOUS COMMUNICATIONS DATA ORGANIZATION

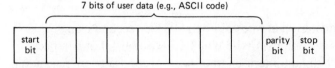

Figure 41. Sample organization of information sent via the asynchronous communications protocol. The user defines the number of data, parity, and stop bits.

ard on all Model 50/60/80 System Boards. This allows Model 50/60/80 to attach to additional external devices. The Async Port is one of the most commonly used ports. Many kinds of peripheral equipment (both IBM and non-IBM) can be attached to Model 50/60/80 computers via these ports (e.g., high quality printers, plotters, external modems, dumb terminals, another computer, etc.). The speed with which information is sent over the Async Port is measured in **bits/second.** Information can be transferred over the Dual Async Adapter/A at rates of up to 19,200 bits/second, or twice as fast as the Async Ports used with PCs (maximum 9600 bits/second).

The term **asynchronous** refers to the communications method or **protocol** used by these ports to move information. Individual bytes of information are transmitted one bit at a time with no fixed relationship between bytes. Figure 41 shows one way a byte might be packaged before it is sent over the Async Port. The start bit tells the receiving Async Port that information is coming down the line. The user's data follows the start bit. The parity bit is used by the receiving end to check for transmission errors in the user's data. Finally, the stop bit signifies the end of the byte. This is just one example of how information might be transmitted over the Async Port. The user can select other organizations including eight user data bits and no parity bit, two stop bits, and so on. These different organizations exist primarily because of the many types of equipment that have used this protocol over the years. The specific organization one uses must be established at both ends of the communications link before communications can begin.

The Dual Async Adapter/A provides an interface based on the widely used EIA RS-232C electrical standard, which defines things such as voltage levels and signal definitions. Two 9-pin male D-shell connectors are provided to allow the attachment of the necessary cables.

300/1200 Internal Modem/A

The IBM Personal System/2 300/1200 Internal Modem/A provides a means for Model 50/60/80 computers to send and receive information over public telephone lines used in the United States. A cable directly connects the Internal Modem/A to a standard telephone line jack. Through this modem, Model 50/60/80 computers can communicate with any distant computer equipped with a modem. (Chapter

6 covers certain uses for modem communications, including access to the many information services that can provide everything from stock market quotes to electronic mail.)

Information can be transferred at rates of up to 300 bits/second using the Bell 103 Standard, and 1200 bits/second using the Bell 212A standard. For perspective, 1200 bits/second is about 120 alphanumeric characters per second. The average adult reads at a rate of about 20 or 30 characters/second.

Why do computers need a modem for this type of communications? Telephone lines were originally designed to carry electronically encoded voice messages from one point to another. A device (the telephone) is therefore necessary to convert the speaker's voice into electronic signals suitable for phone line transmission. Although the information in a computer is already electronically encoded, it is not in a form that can be transmitted over the phone lines. For this reason, a device is needed to convert the electronically encoded computer information into electronic signals suitable for telephone line transmission. A modem can be thought of as a telephone for a computer. Just as both parties need their own telephone to hold a conversation, both computers must have their own modem to transfer information over the phone lines.

The 300/1200 Internal Modem/A is said to be "intelligent" because it can accept high-level commands from the computer to perform various modem functions. For example, the modem adapter can be instructed to automatically place or answer a telephone call. These capabilities are called **auto-originate** and **auto-answer,** respectively. This modem adapter is compatible with the "AT Command Set" used with the popular Hayes® modem. This compatibility allows most programs written for use with earlier modems to work with the adapter.

The 300/1200 Internal Modem/A sends and receives information via the same asynchronous protocol used by the Dual Async Adapter/A just discussed. As a matter of fact, the modem adapter's communication path is simply an Async Port with extra circuits to convert the port's output signals to those suitable for telephone line transmission.

IBM PC Network Adapters

The IBM PC Network is a **Local Area Network (LAN)** in which Model 50/60/80 computers can participate. LANs allow a group of computers in close proximity to one another (e.g., in the same building or campus) to easily share information, programs, and computer hardware. Model 50/60/80 computers can participate in an IBM PC Network environment through the installation of one of two PC Network Adapters: IBM PC Network Adapter II/A, shown in Figure 42, or the IBM PC Network Baseband Adapter/A, shown in Figure 43.

The PC Network Adapter II/A allows Model 50/60/80 computers to participate in a **broadband** IBM PC Network. The network is called broadband because many different types of signals can share the same coaxial cable used with this network. That is, the same coaxial cable used for the broadband PC Network can simultaneously be used to carry television signals, voice signals, and other infor-

$$\begin{bmatrix} \text{Data rate:} & \text{2 MBits/second} \\ \text{Type:} & \text{Broadband} \end{bmatrix}$$

Figure 42. PC Network Adapter II/A. This adapter allows Model 50/60/80 to participate in a broadband PC Network with other Model 50/60/80s, PC/XTs, Personal Computer ATs, etc.

mation without disturbing network operation. The IBM PC Network Protocol Driver provides a programming interface compatible with that of the original PC Network Adapter (NETBIOS). The IBM Network Support Program provides support for more advanced programming interfaces such as IEEE 802.2 and APPC/PC.

The IBM PC Network Baseband Adapter/A allows the adapter to communicate over the less expensive twisted-pair cable which cannot be shared by other signals (television, voice, etc). That is, this network is not a broadband network but a **baseband** IBM PC Network allowing only one type of signal at a time to use the network cable. The IBM PC Network Support Program provides a programming interface compatible with that of the original IBM PC Network Adapter used by PCs (NETBIOS), as well as more advanced programming interfaces. This allows the PC Network Baseband Adapter/A to utilize programs originally written for a PC on the PC Network as well as future programs developed for the new interfaces. For more information about the IBM PC Networks, see Chapter 6.

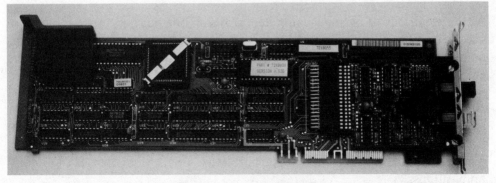

$$\begin{bmatrix} \text{Data rate:} & \text{2 MBits/second} \\ \text{Type:} & \text{Baseband} \end{bmatrix}$$

Figure 43. PC Network Baseband Adapter/A. This adapter allows Model 50/60/80 to participate in a baseband PC Network with other Model 50/60/80s, PC/XTs, Personal Computer ATs, etc.

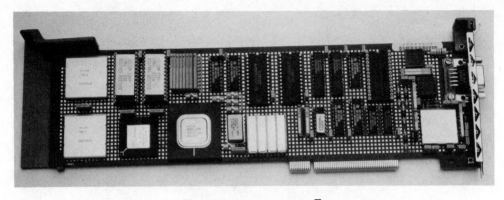

$$\begin{bmatrix} \text{Data rate:} & \text{4 MBits/second} \\ \text{Type:} & \text{Baseband} \end{bmatrix}$$

Figure 44. Token-Ring Network Adapter/A. This adapter allows Model 50/60/80 to participate in the Token-Ring Network with many other PCs as well as larger computer systems.

Token-Ring Network Adapter/A

The IBM Token-Ring Network Adapter/A, shown in Figure 44, allows Model 50/60/80 computers to participate in the Token-Ring Network, a high-function, baseband Local Area Network (LAN). This network allows for the attachment of both small and larger computers for the purpose of sharing information and equipment.

The adapter supports the 4 Mbit/second data rate on the Token-Ring Network. An IBM designed microprocessor and chip set control information movement between the adapter and the network. The adapter is attached to the Token-Ring Network cable via a 9-pin connector. For more information on the Token-Ring Network, see Chapter 6.

Multi-Protocol Adapter/A

As the popularity of personal computers grows among business users, so does the need to transfer information between these personal computers and the larger computer systems commonly found in the business environment. These larger computers are often called **host computers** because they provide computing resources to numerous users. There are many different ways to communicate between a Model 50/60/80 computer and a host computer, as we will see in Chapter 6.

The IBM Personal System/2 Multi-Protocol Adapter/A allows Model 50/60/80 computers to communicate with host computers in one of four different ways depending on the user's needs: asynchronous, BSC, SDLC, or HDLC communications.

When programmed for **asynchronous** communications, the Multi-Protocol Adapter/A provides the same function as the Async Ports provided on Model 50/60/80 System Board and the Dual Async Adapter/A.

As a BSC port, the Multi-Protocol Adapter/A can communicate with a host via the **Binary Synchronous Communications (BSC)** protocol. The "synchronous" in BSC means that special characters preceding the information synchronize the receiver with the incoming information. This synchronization allows many bytes of information to be sent as a single block in contrast to the asynchronous protocol in which a single byte is sent at a time. The ability to send blocks of characters makes BSC more efficient than the asynchronous protocol. Through the BSC capability of this adapter, information can be sent at rates of up to 9600 bits/second. BSC is an older communications protocol used by terminals and other equipment to exchange information with large host computers such as IBM's System 360/370 mainframes. As a result of its past popularity, many of today's host computer systems still use this protocol.

The last two protocols supported by the Multi-Protocol Adapter/A are the **Synchronous Data Link Control (SDLC)** and the **High-level Data Link Control (HDLC)**. These two protocols differ only in the detailed bit patterns used to control the link. Which one you will use will depend on the particulars of your host computer system. As with BSC, SDLC and HDLC are synchronous communication protocols as the names imply. SDLC and HDLC, however, are newer and generally more flexible protocols that are used in IBM's Systems Network Architecture (SNA), discussed further in Chapter 6. Through the SDLC/HDLC capability of this adapter, information can be sent at rates of up to 9600 bits/second.

When used in SDLC/HDLC protocols, the Multi-Protocol Adapter/A can be programmed to use the direct memory access (DMA) method of exchanging information with Model 50/60/80 systems (see Chapter 1). It is the use of DMA that allows the Multi-Protocol Adapter/A to communicate at speeds of up to 9600 bits/second. The single 25-pin D-shell connector supports the attachment of the necessary cables.

3270 Connection

The IBM 3270 Connection allows Model 50/60/80 computers to **emulate** or act like an IBM 3278/79 display terminal or 3287 printer. These devices are commonly used to interact with many larger IBM computer systems, e.g., System/370. This feature card, shown in Figure 45, allows Model 50/60/80 computers to be attached via a coaxial cable to larger host computers. With the appropriate software, Model 50/60/80 computers can then interact with the larger computer as if they were the emulated display or printer.

System 36/38 Workstation Emulation Adapter

The IBM System 36/38 Workstation Emulation Adapter allows Model 50/60/80 computers to emulate an IBM 5250 Information Display System. This is a family of workstations used for interaction with the System/36 or System/38 mid-sized

Emulates: 3279/79 terminal or 3287 printer
Cable type: Coaxial

Figure 45. The 3270 Connection. This adapter allows Model 50/60/80 to act like a 3278 or 3279 terminal. These terminals are commonly used to interact with IBM's mainframe computers.

computer systems. Model 50/60/80 computers can therefore be an intelligent workstation in these environments. The adapter allows Model 50/60/80 computers to conduct up to four independent conversations or **sessions** with the host computer. The 15-pin connector provided allows for direct attachment to the twinaxial cable system used by System 36/38 computers.

In addition, a Convenience Kit is available that comes with the IBM System 36/38 Workstation Emulation Adapter, the IBM System 36/38 Emulation Program, and the IBM System 36/38 Emulation Attachment Cable. Elements of the Convenience Kit may also be purchased separately.

OTHER OPTIONS

Before leaving this chapter, we will cover four other options for Model 50/60/80:

- ◻ IBM Personal System/2 Mouse
- ◻ IBM Personal System/2 Data Migration Facility
- ◻ IBM Personal System/2 80287 Math Co-processor
- ◻ IBM Personal System/2 80387 Math Co-processor

Mouse

The IBM Personal System/2 Mouse is an optional input device that attaches to the Pointing Device Port provided on all Model 50/60/80 computers. This Mouse is shown in Figure 46. The user slides the Mouse on a flat surface to control cursor movement or to draw images. The two buttons provided on the Mouse are typically used to select a menu item or take some other action after the cursor is positioned on the screen. The Mouse augments the keyboard as a means of interacting with Model 50/60/80. The Mouse is compatible with the Microsoft® Mouse, allowing application programs written for that mouse to be used with the IBM Mouse.

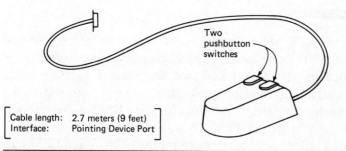

Figure 46. The IBM Mouse. This device provides another method for the user to interact with Model 50/60/80. It is used in conjunction with a normal keyboard.

Data Migration Facility

Current PC users will need a way to migrate information on PC fixed disks and diskettes to their Model 50/60/80 system. One option is to transfer the information from a PC Printer Port to the Model 50/60/80's Parallel Port (also called a Printer Port) using the IBM Personal System/2 Data Migration Facility. This accessory comes with a cable adapter and a Send program that works with DOS. To transfer information using this facility, attach a standard printer cable between the ports using the cable adapter on the Model 50/60/80 end of the cable. The complementary Receive program provided on the Model 50/60/80 Reference Diskette is then loaded into the Model 50/60/80. The Send program provided on the 5.25-inch diskette is loaded into the PC. The commands used with the Send program are similar to the DOS COPY command. (Transfer in the other direction is not supported).

The rate of information transfer via the Data Migration Facility varies largely depending on whether the transfers involve fixed disks or diskettes as well as on the system performance of the computers involved. As a reference point, transferring 5 MB from a PC/XT's fixed disk to a Model 50's 3.5-inch fixed disk takes about 25 minutes.

Non-DOS files or copy protected files cannot be transferred using this option. Chapter 7 discusses the use of the Data Migration Facility further, as well as other PC-to-Model 50/60/80 migration tools.

80287 Math Co-processor

The IBM Personal System/2 80287 Math Co-processor operates at 10 MHz and can be installed into a special socket provided in all Model 50/60 System Boards. It is designed to perform floating-point mathematical functions efficiently and to work hand-in-hand with the 80286 microprocessor to improve system performance. In order to enjoy this improved system performance, however, the program being executed must be specially written to use the capabilities of the 80287. Since the Personal Computer AT also supports this chip, many programs exist that take advantage of its capabilities. The 80287 is not supported in Model 80.

80387 Math Co-processor

The IBM Personal System/2 80387 Math Co-processor can be installed into a special socket provided in all Model 80 System Boards. This chip operates at the same speed as the 80386 microprocessor. It is also designed to perform floating-point mathematical functions efficiently and to work hand-in-hand with the 80386 microprocessor to improve the computer's performance. The 80387 is software compatible with the 80287 used in earlier PCs. This allows Model 80 to execute mathematical intensive applications originally written for the 80287. The 80387 Math Co-processor is not supported in the Model 50/60 computers.

OPTION COMPATIBILITY MATRIX

With the many options and peripherals available for Model 50/60/80 computers, users can easily become confused as to what options work with which computers. Figure 47 summarizes what works with what.

OPTION COMPATIBILITY MATRIX

	Model 50	Model 60	Model 80
Monochrome Display 8503	yes	yes	yes
Color Display 8512	yes	yes	yes
Color Display 8513	yes	yes	yes
Color Display 8514/adapter	yes	yes	yes
Proprinter II (4201)	yes	yes	yes
Quietwriter III (5202)	yes	yes	yes
80286 Memory Expansion Option	yes	yes	no
80286 Expanded Memory Adapter	yes	yes	no
80386 System Board Memory Expansion Kit (1 MB)	no	no	44 MB Model 80
80386 System Board Memory Expansion Kit (2 MB)	no	no	115 MB Model 80
80386 Memory Expansion Option	no	no	yes
Second 1.44 MB diskette drive	yes	yes	yes
External 5.25″ diskette drive	yes	yes	yes
Second 44 MB fixed disk	no	44 MB Model 60	44 MB Model 80
Second 70 MB fixed disk	no	70 MB Model 60	70 or 115 MB Model 80
Second 115 MB fixed disk	no	70 MB Model 60	70 or 115 MB Model 80
6157 Streaming Tape Drive/adapter	yes	yes	yes
Internal Optical Disk Drive	no	yes	yes
3363 Optical Disk Storage Unit	yes	yes	yes
Dual Async Adapter/A	yes	yes	yes
300/1200 Internal Modem/A	yes	yes	yes
PC Network Adapter II/A	yes	yes	yes
PC Network Baseband Adapter/A	yes	yes	yes
Token-Ring Network Adapter/A	yes	yes	yes
Multi-Protocol Adapter/A	yes	yes	yes
3270 Connection Adapter/A	yes	yes	yes
System 36/38 Work Station Emulation Adapter/A	yes	yes	yes
Mouse	yes	yes	yes
Data Migration Facility	yes	yes	yes
80287 Math Co-processor	yes	yes	no
80387 Math Co-processor	no	no	yes

Figure 47. Option compatibility matrix. This table indicates which options discussed in the chapter work with which computers.

3

Using Your Model 50/60/80 Computer

The previous chapters closely examined the System Units and optional equipment of the Model 50/60/80 computers. This chapter begins our look at how that hardware is put to work, namely, by the all important **software.** Software is a general term for the many programs that execute in computers. It is software that harnesses Model 50/60/80's computational power and allows you to perform so many diverse and useful tasks. The chapter begins by taking you step by step through the programs provided with all Model 50/60/80 computers. This serves as a good introduction and allows you to actually use your computer even if you never have before.

Later in the chapter, you are introduced to the kinds of software employed to perform useful work. We discuss the three general categories of software along with the job each performs. Finally, we discuss Model 50/60/80's compatibility with software written for PCs.

GETTING YOUR FEET WET

Every Model 50/60/80 computer comes with certain special purpose programs. Some of these programs are permanently stored in the Read Only Memory (ROM) chips resident on the System Board. Other programs reside on the **Reference Diskette** provided with every system. One easy way to learn more about the programs provided is to run them. The steps that follow will help you learn by doing just that. If you haven't yet unpacked and set up the hardware components of your Model 50/60/80 computer, this would be a good time to do so. Follow the unpacking and installation instructions provided with your system. This should only take a few minutes. Keep the Reference Diskette handy. If you don't have a Model 50/60/80 computer nearby, you can simply read along. For your convenience, all computer elements

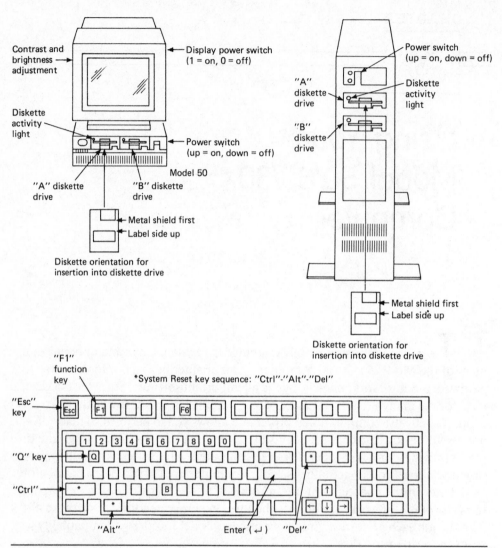

Figure 48. Reference diagram for procedures provided in this chapter.

referred to in the procedures that follow are labeled in Figure 48. If your computer does not respond as described in the procedures that follow, refer to the "Solving Computer Problems" section of the Quick Reference manual for assistance.

Greetings from POST

The first program we will explore is one that, whether you know it or not, is automatically started every time you turn on your computer. It is called the **Power-On Self Test (POST)** program, and is permanently stored in your computer. The first thing POST does is test the health of your computer system. It exercises the microprocessor and support chips, the diskette drive, the graphics circuitry, the ports,

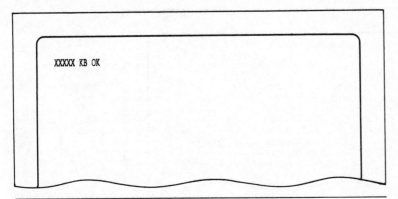

Figure 49. Location of memory count kept by POST during the memory test.

the memory, etc. It's like having a resident service technician that tests your computer every day. The only indication you get of all this activity is during the memory test portion of POST, which takes the most time to perform. The more memory in the system, the longer this system checkout takes, since every memory location is tested. During this test, POST keeps a count in the upper left corner of your display. To see this memory count, perform the following steps:

⇨ If a diskette is in drive "A," remove it from the drive.

⇨ Turn the display's switch to the on ("1") position.

⇨ If your computer is off, turn the power switch to the on (switch up) position.

⇨ If your computer is already on, simply turn it off, pause five seconds, and then turn it back on.

Figure 49 shows where the memory count appears on your display screen.

After POST finishes checking the health of the system, it sets the **system configuration** of the computer based on the information stored in the CMOS memory. The system configuration is the basic settings and arrangement of the internal computer elements. This configuration chore includes setting Programmable Option Select (POS) switches on the System Board and feature cards. (POS was discussed in Chapter 1.) This activity is not detectable by the user. If POST successfully completes these chores, you will hear a single beep signaling that everything is OK and ready to go. Then POST will check to see if the power-on password feature is enabled. If it is, a small key-shaped image will be displayed in the upper left corner of the screen, as shown in Figure 50. This indicates that the user-defined password must be entered before operation can continue. If password security is not enabled or if the user enters the correct password, POST will terminate and pass control to some other program. This other program can be on your fixed disk (e.g., the operating system) or a program on a diskette in drive "A" (e.g., the Reference Diskette). If you don't have any programs on either the fixed disk or a diskette in drive "A," you will be presented with the screen shown in Figure 51. This screen is asking you to insert the Reference Diskette into drive "A" and press the "F1" function key to resume. Don't do this yet, we will get to the Reference Diskette later.

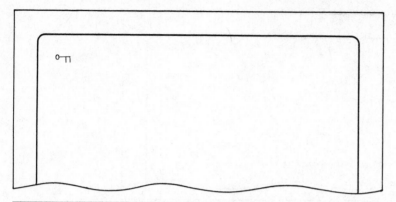

Figure 50. Password prompt. When you are presented with this key-shaped emblem, you must type in the user-defined password before operation can continue.

What If POST Finds an Error?

The above scenario assumes that POST finds no problems with the computer system, which will normally be the case. But what happens if POST does find a problem? Indeed, unless someone has previously set up your computer, a POST error will notify you that the system has not yet been configured and that the time/date has

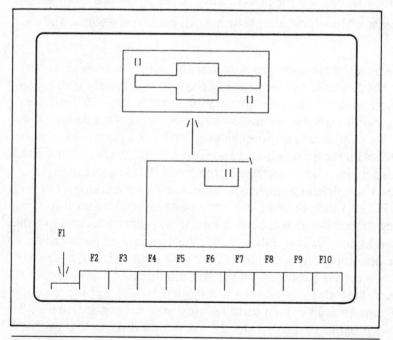

Figure 51. Screen presented when no programs are on the fixed disk and no diskette is in drive "A". This screen is asking you to put a diskette in drive "A" and press the "F1" function key.

not been set. To see how you can easily handle POST errors of any kind, let's intentionally cause a harmless problem and see how we can resolve that problem. The following steps simulate a stuck key on the keyboard:

⇨ Turn the System Unit's power switch off.

⇨ If a diskette is inserted in a drive, remove it.

⇨ Press and hold down the "Q" key on the keyboard.

⇨ Turn on the computer (continue to hold the "Q" key until you hear two beeps, then release the "Q" key).

POST again begins its checkout of the computer. The "memory test" portion of POST displays the memory count as before. When POST gets around to checking out the keyboard, however, it detects that the "Q" key is stuck. The POST program responds by displaying a "10 301" **error code** (Figure 52) and sounding two beeps. Two beeps indicate that POST has found a problem. If your system has not yet been set up, you may also get other error codes—fear not. Here is how you can handle any POST error that arises without having to know what any of the POST error codes mean:

⇨ Insert the Reference Diskette into the "A" diskette drive as shown in Figure 48.

⇨ Press the "F1" function key.

Note: Memory count may be different depending on how much memory is contained in your system.

Figure 52. Error code presented by POST when a key is stuck down.

⇨ If the " ⊶ " symbol does not appear on your screen, ignore this step. If the " ⊶ " symbol does appear on your screen, this indicates that password security is enabled. Type in the necessary password and depress "Enter" (↵).

The first thing the Reference Diskette programs do is notify you that they are now in control by displaying the Reference Diskette title screen shown in Figure 53. When you see this title screen, you know the computer is ready to help you resolve any problems through the POST Error Processor, or the diagnostic programs we will discuss later in the chapter. If you do not get to this title screen, refer to the "Problem Determination" section of the Quick Reference manual.

⇨ Press "Enter" (↵).

Any POST error codes are now passed to the **POST Error Processor** program on the Reference Diskette. The POST Error Processor program looks at the errors detected by POST and displays the appropriate error messages, each in turn. These messages explain the nature of the problem and recommend the appropriate action. Figure 54 shows the error message resulting from the "10 301" error we caused by holding down the "Q" key. This message tells you that POST has detected the stuck key. It also recommends that you check for anything resting on the keyboard. Since you have already resolved the problem (you took your finger off the "Q" key), we will continue.

⇨ Press "Enter" (↵).

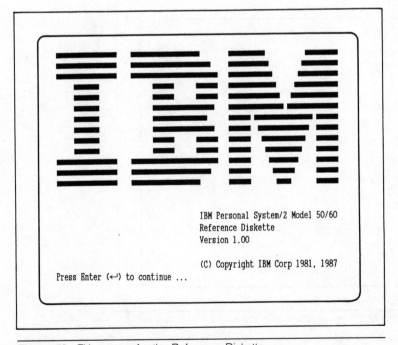

Figure 53. Title screen for the Reference Diskette.

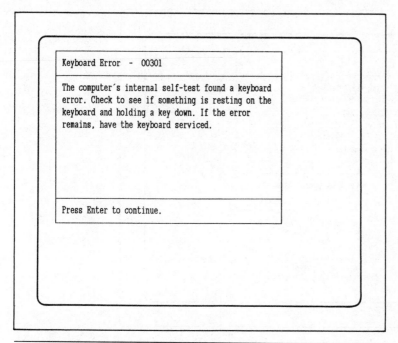

```
Keyboard Error  -  00301

The computer's internal self-test found a keyboard
error. Check to see if something is resting on the
keyboard and holding a key down. If the error
remains, have the keyboard serviced.




Press Enter to continue.
```

Figure 54. Error message presented by the POST Error Processor program resulting from the stuck key detected by POST.

If additional error codes were generated during POST, the POST Error Processor program would now display each error message in turn. If you follow the instructions that appear on your screen, you should be able to handle any POST error that arises. After you resolve any additional errors, you will find yourself at the Reference Diskette Main Menu shown in Figure 55.

Why didn't IBM simply store the POST messages in ROM with the POST rather than having a separate POST Error Processor program on the Reference Diskette? The reason lies in the fact that the Model 50/60/80 computers are designed for worldwide use. If the message were automatically displayed in English, it wouldn't be very useful to someone who speaks French or Spanish. Having a separate version of ROM for every national language is not logistically practical. Since the Reference Diskette is translated into the various national languages, it is possible to provide complete translated POST error messages on this diskette.

Referring to the Reference Diskette

A Reference Diskette is included with every Model 50/60/80 computer system. This diskette contains many specialized programs that can teach you about your Model 50/60/80 computer as well as help you use it. A very simple and effective way to explore the programs provided on this diskette is to run them. The following steps will help you explore the programs on the Reference Diskette. The original Reference Diskette is permanently **write protected,** which means you can't overwrite the pro-

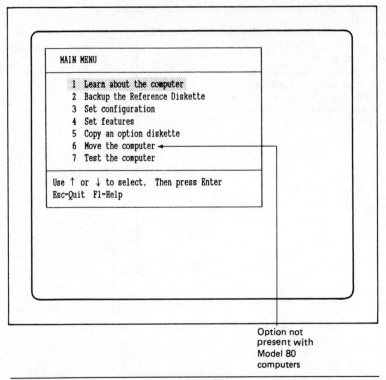

```
MAIN MENU

    1 Learn about the computer
    2 Backup the Reference Diskette
    3 Set configuration
    4 Set features
    5 Copy an option diskette
    6 Move the computer ◄
    7 Test the computer

Use ↑ or ↓ to select.  Then press Enter
Esc=Quit  F1=Help
```

Option not
present with
Model 80
computers

Figure 55. The Reference Diskette Main Menu.

grams on the diskette either accidentally or on purpose. Since the information on diskettes can be lost in other ways (e.g., physical damage, magnetic fields, etc.), it is a good idea to make a backup copy of the Reference Diskette soon if you haven't already. If you wish to do so now, get a blank 1.44 MB diskette, start the Reference Diskette programs, and then skip to the section entitled "Menu Option 2: Backup the Reference Diskette."

Let's begin exploring the programs on the Reference Diskette. If you followed the above POST procedure, the Reference Diskette Main Menu, shown in Figure 55, is currently on your screen and you can skip to the next section if you wish.

Starting the Reference Diskette

If the Computer Is Already Turned On:

⇨ Insert the Reference Diskette into the "A" diskette drive as shown in Figure 48.

⇨ Perform a System Reset by pressing and holding the "Ctrl" and "Alt" keys, and then pressing the "Del" key simultaneously.

If the Computer Is Turned Off:

⇨ Insert the Reference Diskette into the "A" diskette drive as shown in Figure 48.

⇨ Turn the display switch to the on ("1") position.

⇨ Turn the computer's power switch on (the "up" position).

⇨ If the " ⌐ " symbol does not appear on your screen, ignore this step. If the " ⌐ " symbol does appear on your screen, this indicates that password security is enabled. Type in the necessary password and press "Enter" (↵).

You will then see the diskette activity light turn on, indicating that the Reference Diskette is being read by the computer. After performing the preceding steps, you will be presented with the Reference Diskette title screen shown in Figure 53. This screen identifies the diskette as the Reference Diskette and indicates the revision level of the diskette and which Personal System/2 model(s) the diskette is for.

⇨ Press "Enter" (↵).

The Reference Diskette Main Menu then appears as shown in Figure 55.

Strolling through the Main Menu

There are either six or seven choices provided on the Reference Diskette Main Menu depending on which Personal System/2 model you are using. Model 50 and Model 60 use the exact same Reference Diskette, which has seven choices as shown in Figure 55. The only thing different about the Model 80 Reference Diskette is that there is no "Moving the Computer" option in the menu. This option is not necessary with Model 80 and is simply omitted.

The menu choices are selected by typing in the corresponding number or by moving the highlight bar to the selection by using the up and down arrow keys and then pressing "Enter." When a menu item is selected, either the desired action will be performed or you will be presented with instructions or a submenu that provides more detailed items from which to choose. For simplicity, the following step-by-step procedures will ask you to enter the number to select the menu item. If at any point in the following procedures you get lost, repeatedly press the "Esc" key until you see the Main Menu in Figure 55 and start that section of the procedure over again. If you press the "Esc" key too many times, the message shown in Figure 56 will appear. Just hit the "Esc" key once more and the window will disappear, leaving only the Reference Diskette's Main Menu.

At most points during Reference Diskette interaction, you can get **contextual help** messages by pressing the "F1" function key. These messages will provide further explanation or instructions related to the particular place you are in the Reference Diskette programs. If no help is available at a given point in the program, pressing "F1" will result in a single beep. At any point during the following procedures, feel free to press "F1" to review any help information available. Simply press the "Esc" key to get rid of the help message and you will be right where you started. With the information given in these contextual help messages, you can take self-guided tours through any of the programs in the Reference Diskette. The procedures that follow will introduce you to each item in the Reference Diskette Main Menu to help get you started.

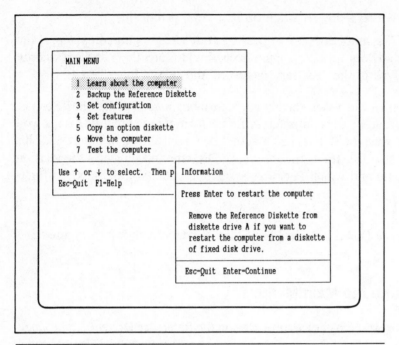

Figure 56. Screen presented if you press the "Esc" key when the Reference Diskette Main Menu is shown.

Menu Option 1: Learn About the Computer

This menu item starts the interactive Tutorial program on the Reference Diskette. This Tutorial provides a guided tour of Model 50/60/80.

⇨ Press "1."

A message appears indicating that the Tutorial is being loaded into memory. Then the Tutorial title screen appears followed by a welcome message. Lastly, the Tutorial's table of contents appears as shown in Figure 57, and the program pauses.

The Tutorial program is organized just like a book, with chapters, a glossary, and an index. You can review any Tutorial chapter by pressing the Tutorial chapter number or moving the highlight bar to the Tutorial chapter and pressing "Enter" (◄┘). You can view the Tutorial chapters in any order at your own pace. It is recommended, however, that new users view the chapters in order. The following is a summary of the topics covered in each Tutorial chapter:

Chapter 1: How to Use This Program explains how you can step through the Tutorial program by pressing the "PgDn" key to move forward in the chapter one screen at a time, or the "PgUp" key to move backward in the chapter one screen at a time. This chapter also explains how to look up information in the Tutorial's glossary and index.

Chapter 2: Hardware describes the System Unit, keyboard, display, diskettes, and options.

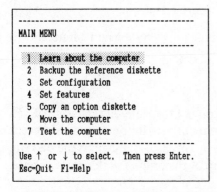

```
------------------------------------------
MAIN MENU
------------------------------------------
 1  Learn about the computer
 2  Backup the Reference diskette
 3  Set configuration
 4  Set features
 5  Copy an option diskette
 6  Move the computer
 7  Test the computer
------------------------------------------
Use ↑ or ↓ to select.  Then press Enter.
Esc=Quit  F1=Help
```

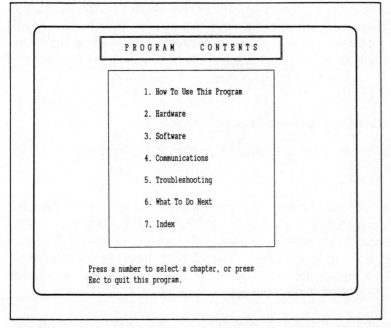

```
          PROGRAM     CONTENTS

              1. How To Use This Program

              2. Hardware

              3. Software

              4. Communications

              5. Troubleshooting

              6. What To Do Next

              7. Index

     Press a number to select a chapter, or press
     Esc to quit this program.
```

Figure 57. Tutorial "Program Contents" screen, which tells you what is covered in the Tutorial.

Chapter 3: Software provides overviews and demonstrations of the different types of application programs commonly used.

Chapter 4: Communications covers different methods of transferring information between computers. Methods discussed include local area networks, modems, and so on. This chapter also describes the information services available over the telephone lines and provides a simple demonstration.

Chapter 5: Troubleshooting covers problem determination methods available to you if you experience a problem.

Chapter 6: What to Do Next provides a checklist of things to do when first setting up your computer.

Chapter 7: Index helps you find particular topics covered in the Tutorial.

When you are done exploring the Tutorial program:

⇨ Press the "Esc" key to get back to the Reference Diskette Main Menu shown in Figure 55.

Menu Option 2: Backup the Reference Diskette

This menu item allows you to make a working copy of the Reference Diskette. Even though the original Reference Diskette is permanently write protected to prevent accidental erasure, the information can be lost by physical damage to the diskette or strong magnetic fields. After making a backup of the original Reference Diskette, store it in a safe place.

If you have already made a backup copy or don't wish to right now, skip to the next section. If you have not yet made your backup copy, get a blank 1.44 MB diskette and we will do it now. Insure that the write protect switch in the corner of the blank diskette is such that the square hole is blocked, as shown in Figure 58.

⇨ Press "2."

If You Have a Single Diskette Drive System:

You will be presented with the screen shown in Figure 59. To begin the copy procedure:

⇨ Press "Enter" (↵).

You will now be presented with a series of instructions that tell you to either put the blank diskette (target diskette) or the original Reference Diskette into the "A" drive and press "Enter." This "diskette swapping" is necessary because the memory used by the Copy program is not large enough to hold the entire contents of the Reference Diskette. It must therefore be copied a section at a time. You will be asked to swap diskettes four times before the copy is complete.

⇨ Follow the swapping instructions that appear on the screen.

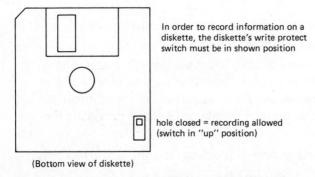

In order to record information on a diskette, the diskette's write protect switch must be in shown position

hole closed = recording allowed (switch in "up" position)

(Bottom view of diskette)

Figure 58. Write protect switch position necessary to allow writing information on the diskette. The square hole should be blocked by the switch.

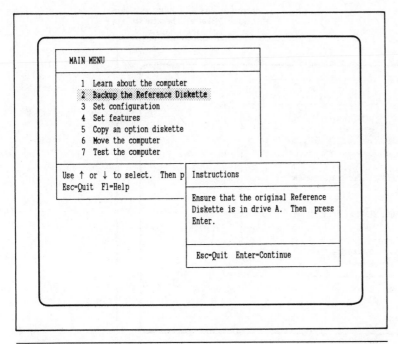

Figure 59. Screen presented if you have a single diskette drive system and you select Option 2.

If You Have a Dual Diskette Drive System:

You will see the screen shown in Figure 60. This screen allows you to indicate which diskette drive will contain the original Reference Diskette and which drive will contain the blank diskette. The easiest way to make your backup on a two-diskette drive system is to:

⇒ Insure that the original Reference Diskette is in the "A" drive.

⇒ Place the blank diskette in the "B" drive.

⇒ Press the " ↓ " key to position the highlight bar over the "target diskette" field on the screen.

⇒ Press "B" to indicate that the blank diskette will be in drive "B" (see Figure 61).

⇒ Press "Enter" (↵).

You will now be presented with the screen shown in Figure 62, which tells you to verify that the diskettes are in the drives you indicated in Figure 61. To begin the copying:

⇒ Press "Enter" (↵).

When a "Copy Complete . . ." information message appears on the screen, your backup copy is ready to use:

⇒ Label the new backup copy of the Reference Diskette.

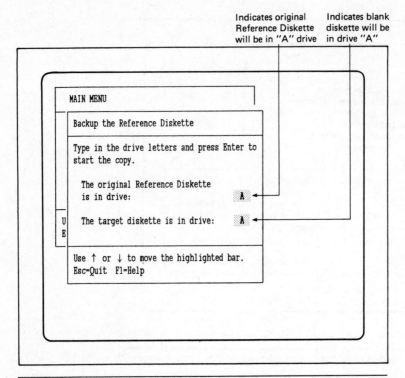

Figure 60. Screen presented if you have a dual diskette drive system and you select Option 2.

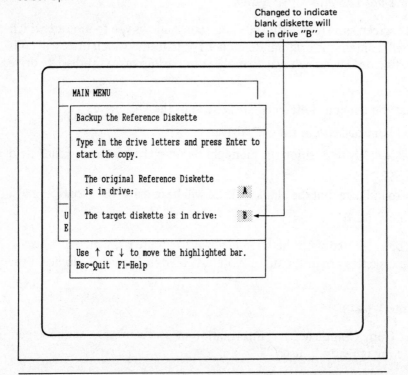

Figure 61. Screen after you have indicated that the target diskette will be in drive "B".

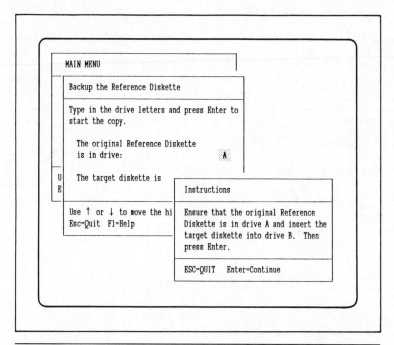

MAIN MENU

Backup the Reference Diskette

Type in the drive letters and press Enter to
start the copy.

   The original Reference Diskette
   is in drive: A

U   The target diskette is
E

                          Instructions

Use ↑ or ↓ to move the hi| Ensure that the original Reference
Esc=Quit F1=Help   Diskette is in drive A and insert the
                       target diskette into drive B. Then
                       press Enter.

                       ESC=QUIT   Enter=Continue

Figure 62. Message asking you to ensure you have the diskettes in the correct positions.

⇨ Store the original Reference Diskette in a safe place.

⇨ Insure that the backup copy of the Reference Diskette is back in drive "A."

⇨ Press "Enter" to return to the Main Menu.

Menu Option 3: Set Configuration

This menu item starts the setup program that allows you to examine or modify your "system configuration." The system configuration is the setting of any switches or optional features inside the computer system.

⇨ Press "3."

A secondary menu appears on the screen as shown in Figure 63. There are five items on this menu:

1. **View configuration** allows you to examine the current system configuration but will not let you change the configuration.

2. **Change configuration** allows you to examine and change the system configuration.

3. **Backup configuration** provides a way to save the current system configuration to the Reference Diskette. Note: A non-write protected backup copy of the Reference Diskette must be used to back up the configuration.

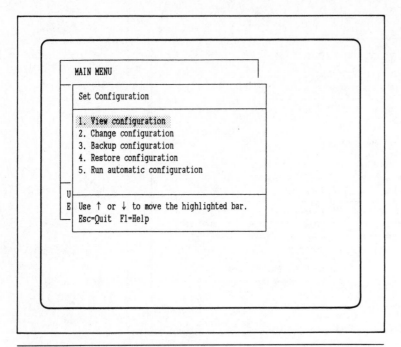

```
MAIN MENU

  Set Configuration

  1. View configuration
  2. Change configuration
  3. Backup configuration
  4. Restore configuration
  5. Run automatic configuration

U
E  Use ↑ or ↓ to move the highlighted bar.
   Esc=Quit F1=Help
```

Figure 63. "Set Configuration" submenu.

4. **Restore configuration** allows you to reconfigure your system using the configuration information on a diskette saved with Option 3, "Backup configuration." This is handy if you lose the system configuration in formation stored in CMOS memory when, for example, you change the battery in the computer.

5. **Run automatic configuration** automatically sets your System Board and feature cards to their normal or **default** configuration. Any time you add or remove a feature card or option, you must run this program to configure the new item(s). If this program cannot resolve any configuration conflicts that may arise, you will be instructed to choose Menu Item 2, "Change configuration," and manually resolve the conflicts.

To explore your system configuration

⇨ Press "1."

Figure 64 shows a sample system configuration on a Model 50. Your configuration may vary. The "Total System Memory" area of the screen has two lines under it: "Installed Memory" and "Usable Memory." "Installed memory" is the amount of built-in memory on the System Board (1 MB) plus any memory on Memory Expansion Options in feature card slots (none are installed in our example). "Usable memory" is the portion of the installed memory that was tested and found to be in good working order. If these numbers do not match, you have some defective

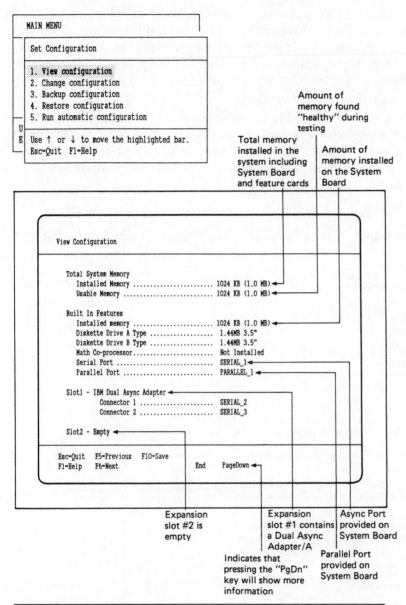

```
┌─────────────────────────────────────────────┐
│ MAIN MENU                                     │
│ ┌───────────────────────────────────────────┤
│ │ Set Configuration                          │
│ ├────────────────────────────────────────────┤
│ │ 1. View configuration                       │
│ │ 2. Change configuration                     │
│ │ 3. Backup configuration                      │
│ │ 4. Restore configuration                     │
│ │ 5. Run automatic configuration               │
│U│                                             │
│E│ Use ↑ or ↓ to move the highlighted bar.     │
│ │ Esc=Quit  F1=Help                           │
└─┴─────────────────────────────────────────────┘
```

Amount of memory found "healthy" during testing

Total memory installed in the system including System Board and feature cards

Amount of memory installed on the System Board

```
    View Configuration


      Total System Memory
         Installed Memory ..................... 1024 KB (1.0 MB)◄
         Usable Memory ........................ 1024 KB (1.0 MB)◄

      Built In Features
         Installed memory ..................... 1024 KB (1.0 MB)◄
         Diskette Drive A Type ................ 1.44MB 3.5"
         Diskette Drive B Type ................ 1.44MB 3.5"
         Math Co-processor..................... Not Installed
         Serial Port .......................... SERIAL_1◄
         Parallel Port ........................ PARALLEL_1◄

      Slot1 - IBM Dual Async Adapter ◄
               Connector 1 .................... SERIAL_2
               Connector 2 .................... SERIAL_3

      Slot2 - Empty ◄


      Esc=Quit   F5=Previous   F10=Save
      F1=Help    F6=Next              End    PageDown ◄
```

Expansion slot #2 is empty

Expansion slot #1 contains a Dual Async Adapter/A

Async Port provided on System Board

Indicates that pressing the "PgDn" key will show more information

Parallel Port provided on System Board

Figure 64. The "View Configuration" screen allows you to examine the configuration of your system but will not let you make any changes.

memory and should get the computer serviced. Dynamic Memory Relocation, discussed in Chapter 2, will permit you to disable any bad memory, thus allowing you to restart operation with the remaining good memory.

The "Built In Features" area tells you the devices currently installed in your system. The amount of built-in memory residing on the System Board is indicated as 1024 KB (1 MB). Two 1.44 MB diskette drives are installed and the optional Math Co-processor is not installed. The standard Async Port, also called a Serial Port, is configured as "SERIAL__1" or the primary Async Port. This identifies the address at which a computer program can find the port. The Parallel Port is configured as the "PARALLEL__1" or primary Parallel Port. Next, information is provided about any feature cards installed in the Micro Channel expansion slots. In our example system, a Dual Async Adapter/A is installed in "Slot1," and no feature card is in "Slot2." Pressing "PgDn" and "PgUp" allows you to see information on the additional Micro Channel expansion slots.

Let's see how you would change the configuration of the Serial Port, for example. This might be desirable if you wish to use the Serial Port on the System Board as "SERIAL__2" due to the special needs of a program. To change the configuration of the System Board Serial Port, perform the following steps (don't worry, we won't save any of the changes we make):

⇨ Press the "Esc" key one time to get back to the menu in Figure 63.

⇨ Select Menu Item 2, "Change configuration," from the menu by pressing "2."

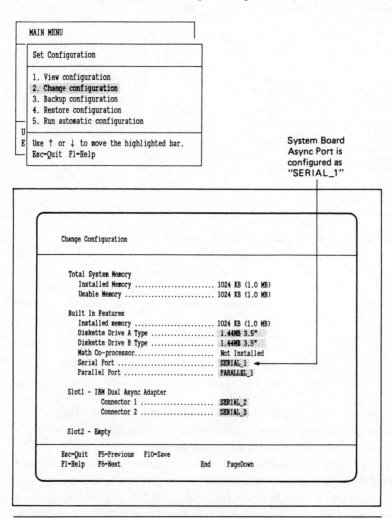

Figure 65. The "Change Configuration" screen allows you to modify your system's configuration.

You are now presented with the screen shown in Figure 65. From this screen, you can change the configuration as indicated in the upper left corner. The specific items you can change are indicated by brackets, [ ]. Items not in brackets cannot be changed. If your configuration has not already been modified, the Serial Port will be configured as the primary serial port "Serial__1."

⇨ Use the " ↓ " key to position the highlight bar over the field associated with the "Serial Port" under the "Built In Features."

⇨ Press the "F6" function key.

The Serial Port is now configured as "SERIAL__2," as shown in Figure 66. In our example, we have created a **configuration conflict,** indicated by the asterisk. We have configured both the System Board Serial Port and one of the Dual Async Adapter/A ports as "SERIAL__2." In order for a program to tell one port from

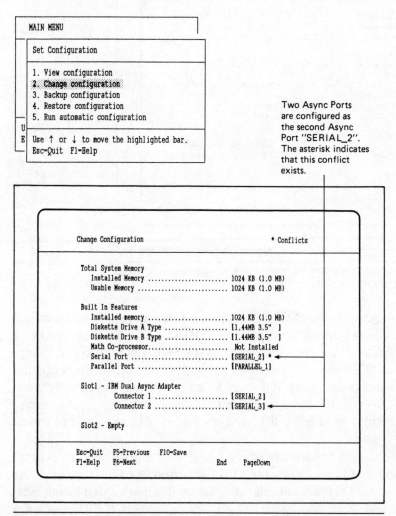

MAIN MENU

Set Configuration

1. View configuration
2. Change configuration
3. Backup configuration
4. Restore configuration
5. Run automatic configuration

Use ↑ or ↓ to move the highlighted bar.
Esc-Quit F1-Help

Two Async Ports
are configured as
the second Async
Port "SERIAL_2".
The asterisk indicates
that this conflict
exists.

Change Configuration   * Conflicts

Total System Memory
    Installed Memory .... 1024 KB (1.0 MB)
    Usable Memory .... 1024 KB (1.0 MB)

Built In Features
    Installed memory .... 1024 KB (1.0 MB)
    Diskette Drive A Type .... [1.44MB 3.5"]
    Diskette Drive B Type .... [1.44MB 3.5"]
    Math Co-processor........................ Not Installed
    Serial Port .... [SERIAL_2] * ←
    Parallel Port .... [PARALLEL_1]

Slot1 - IBM Dual Async Adapter
    Connector 1 .... [SERIAL_2]
    Connector 2 .... [SERIAL_3] ←

Slot2 - Empty

Esc-Quit   F5-Previous   F10-Save
F1-Help   F6-Next   End   PageDown

Figure 66. The System Board Async Port is now configured as "SERIAL__2," but a configuration conflict exists.

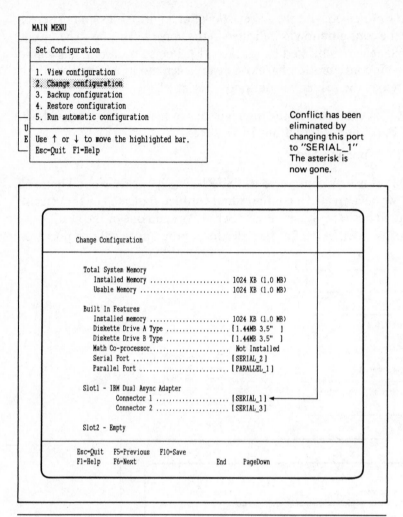

```
MAIN MENU

   Set Configuration

   1. View configuration
   2. Change configuration
   3. Backup configuration
   4. Restore configuration
   5. Run automatic configuration
  U
  E  Use ↑ or ↓ to move the highlighted bar.
     Esc=Quit  F1=Help
```

Conflict has been
eliminated by
changing this port
to "SERIAL_1"
The asterisk is
now gone.

```
      Change Configuration


         Total System Memory
            Installed Memory ....................... 1024 KB (1.0 MB)
            Usable Memory .......................... 1024 KB (1.0 MB)

         Built In Features
            Installed memory ....................... 1024 KB (1.0 MB)
            Diskette Drive A Type .................. [1.44MB 3.5"  ]
            Diskette Drive B Type .................. [1.44MB 3.5"  ]
            Math Co-processor...................... Not Installed
            Serial Port ........................... [SERIAL_2]
            Parallel Port ......................... [PARALLEL_1]

         Slot1 - IBM Dual Async Adapter
            Connector 1 ..................... [SERIAL_1] ◄
            Connector 2 ..................... [SERIAL_3]

         Slot2 - Empty


      Esc=Quit   F5=Previous   F10=Save
      F1=Help    F6=Next                    End    PageDown
```

Figure 67. The configuration conflict has been resolved by changing the first
Async Port on the Dual Async Adapter/A to "SERIAL__1."

another, only one port can be "SERIAL__2" at a time. To resolve this conflict,
we could move the highlight bar down to the "SERIAL__2" field associated with
the Dual Async Adapter/A and repeatedly press the "F6" function key to change
its configuration to "SERIAL__1," as shown in Figure 67. Changing the configuration of other elements in the system is done in a similar fashion. Continually pressing function key "F6" will step through all configuration possibilities for the selected
item. When all options have been displayed, they start over in a "round robin"
fashion.

If you really wanted to save any changes that you've made in your system's
configuration, you would now press the "F10" function key. Once the new configuration was saved, POST will automatically set up this new configuration every
time you turn on your computer. Since this is just an exercise, we will not save any
configuration changes. To leave things the way they were before we started:

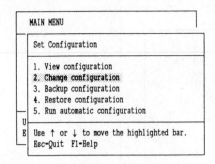

```
MAIN MENU
┌─────────────────────────────────────────────────┐
│ Set Configuration                                 │
│                                                   │
│ 1. View configuration                             │
│ 2. Change configuration                           │
│ 3. Backup configuration                           │
│ 4. Restore configuration                          │
│ 5. Run automatic configuration                    │
U                                                    │
E  Use ↑ or ↓ to move the highlighted bar.          │
│  Esc-Quit  Fl-Help                                │
└─────────────────────────────────────────────────┘
```

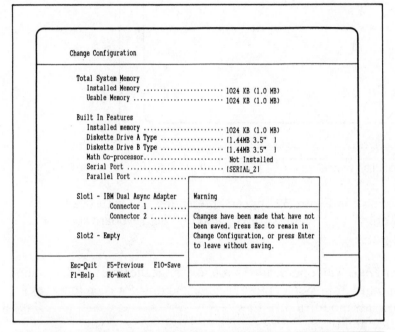

```
Change Configuration

  Total System Memory
    Installed Memory ..................... 1024 KB (1.0 MB)
    Usable Memory ........................ 1024 KB (1.0 MB)

  Built In Features
    Installed memory ..................... 1024 KB (1.0 MB)
    Diskette Drive A Type ................ [1.44MB 3.5"  ]
    Diskette Drive B Type ................ [1.44MB 3.5"  ]
    Math Co-processor..................... Not Installed
    Serial Port .......................... [SERIAL_2]
    Parallel Port ...............┌─────────────────────────────┐
                                 │ Warning                     │
  Slot1 - IBM Dual Async Adapter │                             │
          Connector 1 ..........│ Changes have been made that have not
          Connector 2 ..........│ been saved. Press Esc to remain in
                                 │ Change Configuration, or press Enter
  Slot2 - Empty                  │ to leave without saving.    │
                                 │                             │
  Esc-Quit   F5-Previous  F10-Save                             │
  Fl-Help    F6-Next     └─────────────────────────────┘
```

Figure 68. Warning message indicating configuration changes have been made but not saved.

⇨ Press "Esc."

A warning message appears indicating that you have made configuration changes but have not saved the changes, as shown in Figure 68. Since we don't want to save the changes:

⇨ Press "Enter" (⏎) to leave this menu without changing anything.

⇨ Press "Esc" to get back to the Reference Diskette Main Menu.

Menu Option 4: Set Features

This menu item allows you to change some other settings inside the computer system.

⇨ Press "4."

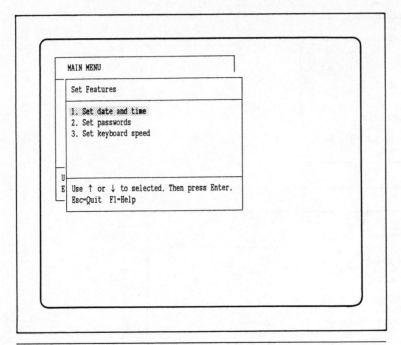

```
  MAIN MENU

    Set Features

    1. Set date and time
    2. Set passwords
    3. Set keyboard speed



  U
  E  Use ↑ or ↓ to selected. Then press Enter.
     Esc=Quit  F1=Help
```

Figure 69. "Set Features" submenu.

The screen shown in Figure 69 appears, presenting you with three options: (1) "Set date and time," (2) "Set passwords," and (3) "Set keyboard speed." Let's explore each option.

Set Date and Time: This option allows you to change the time and date maintained by the computer. Your system uses this date and time for such things as indicating when you last modified disk files.

To set the date and time:

⇨ Press "1."

The screen in Figure 70 is then displayed.

⇨ Type in the current date in the following format: MM-DD-YYYY, for example, "04-02-87" is April 2, 1987.

⇨ Press the " ↓ " key to position the highlight bar over the time area.

⇨ Type in the current time in the following format: HH:MM:SS, for example, "18:30:00" is 6:30 P.M.

⇨ Press "Enter" (↵) to save the new date and time.

Figure 71 shows the message that appears indicating that the date and time have been updated. Your computer will keep track of the time and date from now on. To get back to the "Set Features" menu:

⇨ Press "Enter" (↵).

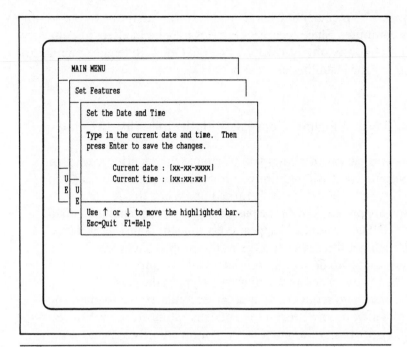

Figure 70. Screen used to change the date and time kept by the computer.

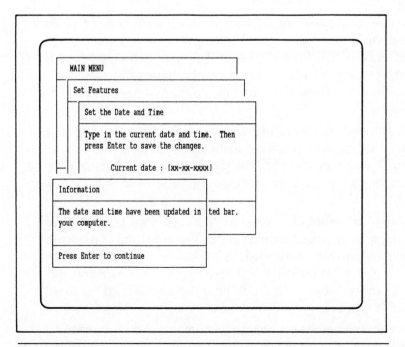

Figure 71. Message indicating that the new time and date are in effect.

Set Passwords: This menu option allows you to work with the password security features of your computer. Since security practices may be in effect in your area, we will not actually modify any passwords. See the Quick Reference manual for detailed instructions for installing any passwords.

⇨ Press "2."

The screen shown in Figure 72 appears with the following five choices:

1. **Set power-on password** allows you to enable the security feature of your computer that will require you to type in a password that you define every time the computer is turned on. When this feature is enabled, you are presented with the password prompt resembling a small key " o⊓ ". This prompt will appear every time the computer is turned on. You then get three tries to type in the proper password. If after three tries you fail to do so, the computer will halt and must be turned off and then back on before you may try to type in the password again. Since the power-on sequence takes a few seconds, trying to guess the password will be a time-consuming and frustrating effort. When you type the proper password, an "OK" will momentarily appear on the screen and then normal operation will commence.

   What if you forget your password? You must then disassemble your computer system and remove the battery for a few minutes. This will destroy the password stored in CMOS memory and disable the power-on password feature, leaving evidence of the intrusion (i.e., no password or different password).

2. **Change power-on password** provides you with instructions on how to change the power-on password. The power-on password can be changed only at the " o⊓ " password prompt. This password is changed by typing in the current password followed by a slash ("/") and then the new password. From then on, the new password will be in effect.

3. **Remove power-on password** provides you with instructions on how to disable the power-on password feature. This can only be done at the " o⊓ " password prompt. The password feature is disabled by typing in the current password followed by a slash and then no new password.

4. **Set keyboard password** allows you to "lock up" your keyboard and Mouse input while your computer is on. This is helpful if you leave your computer on but unattended, as is common in the business environment. Once this feature is activated, typing "KP" prevents further keyboard or Mouse interaction until the user-defined keyboard password is typed in.

5. **Set network server mode** is a security feature that allows your Model 50/60/80 computer to automatically start up (e.g., after a power failure)

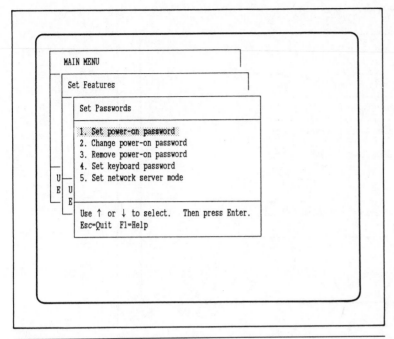

```
  MAIN MENU

    Set Features

      Set Passwords

        1. Set power-on password
        2. Change power-on password
        3. Remove power-on password
        4. Set keyboard password
   U    5. Set network server mode
   E  U
      E

        Use ↑ or ↓ to select.   Then press Enter.
        Esc=Quit  F1=Help
```

Figure 72. "Set Passwords" submenu.

from the fixed disk with the keyboard/Mouse password lock in effect. This allows the computer to be used as a secure unattended network server sharing its fixed disks and printers with other computers in a Local Area Network (discussed in Chapter 6). The server is secure because all keyboard/Mouse input is prevented, even if power is turned off and back on, until the keyboard password is provided.

⇨ Press the "Esc" key to get back to the "Set Features" Menu.

Set Keyboard Speed: This menu item allows you to change the **typematic** rate of the keyboard based on your personal preference. This is the rate at which characters appear on the screen if you press and hold down a key on the keyboard. To explore this item:

⇨ Press the "3" key.

Figure 73 shows the resulting screen. The keyboard can be set to one of two speeds, normal or fast. The normal speed puts characters on the screen at a rate of 15 per second while the fast speed results in 30 characters per second.

⇨ Use the " ↓ " key to move the highlight bar over the desired speed.

⇨ Press "Enter" (⏎) to save the new keyboard speed.

A message appears indicating that the new keyboard speed is now in effect, as shown in Figure 74. To get back to the "Set Features" Menu:

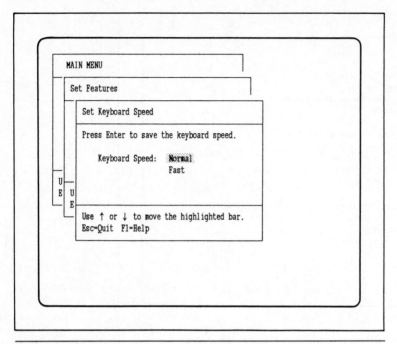

Figure 73. Screen used to change the keyboard's typematic speed.

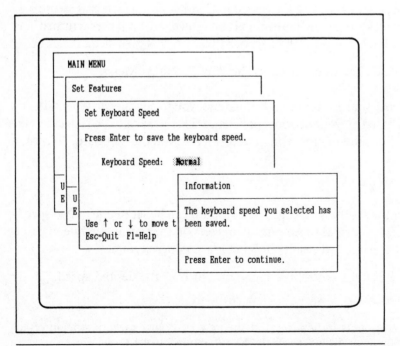

Figure 74. Message indicating the new keyboard speed is now in effect.

⇨ Press "Enter" (↵).

To get back to the Reference Diskette Main Menu:

⇨ Press the "Esc" key.

Menu Option 5: Copy an Option Diskette

Some of the feature cards available for Model 50/60/80 computers come with their own diskette containing diagnostic programs, error messages, configuration information, and so on. Menu Item 5 automatically copies the feature card's configuration information and diagnostic programs onto your backup copy of the Reference Diskette. You can't use the original Reference Diskette here because it is permanently write protected. This is necessary so that the "Set configuration" and "Test the computer" items in the Reference Diskette Main Menu can manage the feature card.

⇨ Press "5."

An information message appears on your screen. If you have a dual diskette system, the message in Figure 75 will appear, which tells you to place the backup copy of the Reference Diskette in drive "A" and the Option Diskette in drive "B." If you have a single diskette drive system, the message will tell you to swap between the New Option Diskette and the Reference Diskette until all copying is complete. If you are actually going to copy an option diskette, follow the instructions that appear on your screen until a message indicates that the copying is complete. The Reference Diskette is then ready to configure and test the new feature card.

⇨ Press the "Esc" key to get back to the Reference Diskette Main Menu.

Figure 75. Message that appears when you start to copy an option diskette in a dual drive system.

Menu Option 6: Move the Computer

This menu option prepares Model 50/60's fixed disk(s) for relocation. Fixed disks consist of a magnetic disk and a reading head that senses the information stored on the magnetic disk surface. While the spinning disk surface is extremely close to the reading head, there is no actual contact between the disk surface and the reading head. When the computer is turned off for the move, the head will remain close to the disk surface. Due to this closeness, a mechanical shock could cause the head to hit the disk surface. This is called a **head crash** and may result in the loss of stored information.

To reduce the chances of a head crash, a program is provided that positions the head in a safety zone away from any information. This is known as *parking the head* of the fixed disk. While a sufficiently large shock may still damage Model 50/60's fixed disks, the chances of damage are reduced when the head is parked. Since the probability of shocking the fixed disk is higher when the system is being relocated, it is strongly recommended that the heads be parked immediately prior to turning off the computer for the move. The head is automatically unparked when you begin to use your computer again, making normal operation possible. The fixed disks used in Model 80 automatically park themselves, which is why this menu item was not provided on the Model 80 Reference Diskette.

To park the fixed disk in Model 50/60 computers:

⇨ Press "6."

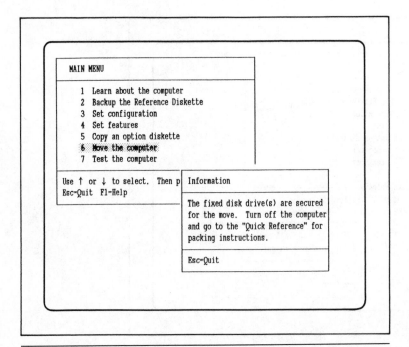

Figure 76. Message indicating that the fixed disks have been parked.

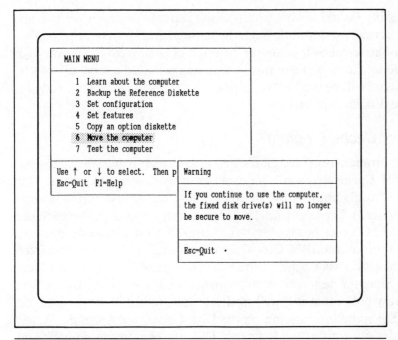

Figure 77. Warning message indicating the fixed disks will no longer be parked if you continue operation.

You are presented with an information window notifying you that the fixed disk(s) have been parked, as shown in Figure 76. If we were actually moving, you would now turn off the computer and go to the Quick Reference manual for packing instructions. Since we are not actually moving the computer in our exercise, we will continue:

⇨ Press the "Esc" key.

A warning message (Figure 77) appears, stating that if you continue operation, the fixed disk(s) will no longer be parked and therefore will not be ready for moving. Since we are not moving the computer, this is all right.

⇨ Press the "Esc" key again.

You are now back to the Reference Diskette Main Menu.

Menu Option 7: Test the Computer

This last menu option executes the diagnostic programs that reside on the Reference Diskette. These programs conduct a physical examination of the Model 50/60/80 hardware elements, as does the POST program discussed earlier in the chapter. The exam performed by this testing program, however, is more complete than the one performed by POST and also allows you to directly control the testing. The user will typically conduct this testing to isolate some type of problem he or she is experiencing.

Since this testing should rarely be needed and can take quite a while to complete, we will not actually step you through the testing here. However, the instructions provided on the screen will guide you through the complete test if you wish to do so. If you do intend to perform this testing, you will need a scratch 1.44 MB diskette. This diskette will be used in the testing of the diskette drives, and any information on the diskette will be lost.

What Is the Disk Cache Program?

There is one other program provided on the Reference Diskette that we will discuss here. The **IBM Disk Cache** program is provided on every Reference Diskette. This program can significantly improve the speed of your fixed disk(s) during normal operation (see Chapter 1). The Disk Cache program does not appear in the Reference Diskette menus and can't even be seen on the diskette's directory. However, it is easy to install after you install the IBM Disk Operating System (DOS) on your fixed disk. Refer to "The IBM Disk Cache" instruction sheet provided with your Model 50/60/80 system. Since the performance improvements afforded by the Disk Cache program can be very noticeable, it is well worth the time to install the program on your fixed disk. For more information on the Disk Cache, see Appendix A.

This concludes our tour of the Reference Diskette. Feel free to go back and review any area of the Reference Diskette. Use the help messages, the "F1" key, to get further information on any topic.

THE REAL SOFTWARE—A MODEL

The term software is analogous to the term "publication." Newspapers are a category of publication. Annual reports, novels, and Who's Who directories are some other categories of publications. These different categories fill very different needs. The

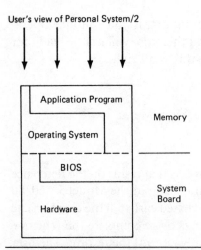

Figure 78. Conceptual software model of Model 50/60/80's basic software structure. The three layers of the software model work together to perform useful work for the user.

same situation exists with software. The different categories of software are diverse in function and purpose. We have just explored some special-purpose programs provided with all Model 50/60/80 computers. These programs, however, do not allow you to perform useful work.

The basic categories of real software used to perform useful work can be understood through the simple software model shown in Figure 78. There are three basic categories or software layers commonly used with Model 50/60/80 computers: the **application program** layer, the **operating system** layer, and the **Basic Input Output System (BIOS)** layer. While each software layer performs a completely different job, all three work closely together to perform useful work for the user. While there are some special-purpose programs that don't fit neatly into any of the three categories, the majority of software commonly used to perform business tasks does. Later chapters focus on the application and operating system layers. For now, let's briefly look at each of the three layers in our software model.

Application Programs

The top software layer in the software model is the application program layer, highlighted in Figure 79. The programs in this layer apply Model 50/60/80 to specific tasks such as word processing and communications. Thus they are called application programs. They actually perform the task the user purchased the computer for while the other two layers play important support roles.

The "User's View" arrows in Figure 79 indicate that the user usually interacts with the application program layer and less frequently interacts with the operating system. By working closely with the other software layers, the application program processes the various keystrokes made by the user and responds by displaying information on the computer's display or some other output device.

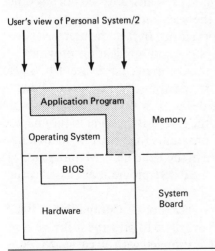

Figure 79. The application program software layer of the software model. It is the application program that defines the particular task the computer is performing for the user.

As we will see later in the chapter, Model 50/60/80 can execute most of the application programs written for PCs. This allows Model 50/60/80 users to capitalize on the thousands of application programs available for PCs today. There is an application program that can help the user with just about anything he or she wishes to do. Do you want a program that computes the number of eggs needed to completely fill a swimming pool? Look around, it may be hard to find, but it probably exists. Some more common functions that application programs perform in the business environment are accounting, financial modeling, word processing, data base management, communications, and computer graphics. Chapter 4 is devoted to discussing various application programs.

Operating Systems

The next layer in our software model is called the operating system, highlighted in Figure 80. The operating system must manage the hardware resources of the computer system and perform tasks under the control of application programs and keyboard commands typed by the user. The application program can rely on the operating system to perform many of the detailed housekeeping tasks associated with the internal workings of the computer. Thus, the operating system is said to provide the environment in which application programs execute. Operating systems also accept commands directly from the user to perform such tasks as formatting diskettes and clearing the screen. Model 50/60/80 users have a choice of operating systems as we will see in Chapter 5.

BIOS

The third and final layer of software in our software model is called the **Basic Input Output System** layer, highlighted in Figure 81. BIOS is a set of specialized programs that, unlike application programs or operating systems, are used only by other programs. BIOS never interacts directly with the user and exists only to help application programs and operating systems perform tasks. In fact, the user never even knows it's there. BIOS assists the operating system and application programs in performing tasks directly involving details of the computer hardware. BIOS also shields a computer program from the hardware specifics of computers, allowing these specifics to evolve as new computers are designed without causing software compatibility problems. We will further discuss the role of BIOS later in the chapter.

Unlike operating systems or application programs that must be loaded into memory from disk, BIOS is permanently stored in the Read Only Memory (ROM) on Model 50/60/80 System Boards along with the POST program discussed earlier in the chapter.

Model 50/60/80 computers are the first to have both a **Compatibility BIOS** and an **Advanced BIOS.** Compatibility BIOS is provided to preserve software compatibility with PCs. This is the same type of BIOS supplied with all earlier PC computers.

Advanced BIOS is a new and completely independent set of programs also stored in Model 50/60/80's ROM. Advanced BIOS sets a new standard for operating

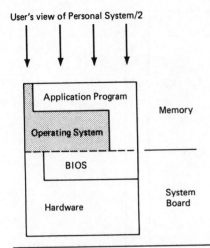

Figure 80. The operating system software layer of the software model. The operating system provides the environment in which the application programs run.

system programmers and provides specific support for the multi-application environment discussed in Chapter 5.

How the Layers Work Together

In order to get a feel for how these three software layers work together to perform tasks for the user, let's quickly trace a typical series of events that might occur when you strike a key during a computer session.

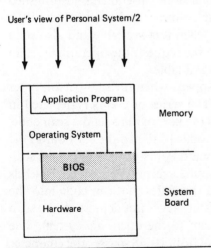

Figure 81. The BIOS software layer of the software model. BIOS directly controls the hardware elements of Model 50/60/80 and shields application programs and operating systems from hardware details.

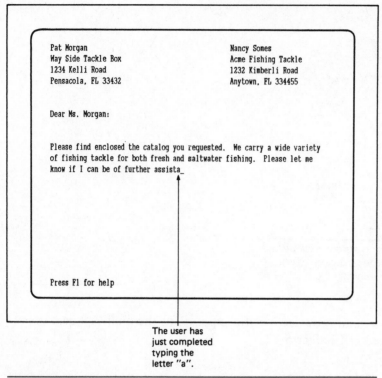

Press F1 for help

The user has
just completed
typing the
letter "a".

Figure 82. Salesperson typing a memo using a word processing application program. The salesperson is about to strike the "n" key on the keyboard, which is the next letter in the word "assistance."

In our example depicted in Figure 82, a salesperson is using a word processing program to type a memo to a prospective customer. Here is what the various software layers are doing: The word processing application program has just finished processing the latest letter typed, an "a" in our example, and has instructed the operating system to provide the next keystroke when it is available and also send the keystroke to the display. In compliance with the request, the operating system asks BIOS to provide the next keystroke when available.

Now that the stage is set, let's see what happens when the salesperson types the next letter, "n," in the word "assistance." The series of events is depicted in Figure 83. The depression of the "n" key causes the keyboard to send a **scan code,** corresponding to the depressed key, over the keyboard cable to the Keyboard Port on the Model 50/60/80 System Board. The Keyboard Port signals BIOS that a scan code has been received. The keyboard BIOS routine accepts the scan code, sends an acknowledgment back to the keyboard, and translates the scan code into the intended meaning. Since BIOS can tell that the shift key is not depressed, the scan code is interpreted as the lowercase "n" and sent to the operating system. The operating system accepts the translated keystroke from BIOS, passes the character to the word processing program, and then sends the character to the user's display (Figure 84). The word processing program then tells the operating system to monitor for the next keystroke, and it starts all over again.

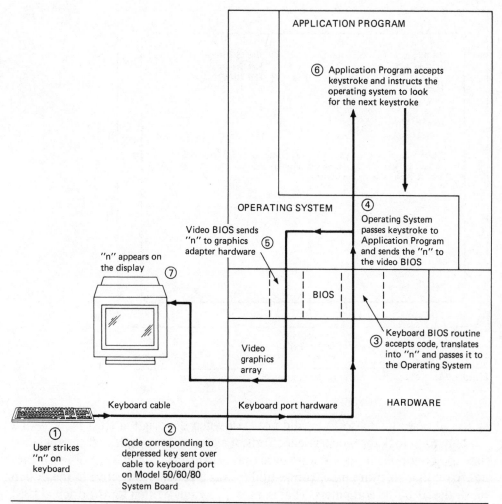

Figure 83. Flow of a typical keystroke through the software layers in our software model.

For simplicity, I have glossed over many of the detailed steps that the computer must perform simply to interpret and display a single keystroke. As complicated as this process may be, computers easily perform these steps in small fractions of a second. You can begin to get a feel for the speed at which computers operate.

Similar but more complicated cooperation among the three software layers occurs for most functions performed by the computer, such as reading or writing a file on a disk, communicating over the Async Port, and so forth.

SOFTWARE COMPATIBILITY—WILL PC PROGRAMS WORK?

The popularity enjoyed by PCs is largely a result of the wide variety of programs that have been developed for these computers. The flexibility afforded by virtue of this large and diverse software base allows PCs to fill many different needs. Of

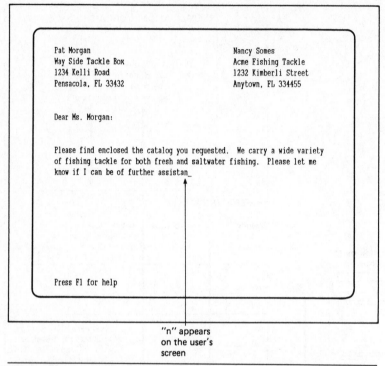

Figure 84. Salesperson's computer screen after typing the "n".

course, this sea of PC software did not exist when the original IBM PC was first announced. It took the independent efforts of a great many people over several years' time to develop the large software base that exists today for PCs. In order to capitalize on that software base, compatibility was a primary objective in the design of Model 50/60/80 computers. That is, most programs written for the original IBM PC will run on Model 50/60/80 computers. While many things were changed in Model 50/60/80 computers, they still possess a high degree of software compatibility with PCs.

What Is Meant by "PC Compatibility"?

Computers that can execute most programs originally written for PCs are said to be **PC compatible.** Notice the definition says *most* programs. The changes in hardware components, speed, or architectures necessary to evolve computers to new levels of performance may introduce some level of incompatibility.

It is important to understand that of the three software layers in our software model, compatibility with programs in the application programs layer is important. Why? First of all, application programs typically represent the lion's share of a user's software investment. Further, being forced to abandon an application program due to incompatibilities may make the user throw away whatever data and training/experience that has accumulated with the application program—both of which can be substantial. Some users have developed custom application programs at considerable cost in development time and money. Incompatibility at the application program level would render these programs useless. Finally, and perhaps most importantly, application layer compatibility allows Model 50/60/80 users to select from the thousands of application programs that have appeared for PCs.

What about the operating system and BIOS layers? Maintaining compatibility with earlier versions of operating system software is not as important for several reasons. Operating systems typically represent only a small fraction of the user's software investment. Further, it is usually necessary to purchase a new version of a given operating system when migrating to a new computer in order to fully enjoy the new hardware features. For example, the Disk Operating System 3.3 (DOS 3.3) is a new version of the existing DOS operating system enhanced to support Model 50/60/80's new 1.44 MB diskette drives among other things. Of course the user is automatically supplied with a new BIOS layer in Model 50/60/80's ROM that fully supports the new hardware while maintaining the important software compatibility layer.

What Affects "Compatibility"?

Given the importance of PC compatibility at the application program level, what was required to maintain this compatibility in Model 50/60/80? Basically, the application must be presented with the same view of the computer system as earlier PCs. That is, the **Application Program Interface (API)** presented by Model 50/60/80 computers must be the same as that of the earlier PCs. This API consists of multiple components, as shown in Figure 85. It consists of all elements that interact with the application program. From the figure we can see that the application program interacts with both the operating system and BIOS layers. These comprise the major parts of the API that must be preserved to maintain software compatibility with application programs. Model 50/60/80 operating systems maintain a high degree of compatibility with earlier DOS releases. We will examine compatibility issues of the operating systems more closely in Chapter 5. Model 50/60/80's BIOS also maintains compatibility with earlier versions of BIOS.

Through examination of our software model, it seems that maintaining the operating system and BIOS compatibility is all that is necessary to maintain compatibility at the application program level. In reality, however, application programs don't always follow the conventional interaction illustrated in our software model. Instead, these application programs bypass the other software layers and interact directly with the hardware elements of the computer. This interaction is depicted in Figure 86. When an application program interacts directly with the hardware, the hardware becomes part of the API and therefore must be precisely preserved to maintain compatibility with that application program. Why do application programmers choose to manipulate the hardware elements directly? Often, direct interaction with hardware elements can enhance speed or help implement copy pro-

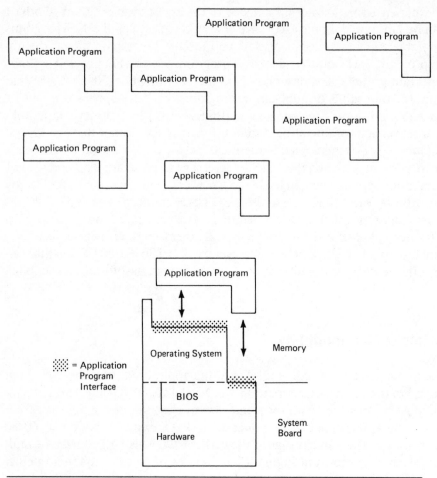

Figure 85. The operating system and BIOS are the major elements of the Application Program Interface.

tection. To maintain compatibility with application programs that directly manipulate the hardware, Model 50/60/80 computers have preserved critical hardware interfaces as they existed in PCs. These include graphics circuitry registers, Async Port registers, and many other hardware details.

One final compatibility issue revolves around the 3.5-inch diskette used in Model 50/60/80. Up until the introduction of the IBM PC Convertible in 1986, PCs used 5.25-inch diskettes exclusively, so of course programs for PCs were distributed on 5.25-inch media. Model 50/60/80 computers use 3.5-inch diskette drives. While many programs are now available on 3.5-inch media, there are still some programs that aren't. Further, the programs that users have already purchased for earlier PCs may be on 5.25-inch diskettes. Finally, the data and programs created by the PC user may be on 5.25-inch diskettes. Clearly, there is a need for a way to transfer programs and data from 5.25-inch diskettes to 3.5-inch diskettes. Similarly, the user may have a need to transfer programs and data from the fixed disks of PCs to a

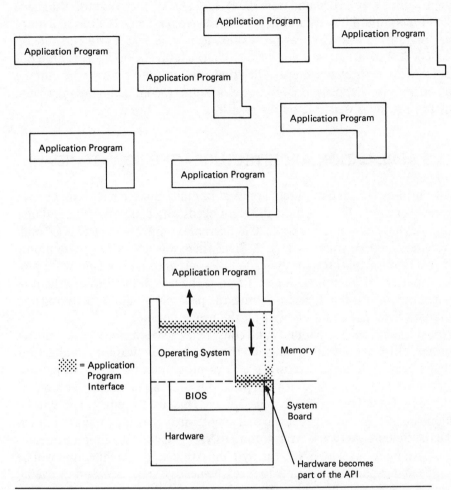

Figure 86. When an application program interacts directly with hardware elements, the hardware also becomes part of the API.

Model 50/60/80. There are many ways to transfer programs and data from PCs to Model 50/60/80. The method you will use will depend on your particular computer environment and the nature of the information (programs or data) you must transfer. Chapter 7 covers the various methods available to handle the transition from 5.25-inch diskettes to 3.5-inch diskettes.

Which Programs Are and Are Not Compatible?

A general discussion of compatibility is good for understanding the issues, but business users want to know exactly which programs are and are not compatible with Model 50/60/80. The best way to determine Model 50/60/80's compatibility with a given application program is through exhaustively executing the program under a variety of conditions. This is exactly what was done for many popular application programs (both IBM and non-IBM). For a list of the programs that have been tested for compatibility as of this writing, see Appendix D. If a particular application program does not appear in this list, it may be that it will run fine on Model 50/60/80 and simply was not included in the test. The best way to find out is to contact the software publisher of the application of interest or try to run the program and see what happens. Beware, however; subtle incompatibilities may cause problems not readily observable by the user in a casual check.

SYSTEMS APPLICATION ARCHITECTURE—THE NEW STANDARD

In today's business world, computers are used in many diverse environments for a wide variety of tasks. To meet these different needs, three major IBM computer system families have evolved: System/370 mainframe computers, System/3X mid-sized computers, and Personal System/2. Since there was no single programming standard that covered all three computer families, programmers would write programs for a particular computer family. Later, if the user wanted to use the program on a computer from a different family, the program would have to undergo major changes before it could be used on the new computer.

To provide program compatibility and consistency across its three main families of computers, IBM has recently published the **Systems Application Architecture.** The Systems Application Architecture is a set of programming rules that provide a base for the development of application programs that can be used on computers from all three families: System/370, System/3X, and Personal System/2. The Systems Application Architecture is the beginning of a long-term application program strategy much like the **Systems Network Architecture (SNA),** which is the long-term communications strategy. As with SNA, the Systems Application Architecture will be implemented and expanded over time to meet the needs of the users and its overall goal—consistency across the major IBM computer families.

When a program conforms to the Systems Application Architecture, three nice things happen:

> **Program portability:** An application program conforming to the Systems Application Architecture can be easily moved across family boundaries (e.g., from a Model 50/60/80 to a System/370 mainframe) with only minor changes. This allows the user to migrate his or her favorite application programs to larger (or smaller) computers as business needs change. Further, a single application program can be used on multiple types of computers that may be found in a single business, bringing common function to all users. Another advantage of program portability is that programmers who follow the conventions of the Systems Application Architecture can offer their programs to users of computers in all three families. This gives users a wider variety of programs from which to choose.
>
> **Communication between programs:** By following the Systems Application Architecture communications conventions, one Systems Applica-

tion Architecture program can communicate directly with other Systems Application Architecture programs running on different computer systems. In other words, the programs running in different families of computers in a network can cooperate directly with one another, providing for a sophisticated computer environment.

User interface consistency: It takes time for a user to learn to use a given application program. Not only must the user understand the basic function provided (e.g., spreadsheet or database) but he or she must also learn the details of interacting with specific programs. This includes user interface details, like function key definitions, how to select a menu item or call up help information, and where commands appear on the screen. The Systems Application Architecture defines standards for these items and many other user interface details. The goal of these user interface standards is to allow for transfer of learning, ease of learning, and ease of use across programs for all three major computer families.

Some of Model 50/60/80's operating systems participate in the Systems Application Architecture, providing a base for the development of application programs conforming to the Systems Application Architecture.

Application Programs

In the last chapter we saw that there are three basic software layers in Model 50/60/80 computers that cooperate to perform useful work for the user. This chapter concentrates on the top layer of the model—the application programs. Application programs actually apply Model 50/60/80's computational power to a particular business task. This chapter discusses the difference between prewritten and custom application programs. It covers the five major functions provided by business application programs and what Model 50/60/80 features apply to each. Finally, the all-important relationship between the application program and the operating system is discussed.

This chapter is by no means a consumers' guide to application programs. Comprehensive coverage of the thousands of business application program products available today would fill many books and would quickly become obsolete. Instead, this chapter provides a general discussion of topics to consider when planning your application program strategy.

APPLICATION PROGRAM ALTERNATIVES

There are two basic alternatives when acquiring application programs to fill your business needs:

- □ Prewritten application programs
- □ Custom application programs

Prewritten application programs are offered as complete off-the-shelf products by various software publishers. Custom application programs are not off-the-shelf products; rather, they are specially developed to the exact specifications defined by a particular customer. Let's examine each of these alternatives more closely.

Prewritten Application Programs

Today's prewritten application programs range from simple programs that concentrate on a very specific task to powerful and very complex groups of programs designed to work together. They perform a myriad of functions as diverse as the environments in which you find computers today.

Despite this diversity, most of the application programs commonly found in business are an implementation or combination of five basic functions that I call the **Big Five**:

1. Word Processing
2. Spreadsheets
3. Data Base Management
4. Business & Presentation Graphics
5. Communications

There are many prewritten application programs that are direct and general implementations of these Big Five functions, resulting in tools that are more flexible than a pencil and paper. Other prewritten applications combine specialized implementations of the Big Five functions, resulting in programs more tailored to the specific needs of a business or industry such as accounting (data base), project scheduling (data base and graphics), and so forth.

Let's examine the Big Five and how Model 50/60/80 computers fill each application need.

Word Processing

Word processing application programs allow Model 50/60/80 computers to generate virtually any kind of document. The user types documents in on the keyboard in much the same way as with a typewriter. Since the document is temporarily stored in memory, it can be easily modified.

Basic capabilities found in even the simplest word processing program include changing, inserting, moving, and deleting text. Today's word processing programs offer other important features such as spell checking, grammar checking, automatic generation of tables of contents, page numbers, and indexes. Still more advanced word processing programs provide for **desktop publishing,** which allows you to combine text and graphics in documents and print "camera ready" results on a high quality printer. The advantages of word processing over manual methods, plus the common need to create documents, has made word processing one of the most popular applications in the business environment.

Model 50/60/80 along with a good word processing application program will quickly spoil anyone used to a typewriter and rival the conventional word processing systems. First of all, the Video Graphics Array provided with every Model 50/60/80 system generates superior alphanumeric characters that are easier to read than those of earlier PCs. The Video Graphics Array also allows for custom type styles, or custom character sets, providing more flexibility. The antiglare screen on all Model 50/60/80 displays is also easier on the eyes during the long hours often associated with word processing. The Enhanced Keyboard is designed for maximum typing ease and efficiency.

After you finish with a document, you can store it on the standard fixed disk or a diskette. The 1.44 MB diskettes used by Model 50/60/80 can hold over 750 double-spaced pages of text and fit in your shirt pocket or purse, providing for easy transport of long documents. The various letter quality printers supported by Model 50/60/80 computers generate clear, crisp documents.

Spreadsheets

Computers were originally developed to do numerical calculations. An extremely popular way of working with numbers on Model 50/60/80 computers is through spreadsheet application programs. These are programs that allow you to enter numbers and equations in a free-form manner. Virtually any calculations you can do on a sheet of paper can be done automatically through the use of a spreadsheet program. Common applications of spreadsheet models include financial analysis, sales monitoring, and forecasting. Through these mathematical models, "what if" questions are quickly answered by changing the parameters (cells) in the model and watching the effects of the change ripple through the entire spreadsheet. Spreadsheets were quick to catch on in the PC marketplace because the blackboard format employed by these programs is very familiar and immediately useful to even novice users.

The large memory capabilities available on Model 50/60/80 computers and their operating systems allow for the construction of extremely complex and powerful spreadsheet models. The improved performance of Model 50/60/80 computers will speed up the many calculations ("recalc"s) associated with large spreadsheet models. The Math Co-processor option available for Model 50/60/80 computers can speed up these calculations even more. Some spreadsheet application programs can take advantage of Model 50/60/80's improved graphics capability to generate high quality graphs.

Data Base Management

In order to deal with large amounts of information efficiently, it is necessary to organize the information in a uniform manner. For example, the information in a telephone book is organized into an alphabetical list of names, addresses, and telephone numbers. If you have ever lifted a Manhatten telephone book, you know that phone books can contain a fair amount of information.

Computers also require information to be organized in some fashion. Data Base Management application programs are the major tool for organizing large amounts of information through computers. Data base managers typically organize information into **files, records,** and **fields.** Don't be intimidated by the words. This is exactly how the information in a phone book is structured. Figure 87 shows a sample telephone book listing and the corresponding computer data base struc-

(a) Information organized in a telephone book		
Telephone book		
(Name)	(Address)	(Phone number)
Packar J. C.	1012 SE 45 St-----	654-8499
Packer O. R.	244 W 13th St-----	878-2443
Pagano B. R.	667 NW 83rd St----	655-0097
⋮		

	(b) Information organized by a data base application program		
	Computer data base file		
	"Name" field	"Address" field	"Phone number" field
Record 1	Packar J. C.	1012 SE 45 St	654-8499
Record 2	Packer O. R.	244 W 13th St	878-2443
Record 3	Pagano B. R.	667 NW 83rd St	655-0097
	⋮		

Figure 87. (a) The information structure used in a telephone book. (b) The same information organized into a data base structure. In order to manipulate large amounts of information efficiently, it is necessary first to organize the information into a consistent format. The organization used by data base application programs is not unlike that used in a telephone book.

ture. The phone book itself is analogous to a file or set of information, also called a **data base.** The information about one person in the phone book would be analogous to a record. The records contain the information for a given entry and all records contain the same information about its respective entry. In this case, a record would contain the name, address, and phone number of a person. Each of these three items would be analogous to a field within a record. For example, the address part of a phone book entry would be called the "address field."

Manually looking up information in a phone book quickly becomes fatiguing. The same is true for manually manipulating any large body of information. Once the information is entered into a data base application program, however, it can be retrieved quickly and easily. Data bases can contain information about a store's inventory, a library's books, personnel records, medical records, or virtually any other type of information. Organizations such as banks, airlines, and insurance companies commonly use extremely large data bases shared by many users. Office workers and executives may use data base application programs to maintain personal telephone books and appointment calendars. Many data base application programs also provide a complete programming language that allows users to customize their data base environments.

The fixed disks standard with Model 50/60/80 computers provide enough storage for the construction of large data bases. For comparison, the 20 MB fixed disk with Model 50 can hold a name/address data base of about 300,000 names and the 70 MB fixed disk with Model 60 can hold over 1 million names and addresses. With the maximum 230 MB of fixed disk storage on a Model 80, you can store over 240 million names and addresses.

The improved performance afforded by the Disk Cache program provided with every Model 50/60/80 computer helps significantly speed up data base activities.

Graphics

Since Neanderthal times, man has drawn images to present and interpret information. Images are native to humans and thus are both enjoyable and powerful communication devices. The greater the amount of information to be conveyed, the greater the need for graphic representations. It is no surprise then that business relies heavily on images to convey information to customers, employees, management, and so on. With the increased use of computers, it is also no surprise that computer generated images, or computer graphics, are common in today's business environment.

Business graphics application programs provide the user with a tool to construct a computer image. These programs vary widely in price and function. Some products accept numerical information from the user and create representative line graphs, bar charts, and pie charts. Others provide the user with a free-form drawing tool with the limitations being only those of the user's imagination. They may have predefined libraries of images such as animals, airplanes, ships, symbols, and state and country outlines. Once an image is defined, it can be saved on disk, printed, or photographed to make full color slide presentations. Some programs can sequence through a series of images and provide automated presentations right on the computer screen.

The Video Graphics Array (VGA) provided with every Model 50/60/80 computer along with the family of displays provide high quality graphics capability. A 320 × 200 PEL image with up to 256 colors can be created. The 256 colors can be selected from over 256,000 available colors. This is useful in presentations when showing a photo-like image of a product. If more complex graphics is required, a 640 × 480 PEL image can be generated with up to 16 colors. This higher resolution can be useful for complex line graphs. The lines generated by the VGA are smoother (less stair-stepped) than those generated by earlier PCs. Further, VGA images have a square aspect ratio, which means that if you rotate the image, the proportions of the image will not be distorted. With the addition of the Color Display 8514 and the Display Adapter 8514/A, even more complex graphics are possible. The 8514 Display and adapter can generate a 1024 × 768 PEL image with 256 colors. This combination of high resolution and many colors is useful in generating attractive business graphics or the complex images associated with engineering/scientific applications such as computer aided design. The high quality printers and plotters that work with Model 50/60/80 can be used to make hard copies of the graphic images.

Communications

Simply stated, it is the job of the communications application program to move information from one computer to another. You can think of communications as the element that ties the other four of the Big Five together. For example, communications allows documents generated by word processing application programs or images created by graphics application programs to be electronically sent anywhere in the world in just minutes. Since communication application programs often work so closely with the other types of application programs, they are often combined with the others into a single product. For example, a spreadsheet or data base application program may be capable of communicating directly with a larger host computer in order to access the large computer's data base. In this case, the user need not be bothered with the details of communication and may not even know it is occurring.

Model 50/60/80 computers have a family of communications feature cards and application programs that provide improvements in performance and function over their PC counterparts. Chapter 6 is devoted to discussing the communication options and application programs that allow Model 50/60/80 computers to participate in many communications environments.

Variations on the Big Five

Many general purpose application programs have been developed by employing combinations and variations of the Big Five functions to perform various tasks. The first and simplest variation of the Big Five application programs is combining several of the Big Five functions into a single all-in-one application program product. Just like all-in-one food processors and all-in-one pocket knives, all-in-one application programs enjoy widespread popularity. All-in-one application programs, also called **integrated** application programs, can be very useful in most any business environment. There are application programs that combine, for example, the spreadsheet, data base, and graphics programs into a single product. Another approach is to provide a **series** of programs designed to work together. The series approach maintains many of the advantages of integrated programs while allowing the user to purchase only the functions he or she needs.

Series and integrated application programs have some advantages over an equivalent collection of independent application programs. First of all, since all the functions are designed by the same person, the user sees a consistent user interface across the different functions. The user doesn't have to remember the different conventions presented by two independent application programs. This consistent user interface advantage is also provided by independent application programs that conform to the Systems Application Architecture discussed in Chapter 3. Another advantage of series and integrated application programs is that they allow the user to easily move information between the different functions within the package. For example, data generated by the spreadsheet part of the integrated program can be transferred to the graphics part to produce graphs of the information. This data transfer may not be so simple between independent application programs. A disadvantage of integrated applications, however, is that you don't select the individual applications; they are chosen for you by the developer of the integrated application program. For example, if you don't like the word processing part of the integrated package, you can't replace it.

Aside from integrated application programs that are direct combinations of the Big Five, programmers have developed other types of application programs by combining more specialized versions of the Big Five. These combinations of the Big Five applications are designed to perform more specific tasks such as appointment calendaring (data base and graphics) and telephone management (data base and communications).

The prewritten application programs discussed up to this point are of a highly general nature and are able to fill the needs of diverse business environments. They were designed to be as general as possible to cover the largest market possible—an "all things to all people" approach. For example, the same data base application program might be used to fill the needs of a tackle shop and a restaurant.

Sometimes these general purpose programs cannot meet the needs of a specific business or professional environment. In these cases, another type of prewritten application program called a **vertical market** application program may be more desirable. Vertical market refers to a subset of computer users with common and very specific application program needs. For example, a real estate office has different application program needs than a dental practice. Each would benefit by an appropriate prewritten, yet highly specialized vertical market application program. Many software publishers have put a great deal of effort into developing vertical market programs for the PCs. As a result, many highly specific business and professional environments are addressed by vertical market application programs. There are vertical market applications designed for insurance companies, real estate offices, medical practices, construction companies, law practices, churches, auto leasing companies, manufacturing companies, and more. The vertical market program approach may be initially more expensive than the general application program approach, but if the former results in more efficient operation of your business, it will save money in the long run.

Custom Application Programs

Prewritten application programs fit many needs the way a mitten fits a hand. They are relatively inexpensive, flexible, and convenient tools. In some cases, however, the user may find that the fit of their application program must be that of a tight glove. This is especially true in environments where Model 50/60/80 is needed to perform unusual and specific tasks or where there is a need to conform to existing company procedures. In these cases, it is often better to develop **custom** application programs written to your exact specifications.

Custom applications also consist of the Big Five functions described above, especially the data base, graphics, and communications functions, but are tailored to your particular hardware/software environment and conform to your existing company policies and procedures.

Custom application programs are usually written either by a programmer within the company or by an outside consulting firm. In either case, the basic development steps are first to define a software specification that describes what the program will do. Then a preliminary version of the program is written demonstrating the function that will eventually be in the final program. This preliminary version is evaluated by the user and the specification is altered to reflect any needed changes. Lastly, the final program is written and then installed at the user's location. Typically, training will be provided by the developer and any problems are ironed out. Once the user accepts the program, additional support is usually on a fee basis.

Custom application program development is initially more expensive and time consuming than the prewritten application program approach. In many environments, however, this additional expense and time can be recovered by the increased productivity that can result from custom applications that precisely fit the needs of the environment. An additional benefit of custom application programs is their ability to change as your company changes. Getting modifications to prewritten application programs may be more difficult or impossible in some cases.

OPERATING SYSTEM DEPENDENCIES

As you may remember from Chapter 3, there is a great deal of interaction between the application program and the operating system layer. This interaction occurs through the Application Program Interface (API) or boundary between the application program and operating system layers as shown in Figure 88. Due to this interaction, application programs have a dependency on the API provided by a particular operating system. That is, application programs are designed to use the specific API provided by a particular operating system and cannot be executed under a dissimilar operating system without change.

In terms of operating systems dependency, there are four types of application programs of primary interest: DOS application programs, Operating System/2 application programs, family application programs, and AIX application programs.

DOS application programs are those originally designed to run with the popular Disk Operating System (DOS) environment supported since the original IBM PC. Historically, the API provided by DOS has defined the standard for PC Compatibility and the majority of today's PC application programs depend on the classical DOS interface. The DOS API has again been maintained in Model 50/60/80's release of DOS (Version 3.3) so that existing DOS applications will run. The main limitations of DOS application programs are that they must usually run in a maximum memory size of 640 KB. This memory limit is inherent in the design of the original

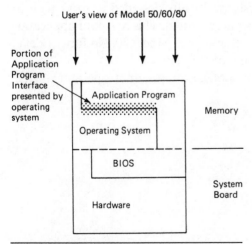

Figure 88. The Application Program Interface (API). Application programs are typically dependent on the specific API presented by an operating system.

PC and still exists in today's DOS environment. Further, DOS applications are primarily designed to allow the user to run only one application program at a time. While there are ways to break both the 640 KB memory limit and run multiple programs in the DOS world as we will see in the next chapter, they are not general solutions to these limitations. Some DOS application programs have been improved to take advantage of new Model 50/60/80 features such as the advanced graphics and the Mouse. Other DOS application programs predated Model 50/60/80 and will provide the same features on either a PC or a Model 50/60/80.

Operating System/2 application programs are named after Operating System/2, which was announced along with Model 50/60/80 computers. Operating System/2 application programs can exploit Model 50/60/80's new features, such as graphics, the Mouse, and so on. Further, Operating System/2 application programs can take advantage of the large 16 MB memory size available in the Operating System/2 environment. This large memory gives the programmer the room to provide richer functions in the application program as well as easier-to-use user interfaces participating in the Systems Application Architecture. In addition, Operating System/2 application programs can use the larger memory to process more data. Finally, the Operating System/2 environment was specifically designed to execute more than one Operating System/2 application program at a time. This ability is called **multi-application** and fits quite naturally into the business environment as we will see in Chapter 5.

Family application programs are those specially designed to work as either a DOS application or an Operating System/2 application. They are written as Operating System/2 applications and fit into Personal System/2's multi-application environment. In order to run as a DOS application, however, the Family application programs must live within the basic limitations of DOS application programs (e.g., 640 KB memory limit). Family application programs can also be written to take advantage of the enhanced graphics and Mouse.

AIX application programs are those specifically designed to work with the Advanced Interactive Executive (AIX) Operating System. This is a multi-application, multi-user operating system for the Personal System/2 Model 80. No further details concerning AIX were available at the time of this writing.

The next chapter will expand on application program/operating system dependencies.

5

Model 50/60/80
Operating Systems

Few areas in personal computers create more confusion and apprehension than the operating system. Never before has the user had more operating system alternatives. This chapter will help remove some of the mystery associated with Model 50/60/80 operating systems. It is designed to familiarize you with operating system topics such as multi-application and Extended Memory and how these concepts apply to the business environment. It will also discuss specific operating system products for Model 50/60/80 computers.

INTRODUCTION TO OPERATING SYSTEM CONCEPTS

The operating system provides the necessary interface that allows the user and application programs to interact with the Model 50/60/80 computers. The user can interact directly with the operating system's user interface to manage files on a disk, prepare a new diskette for use, and initiate application programs, among other things. The operating system also performs tasks directly under the control of the application program without any user assistance. The application program initiates tasks by interacting directly with the operating system through the Application Program Interface (API). The API simplifies the job of the application programmer since he or she need not get involved with the details of hardware interaction. Further, when an application uses the API, it is shielded from changes in the computer hardware as new computers are developed. That is, the operating system can be changed to support new computer hardware while preserving the API, allowing application programs to run on the new computer.

In order to understand the differences between the various Model 50/60/80 operating systems, it is necessary to master a few basic concepts:

- Multi-application
- Real Mode
- Protected Mode

What Is Multi-Application?

Multi-application is the ability of some operating systems to simultaneously run two or more independent application programs. The opposite of multi-application is **single-application,** which means that the computer user must finish using one program before another can be started. Although this is how most early PCs were used, the development of multi-application operating systems is opening new possibilities. We will examine several operating systems for Model 50/60/80 computers that allow various degrees of multi-application.

Many people confuse multi-application with the term **multi-user,** which refers to the ability to share a single computer system between two or more users simultaneously. While a multi-user capability usually implies a multi-application capability, the converse is not true.

How Is Multi-Application Useful?

A multi-application environment offers the user two distinct advantages over a single-application environment:

□ Program switching
□ Background processing

Program switching allows the user to load and start several application programs and instantly move from one to the other with a few keystrokes. The user can also return to the original application program exactly where he or she left off. In order to change applications in a single-application environment, the user must save all work, terminate the current application program, load and start the new application program, and call up the desired file.

Background processing allows the user to initiate a program (e.g., file transfer over communications link, printing a document, etc.) and then switch to another program and start other work while the original program is still performing its tasks unattended. The original program is said to be in the **background**. It will continue to work as long as no user input is required.

Let's look at a typical business environment example to illustrate how multi-application naturally fits in. Meet our typical businessman, Gerald. Gerald is a salesperson for a hardware distributor. He has a Model 50, which he uses for word processing, spreadsheet, data base management, and electronic mail. Gerald's operating system supports multi-application of these four programs.

Gerald comes into work and turns on his Model 50. The system has previously been configured to automatically load and start all four application programs. A menu appears on the screen listing the four application programs that have been started, as shown in Figure 89.

Let's say Gerald decides to compile last month's sales figures using his spreadsheet program. He would select the "Spreadsheet" menu option, immediately bringing the Spreadsheet program from the background to the **foreground.**

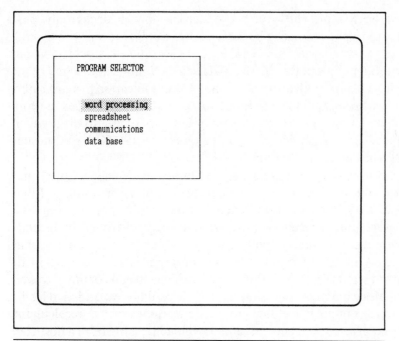

PROGRAM SELECTOR

word processing
spreadsheet
communications
data base

Figure 89. Sample Program Selector used to start, stop, and switch between application programs.

When a program is moved into the foreground, the user can interact with it through the keyboard/Mouse and display in the normal fashion. All of the other application programs are said to be in the background and the user cannot interact with them. Gerald then loads his sales report file and begins compiling this month's figures. A few minutes later, his boss comes in and asks for a preliminary copy of the new sales campaign Gerald had mentioned earlier. Gerald hits a key that places the Spreadsheet program in the background and recalls the application menu. Gerald then selects the "Word Processing" item, bringing his Word Processing program into the foreground. He prints a copy of the sales campaign report for the boss and after some discussion, the boss leaves just as the phone begins to ring. It is the purchasing department, and they want to verify the part number for some bolts Gerald had ordered earlier. Gerald again hits a key, placing the Word Processing program into the background and recalling the application menu. This time Gerald selects the "Data Base" menu item in the list that calls his Data Base Manager program to the foreground. He then queries his data base for information on the particular kind of bolt he ordered. After all questions have been answered, Gerald hangs up and hits a key that places the Data Base program in the background and calls up the application menu. He selects the "Spreadsheet" item and is immediately returned to his sales spreadsheet right where he left off.

The point of this example is to illustrate that the office environment is one in which workers are often interrupted in the middle of one task to perform another. The program swapping capability of multi-application fits naturally into this interrupt driven environment by allowing the user to easily switch back and forth between many application programs as the interruptions occur.

Let's extend the example a little further to examine how the background processing ability of multi-application can be useful. After Gerald is done with the sales figures, he saves the spreadsheet file. Gerald must now send the updated spreadsheet file over a modem link to the district office. Gerald hits a key calling up the application menu. This time, Gerald selects the "Communications" item, calling his Communications program into the foreground. He then establishes the communications link and initiates the transmission of the sales figures to the home office. Since the spreadsheet containing the figures is quite large (512 KB), the transmission will take over an hour at 1200 bps.

If Gerald didn't have multi-application capability, his Model 50 would now be tied up for the duration of this transmission, preventing him from using his Model 50/60/80 for other tasks. However, since Gerald does have multi-application capability, he can place the Communications program into the background by hitting a key. The Communications program will continue unattended until the transmission is complete. While this Communications program is still running in the background, Gerald selects the "Word Processing" menu item and continues to work on his proposed sales campaign. This simple example could be expanded to having additional programs running in the background doing things such as recalculating a large spreadsheet, printing a document, and downloading a file from a host computer.

The program swapping and background processing capabilities available in a multi-application environment fit quite naturally in the business place.

One final note. Since your computer system is running multiple application programs at once, the performance of each individual program will be reduced as compared to a single-application environment. However, program switching and background processing will work to improve the overall productivity of the user.

What Is Real Mode?

Real Mode refers to the environment provided by the 8088 microprocessor used in the original PC. It is called Real Mode because of the characteristics of the 8088 architecture such as straight forward addressing, and no interprocess protection. Real Mode is the definitive IBM PC compatible environment preserved by every PC since the original, including Model 50/60/80 computers. All DOS application programs operate in the Real Mode environment. The main limitations of Real Mode are a maximum memory size of 1 MB (640 KB in the Personal Computer implementation) and a single-application environment emphasis. This means the user typically operates only one application program at a time.

What Is Protected Mode?

Protected Mode refers to the extended architecture environment provided by the 80286 and 80386 microprocessors used in Model 50/60/80 computers as well as the Personal Computer AT and PC/XT 286. It is called Protected Mode because of its ability to prevent one program from interfering with another when more than one program is running simultaneously. Protected Mode also allows a computer to support a very large memory (up to 16 MB for 80286 and 4 GB for 80386). Some Model 50/60/80 operating systems use the protection mechanism and large memory support offered by Protected Mode to provide a powerful multi-application environment. Multi-application provides the capability to execute more than one application program at a time. However, DOS application programs originally written for the PC will not run in Protected Mode unless they have been modified by the programmer.

REAL MODE OPERATING SYSTEMS

Model 50/60/80 computers can be operated in Real Mode to maintain compatibility with earlier PCs. We will discuss three operating environments that allow Model 50/60/80 computers to support Real Mode operation:

- □ IBM Disk Operating System (DOS)
- □ DOS extended with TopView
- □ DOS extended with the 3270 Workstation Program

DOS

The IBM Disk Operating System, commonly called DOS, was the operating system originally offered for the IBM Personal Computer. Since its introduction in 1981, DOS has become widely accepted.

As PCs evolved, DOS was revised to support the enhancements in the computer hardware. While each new version of DOS provided additional functions, compatibility with earlier application programs was maintained. Each version of DOS was numbered to distinguish the different levels. The original DOS was called DOS 1.0.

DOS 3.3 is the entry-level operating system for Model 50/60/80 computers. Earlier DOS versions are not supported by Model 50/60/80 computers. DOS 3.3 provides a PC compatible, single-application environment. It consists of a set of programs designed to perform many diverse hardware housekeeping tasks under the control of either the user or an application program. As the name DOS implies, many of these housekeeping tasks deal with Model 50/60/80's disk system. Other tasks performed by DOS include starting application programs, setting the computer's date and time, sending information to a printer, and managing files.

DOS operates Model 50/60's 80286 and the Model 80's 80386 in Real Mode. In this mode, the 80286/386 microprocessor appears to have the same basic architectural structure as that of the 8088 microprocessor used in the original IBM PC.

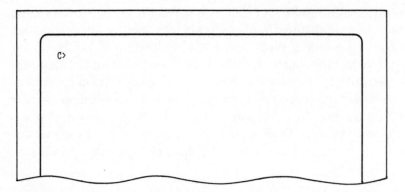

Figure 90. The command drive user interface provided by DOS 3.3. The "C>" is the command prompt from which the user can enter DOS commands or initiate application programs.

The architectural similarities afforded by Real Mode allow Model 50/60/80 (as well as the Personal Computer AT and PC/XT 286) to execute software originally written for the IBM PC.

To initiate DOS tasks, the user types in commands at the DOS command prompt shown in Figure 90. The "C>" indicates that DOS is ready to accept a command from the user. For example, typing "DIR" and pressing "Enter" will cause a list of the files contained on the default drive to be displayed on the computer screen, as shown in Figure 91. This is called the **Directory** of the disk. After all files have been displayed, DOS again presents the "C>" command prompt signifying its readiness to accept the next command. The DOS manual provides comprehensive coverage of all DOS commands available to the user.

DOS 3.3 is functionally compatible with earlier DOS versions. There are, however, three new commands introduced with DOS 3.3: APPEND, FASTOPEN, and CALL. The first two commands provide improved ways to manage disk files. The third command provides an improved way of handling groups of DOS commands.

Still other commands in DOS 3.3 have been enhanced. For example, the BACKUP command supported by previous DOS versions has been improved to format unformatted diskettes automatically during the backup process. DOS 3.3 also has been enhanced to support Model 50/60/80's hardware features such as 1.44 MB diskette drives and large fixed disks.

In addition to performing tasks under direct control of the user, DOS can perform tasks under direct control of an application program. A user can issue DOS commands through keyboard entries. Application programs issue DOS commands through the DOS Application Program Interface (API). This is a defined protocol for passing information directly between the application program and DOS with no user interaction. Often, DOS will subsequently call on the routines of BIOS to affect the desired action. We discussed this interaction between the different software layers in Chapter 3.

The approach to memory management is a large part of the differences between the operating systems that we discuss. Figure 92 shows how DOS 3.3 manages

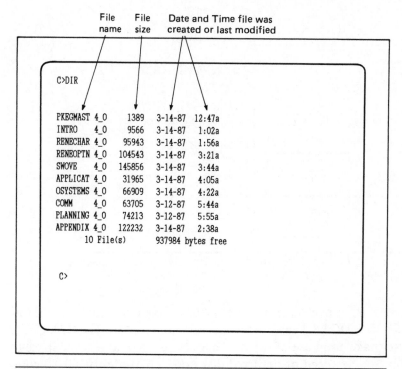

File name	File size	Date and Time file was created or last modified	

```
C>DIR

PKEGMAST 4_0     1389    3-14-87  12:47a
INTRO    4_0     9566    3-14-87   1:02a
RENECHAR 4_0    95943    3-14-87   1:56a
RENEOPTN 4_0   104543    3-14-87   3:21a
SWOVE    4_0   145856    3-14-87   3:44a
APPLICAT 4_0    31965    3-14-87   4:05a
OSYSTEMS 4_0    66909    3-14-87   4:22a
COMM     4_0    63705    3-12-87   5:44a
PLANNING 4_0    74213    3-12-87   5:55a
APPENDIX 4_0   122232    3-14-87   2:38a
         10 File(s)     937984 bytes free


C>
```

Figure 91. The DIR command. The Directory (DIR) command is used to examine the contents of a disk. The names, sizes, and dates of all files contained on the disk are displayed on the screen.

Model 50/60/80's memory. Each byte of memory in Model 50/60/80 resides at a unique **memory address** that distinguishes that byte from all others. The memory address is shown on the scale to the left of the figure. DOS 3.3 itself initially gets loaded into the first part of memory. DOS 3.3 then loads an application program into the next portion of memory. The amount of memory consumed by the application program varies widely. The remaining memory above the application program and below the 640 KB memory address is available for the data to be used by the application program. For example, a memo being generated by a word processing program or a spreadsheet file being manipulated by a spreadsheet program would reside in this area, labeled data space. What about the address range above 640 KB? The system architecture of all PCs is such that the address range from 640 KB to 1 MB is reserved for nonmemory functions such as graphics and BIOS. No user memory can reside in this region. The 1 MB of memory provided as standard on all Model 50/60/80 computers has been divided into two regions, as shown in Figure 92. The first region of memory resides in the 0 to 640 KB address range and the remaining 360 KB of memory starts at the 1 MB address. Together, these two regions of memory comprise the 1 MB of standard memory provided with Model 50/60/80 (640 KB + 360 KB = 1 MB).

What about the memory residing above the 1 MB address? Since DOS 3.3 operates Model 50/60/80 computers exclusively in Real Mode, DOS 3.3 cannot directly use any memory above 1 MB. However, specially written programs including

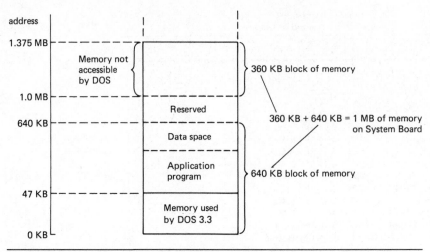

Figure 92. DOS manages Model 50/60/80's memory system. The figure illustrates the organization of the memory in Model 50/60/80 and how it is managed by DOS.

the Disk Cache program provided with Model 50/60/80 computers and the VDISK program provided with DOS 3.3 can use the memory above 1 MB. The Disk Cache program can also make good use of the memory above 1 MB as a work space to significantly improve the speed of the fixed disks used in Model 50/60/80 computers. VDISK allows you to use that memory as if it were a fixed disk, or a **virtual disk.** A virtual disk is a section of memory, usually outside the active 640 KB memory area, that can temporarily store information as if it were a fixed disk. The advantage of a virtual disk over a real fixed disk is that information can be moved between the virtual disk and memory much faster than it can be moved between a real fixed disk and memory. The disadvantage is that you must be sure to save all information on a real disk before you turn off the computer, or all information on the virtual disk will be lost.

Further, extensions to the DOS operating system (some of which are discussed in this chapter) can use the memory above 1 MB as temporary storage areas to help squeeze more programs under the 640 KB ceiling. While these specially written programs are very useful, Protected Mode operating systems are needed to make general use of any memory above 640 KB.

DOS Extended with TopView

TopView is an example of a program that can extend the capabilities of the DOS operating system into the multi-application environment. TopView 1.12 supports the Model 50/60/80 and all of the enhancements in DOS 3.3. It allows you to load and run multiple DOS 3.3 application programs on any Model 50/60/80 computer. You then can switch easily from one program to another (program switching). Top-View also allows certain application programs to continue running unattended in the background (background processing) while you work with another application program in the foreground.

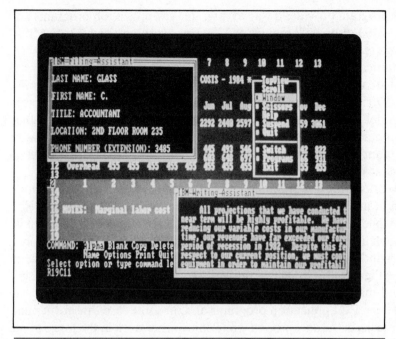

Figure 93. Windowing environment provided by TopView.

TopView lets you divide the screen into sections called windows, shown in Figure 93. Each window can display information about a different application program. TopView lets you transfer text between application programs by copying information from one window to another.

TopView meets your requirements if you can run everything you need to in 640 KB. This means that DOS, TopView, your application programs, and data must all fit in 640 KB of memory. The 640 KB limit can be troublesome for even one business application program and can quickly become a limitation when trying to run multiple application programs. You can run more programs than can fit into 640 KB if you let TopView swap certain programs between fixed disk and memory. While this swapping can significantly reduce performance, the impact can be small if you can use a virtual fixed disk. As mentioned earlier, the VDISK program provided with DOS can turn the memory above 640 KB in your Model 50/60/80 computer into a virtual disk. Even when using a virtual disk, running many large programs simultaneously may stretch TopView to its limits. Since TopView works in Real Mode, there is no built-in protection mechanism that prevents one application program from inadvertently interfering with another. For these reasons, a Protected Mode Operating System may be more desirable in some cases.

DOS Extended with the 3270 Workstation Program

The IBM 3270 Workstation Program can be used to extend the Basic DOS 3.3 functions in the areas of multi-application and communications on Model 50/60/80 computers. This program provides a way to migrate the application programs and functions of the 3270 Personal Computer or 3270 Personal Computer ATs to Model 50/60/80 computers.

The communications capability of the 3270 Workstation Program provides support for local area networks and interacts with a large mainframe computer like the IBM System/370 family. The mainframe communications support allows a properly equipped Model 50/60/80 to emulate a 3270 Display Terminal that is designed for mainframe interaction. In fact, it allows the user to interact with a mainframe as if it were up to four independent terminals, or to interact with four different mainframe computers at once. We will learn more about this in Chapter 6.

The 3270 Workstation Program also provides multi-application capabilities. The user can simultaneously run up to six DOS application programs and two electronic note pads while interacting with mainframe computers. A windowing capability is provided much like that of TopView. In other words, the screen can be divided into sections or windows, each controlled by a PC program or mainframe computer sessions (see Figure 94). This allows the user to simultaneously monitor multiple PC programs and mainframe computer sessions. As with TopView, the user can easily switch between PC application programs and, in some cases, perform unattended computer tasks in the background while doing other work in the foreground.

Since the 3270 Workstation Program operates in Real Mode, it does not provide any protection between the multiple application programs that can be running, and it has the same 640 KB memory size limit to contend with. One way the 3270 Workstation Program can overcome the 640 KB DOS limit is by employing

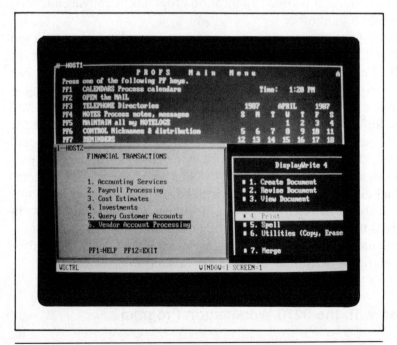

Figure 94. Windowing environment provided by 3270 Workstation Program.

a special memory management technique called **bank switching** to expand the memory limit above the 640 KB limit. The bank switching concept is similar to the program swapping between memory and fixed disk performed by TopView, only the swapping is between active and inactive memory areas. This bank switching allows multiple DOS application programs to be running simultaneously—each thinking they have their own computer. Model 50/60 computers can use the IBM Personal System/2 80286 Expanded Memory Adapter/A discussed in Chapter 2 to increase the memory available to the 3270 Workstation Program above the 640 KB barrier. Since the 3270 Workstation Program takes advantage of the **Virtual 86 Mode** of the 80386, no expanded memory card is necessary in Model 80. The 3270 Workstation Program can perform bank switching using the normal Model 80 memory.

Software provided with the 3270 Workstation Program also allows Model 50/60/80 computers to run application programs specially written to the **Expanded Memory Specification (EMS)** bank switching standard. EMS permits specially written application programs to move blocks of memory in and out of the active 640 KB memory area, allowing dormant portions of programs and data to reside outside the active memory area. This enables an application program to control memory above the 640 KB limit. Application programs not specially written to the EMS cannot make use of this expanded memory capability.

Alternately, the 3270 Workstation Program can use memory on the 80286 Expanded Memory Adapter/A as if it were a high speed fixed disk or virtual disk.

PROTECTED MODE OPERATING SYSTEMS

The full capabilities of Model 50/60/80 computers are not unleashed unless the operating system takes advantage of their Protected Mode capabilities. In Protected Mode, the operating system can exploit large memory sizes and protection schemes to implement a full scale multi-application environment. The cost of these advanced capabilities is a loss of direct compatibility with DOS application programs.

We will cover three operating systems available that allow Model 50/60/80 computers to operate in Protected Mode:

- IBM Operating System/2 (Standard Edition)
- IBM Operating System/2 (Extended Edition)
- IBM Personal System/2 Advanced Interactive Executive

Operating System/2 (Standard Edition)

IBM Operating System/2 (Standard Edition) represents a significant divergence from the traditional DOS. Operating System/2 (OS/2), like DOS, is a set of programs that performs housekeeping tasks based on requests from the user as well as application programs. Unlike DOS, OS/2 can operate Model 50/60/80 computers in Real Mode (called the **DOS Environment**), Protected Mode (called the **OS/2 Environment**), or both simultaneously. While the DOS Environment mimics the DOS 3.3 operating system and thus maintains compatibility with DOS application programs, the OS/2 Environment forfeits DOS compatibility for advanced capabilities. Although OS/2 offers the user complex and sophisticated features, many things have been done to make OS/2 easier to use than earlier operating systems. For example, contextual help and on-line documentation is provided to reduce the need to go to reference manuals when the user needs more information. The initial installation of OS/2 is made easier by the installation program provided.

OS/2 is an initial participant in IBM's Systems Application Architecture discussed in Chapter 3. The Systems Application Architecture is an overall strategy that defines standards in the areas of user interfaces, application program interfaces, and communications methods. It is intended to provide consistency and compatibility across IBM's major product families: System/370, System/3X, and Personal System/2. OS/2 provides a platform for the development of a new generation of application programs consistent with the Systems Application Architecture that exploits large memory and full multi-application. The DOS Environment allows users to run many DOS application programs, which will preserve the user's software investment during the migration to the full OS/2 Environment.

As of this writing, there are two releases of OS/2 (Standard Edition): 1.0 and 1.1. The primary differences between these two releases is in the user interface and the support of graphics. When the user starts OS/2 1.0, he or she is presented with the OS/2 **Program Selector.** This is a menu that allows the user to start, end, or switch between either DOS or OS/2 application programs. The menu of programs is generated from information collected during application program installation. The program selected becomes the foreground program and takes exclusive control of the display.

The ease-of-use features of OS/2 1.1 have again been improved over those of OS/2 1.0. While Version 1.1 provides the same contextual help and on-line documentation features of 1.0, it introduces an improved user interface called the **Presentation Manager.** This improved user interface allows the user to divide the display into windows similar to those in TopView and the 3270 Workstation Program. The window environment provided by OS/2 1.1, however, conforms to SAA, exploits full graphics capability, and is more flexible than the "text-only" window environment provided by TopView and the 3270 Workstation Program. While no photo of the OS/2 1.1 Presentation Manager was available at the time of this writing, Figure 95 shows a Presentation Manager conforming to SAA guidelines.

Each window can be controlled by a separate application program. Alternately, an application program can display multiple windows if appropriate. The user can control the location and size of each window. A **Clipboard** function allows the user to transfer information among application programs by moving the information from one window to another.

OS/2 1.1 also extends the graphics support in its Application Program Interface (API). This allows programmers to write programs for OS/2 that use complex

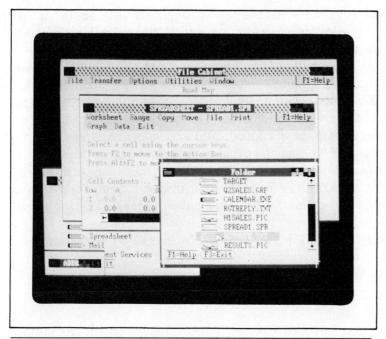

Figure 95. Sample Presentation Manager conforming to SAA guidelines.

graphics. All of the remaining information is true of both versions of OS/2. OS/2 1.1 is a replacement for OS/2 1.0. That is, users who have purchased OS/2 1.0 will be able to get version 1.1 when it becomes available.

Operating System/2's DOS Environment

In order to preserve the user's current software investment, OS/2 provides a way to execute many existing DOS application programs. When OS/2 is operated in its DOS Environment, it acts like DOS 3.3. After the DOS Environment is initiated, the user can perform DOS tasks or start, use, and terminate a DOS application program just as if he or she were using DOS 3.3.

Not all DOS application programs originally written for the PC will work properly with OS/2—especially those that are timing sensitive. Since OS/2 is significantly more complex than DOS, DOS application programs will run slower with OS/2 than with DOS 3.3 on the same computer system. Further, if a DOS application program is switched to the background to bring an OS/2 application program to the foreground, the DOS application program will be suspended by Operating System/2. For these reasons, DOS application programs that have strict time dependencies, such as communications programs, may not work with OS/2's DOS Environment.

Operating System/2 Environment

The OS/2 Environment allows OS/2 to exploit the Protected Mode Extended Memory and inter-program protection features of the 80286 and 80386 microprocessors used in Model 50/60 and Model 80 respectively. The cost of this enhanced capability is a loss of compatibility with DOS application programs originally written for the PC.

The Application Program Interface (API) provided by OS/2 provides a base for developing application programs conforming to the Systems Application Architecture (SAA). While many existing application programs will be migrated to the OS/2 Environment, a new generation of more advanced and functionally richer application programs can also be developed. IBM's open architecture policy and the OS/2 Programmer Tool Kit encourages programmers to embrace the new SAA standard. This tool also allows the programmer to create a Family application program that can run under DOS 3.3 or in the OS/2 Environment. Family application programs, however, cannot exploit the full capabilities of the OS/2 Environment (see Chapter 4).

There are two primary advantages provided by the OS/2 Environment:

- □ Extended Memory
- □ Multi-application

Operating System/2 Extended Memory: The OS/2 Environment exploits the built-in and fully architected capability of the 80286 and 80386 microprocessor called **Extended Memory** to break the 640 KB memory size limit inherent in the DOS Environment. While we have discussed some approaches to breaking the 640 KB limit with DOS 3.3 (i.e., bank switching and information swapping), they are only partial solutions designed to address the shortcomings of the DOS Environment. The Extended Memory feature of the OS/2 Environment provides a consistent and straightforward approach to breaking the 640 KB barrier—once and for all. It allows for use of extended memory for programs, data, multiple application programs, operating systems, and so on. In the OS/2 Environment, the maximum user memory size grows over 24-fold, from the 640 KB maximum of DOS Mode to almost 16 MB.

Figure 96 shows how the extended memory is managed in the OS/2 Environment. OS/2 consumes the first portion of memory. The memory space above OS/2 and below 640 KB is available for Family and OS/2 applications and data if no DOS application programs are to be used. If a DOS application is to be started, some portion of this memory must be reserved for it.

As always, the region from 640 KB to 1 MB is reserved for nonmemory functions and therefore is not usable by application programs or data. However, in the OS/2 Environment, the memory region from 1 MB to nearly 16 MB is accessible by OS/2 and OS/2 application programs.

Why would anyone need or want more than the 640 KB of memory available with DOS 3.3? First of all, if the history of PCs teaches anything, it is that memory size requirements grow quickly. The more memory made available to programmers, the larger and richer their programs can become. The original PC came standard with 16 KB of memory in 1981. At one time, this was thought to be enough memory for many needs. In today's business environment, a PC with 16 KB of memory would

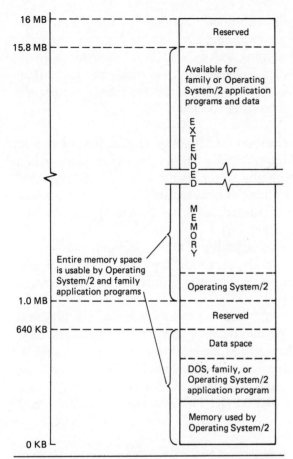

16 MB

15.8 MB

1.0 MB

640 KB

0 KB

Reserved

Available for
family or Operating
System/2 application
programs and data

E
X
T
E
N
D
E
D

M
E
M
O
R
Y

Operating System/2

Reserved

Data space

DOS, family, or
Operating System/2
application program

Memory used by
Operating System/2

Entire memory space
is usable by Operating
System/2 and family
application programs

Figure 96. How Operating System/2 manages Model
50/60/80's memory in Operating System/2 Mode. In
Operating System/2 Mode, application programs can
reside anywhere in the entire 16 MB address space, with
the exception of the reserved areas.

be considered useless. Early in the PC's history, the 640 KB memory ceiling built
into PCs and DOS seemed like an ocean of memory that wouldn't be a limitation
to PC users for a long time to come. That "long time" turned out to be a few short
years because today a growing number of users are finding themselves cramped by
the 640 KB limit. As PCs assume a more important role in the business environment, users demand higher function and easier to use application programs. To
provide more function and easier user interfaces, application programs have con-
tinued to grow in size. The memory requirements of these application programs
and their data areas are bumping up against the 640 KB memory limit more and
more. The problem is greatly compounded if you, as a user, wish to load and run
multiple application programs simultaneously.

One final memory management feature supported by Operating System/2 is
similar to the information swapping performed by TopView. It is called **virtual
memory.** This feature allows Model 50/60/80 to move information quickly between
memory and disk storage "on the fly" in such a way that the application program

seems to have more memory to work with than is actually installed in the computer. However, since this information swapping takes time, performance can be significantly affected by excessive swapping activity. It is therefore better to install enough memory so all programs and data can be held resident simultaneously. Virtual memory is most useful for programs where performance and responsiveness are of limited importance, as in error processing routines.

Operating System/2 Multi-application: Multi-application allows the user to load and start two or more application programs. The user can than easily switch between programs and also allow programs to run unattended in the background while doing other work. Multi-application fits quite naturally into the business environment where workers are often interrupted, requiring them to switch from one task to another.

The need for the program switching capability of multi-application has already been recognized by many DOS users who have purchased TopView, the 3270 Workstation Program, or "Hot-key" application programs that provide their own limited program switching.

OS/2's system approach to multi-application provides program switching and background processing capabilities beyond those of such DOS approaches. First of all, by taking advantage of the Protected Mode hardware features of the 80286 and 80386, the OS/2 Environment can protect one OS/2 application program from interfering with another. This protection is in the form of different "privilege" levels, each with different levels of control over Model 50/60/80 (see Figure 97). OS/2

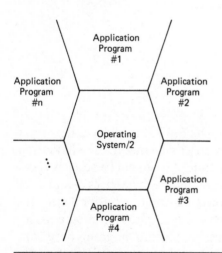

Figure 97. Priority scheme implemented using 80286 and 80386 protection features. Operating System/2 resides at the highest priority level, allowing it the most control over Model 50/60/80's hardware elements. Application programs operate on a subordinate priority level, allowing Operating System/2 to coordinate its activities to prevent interference between separate application programs.

executes at the highest privilege level and watches over all Model 50/60/80 activity. Application programs run at a lower privilege level and are therefore subordinate to OS/2. This priority-based protection scheme provides a more reliable multi-application environment than the DOS approaches discussed.

Another advantage that makes OS/2's multi-application superior to DOS approaches is the Extended Memory capability discussed previously. This allows each OS/2 application program or the combination of all loaded programs to be nearly 16 MB rather than 640 KB as imposed by DOS.

Finally, OS/2 allows the user to set priorities for each program as is done on mainframe computers. This means that the user can allocate the computer's power depending on the needs of each program.

Up to twelve independent OS/2 application programs can be started under OS/2. Alternately, one DOS application program can be started along with up to eleven OS/2 application programs. While the user can interact with only one program at a time, all other OS/2 application programs can continue running in the background as long as no user intervention is required.

Operating System/2 (Extended Edition)

IBM Operating System/2 (Extended Edition release 1.1) is an enhanced version of the IBM Operating System/2 (Standard Edition release 1.1). In addition to providing all the functions of the Standard Edition, the Extended Edition provides extensive capabilities in:

- Communications
- Data Base Management

The Extended Edition is designed to provide a single, flexible solution for users requiring sophisticated communications and data base management capabilities. These capabilities, previously provided by separate application programs, are provided with the Extended Edition operating system. Further, the Extended Edition API's inclusion of these communications and data base features provides a base for the development of sophisticated application programs specifically designed to interact directly with popular mainframe data base application programs. The Extended Edition is also an initial participant in the Systems Application Architecture and offers ease-of-use features similar to those of the Standard Edition. Let's examine the capabilities provided by the Extended Edition that are not included with the Standard Edition.

Communications Capabilities

Through the Enhanced Ease-of-Use Facility, the user can invoke the communications features provided with the Extended Edition. The communication features allow a properly equipped Model 50/60/80 computer to communicate with a variety of different computer systems in a number of different ways. Traditionally, display terminals are used to interact with mainframes and minicomputers. The Extended Edition can make Model 50/60/80 computers appear to be a terminal to the mainframe or minicomputer. In this situation, the Model 50/60/80 computer is "acting like" or emulating a terminal. The Extended Edition allows Model 50/60/80 computers to emulate many popular terminals such as the 3270 Display Terminals, the IBM 3101 and DEC VT100 Asynchronous Display Terminals.

In addition to terminal emulation, the Extended Edition provides support for other communications protocols such as the **Advanced Program-to-Program Communications (APPC)** and the Enhanced Connectivity Facilities (ECF). These protocols allow a Model 50/60/80 computer to interact with larger computers as a peer rather than a subordinate terminal. This allows for the development of more sophisticated communications and productivity applications.

The communications configurations supported by the Extended Edition include SDLC, Async, PC Networks, Token-Ring Networks, and others. Chapter 6 discusses all these communications links and what each offers the business user. The Extended Edition's communications capabilities are only available while operating in Operating System/2 Mode.

Data Base Capabilities

Through the Enhanced Ease-of-Use Facility, the user can initiate the Operating System/2 Extended Edition's data base management capabilities. Data base management is a technique used to organize large quantities of similarly structured information in a computer system. Examples of information commonly found in data bases are telephone directories, inventories, and personnel records.

The Extended Edition's data base management capabilities participate in the Systems Application Architecture (SAA), which makes them similar to data base management application programs used on larger computer systems. The Extended Edition uses the **Structured Query Language (SQL)** familiar to users of the data base application programs used on System/370 mainframes. This is a significant step in achieving the Systems Application Architecture goal of compatibility across the major IBM products. This similarity makes it easier for the user to transfer between data base programs on a mainframe and the Extended Edition data base capabilities on a Model 50/60/80. The Extended Edition provides the foundation from which sophisticated application programs for Model 50/60/80 as well as those for larger computers can cooperate to perform functions for the user. That is, the Extended Edition provides the base from which direct interaction between Model 50/60/80 computers and larger computers can evolve. As with the communications capability, the data base capability of the Extended Edition is only available in the OS/2 Environment.

AIX

IBM has announced its intention to deliver the IBM Personal System/2 Advanced Interactive Executive (AIX). This is a multi-application, multi-user operating system

	DOS	DOS 3.3 w/TopView	3270 Workstation program	Operating System/2 1.0 (Std. Edition)	Operating System/2 1.1 (Std. Edition)	Operating System/2 (Ext. Edition)
Works with 50	yes	yes	yes	yes	yes	yes
Works with 60	yes	yes	yes	yes	yes	yes
Works with 80	yes	yes	yes	yes	yes	yes
Runs DOS programs	yes	yes	yes	many	many	many
Runs Operating System/2 programs	no	no	no	yes	yes	yes
Memory limit	640 KB	640 KB w/swapping	640 KB w/bank switching	16 MB	16 MB	16 MB
Multi-application	no	yes (limited)	yes (limited)	yes	yes	yes
Multi-user	no	no	no	no	no	no
User interface	command prompt	windows (text)	windows (text)	program selector	windows (graphics)	windows (graphics)
On-line help	no	no	no	yes	yes	yes
Built-in communications	no	no	yes	no	no	yes
Built-in data base	no	no	no	no	no	yes

Figure 98. Summary chart comparing the various Model 50/60/80 operating systems covered in this chapter.

for the Personal System/2 Model 80. This product will be a member of the current AIX operating system family developed for the IBM RT Personal Computer. No further details concerning AIX were available at the time of this writing.

OPERATING SYSTEM SUMMARY CHART

Never before has the user had so many operating systems from which to choose. For your convenience, Figure 98 summarizes the differences among the operating systems covered in this chapter. Also, Appendix D provides information on what application programs are compatible with these operating systems.

Model 50/60/80 Communications

Model 50/60/80's standard functions, plus the many communications options and supporting software, provide users with flexibility when configuring Model 50/60/80 for various communications environments. This flexibility, however, can also cause confusion when trying to determine which options and programs are needed for a particular environment. This chapter helps guide you through the different types of business communications available through Model 50/60/80 computers. It examines the most popular types of communications environments and provides a sample configuration for each.

COMPUTER COMMUNICATIONS IN THE OFFICE— AN INTRODUCTION

Just as a woodworker cherishes a solid block of mahogany, businesspeople cherish accurate, timely, and manageable information. If there is one activity that is crucial to any size business, it is the act of communicating information to the proper decision maker. Based on the information available to the decision maker, important choices are made that can have far-reaching effects on the success of the business. Improve communications in a business and you are likely to improve productivity and profitability. Ironically, as a business grows, it becomes more important and more difficult to maintain efficient and accurate communications—the very thing that facilitates business growth in the first place. Communications difficulties grow geometrically with the size of the business.

Today's businesses are quickly finding in computers a communications tool unequaled in significance since Bell invented the telephone. Computers are already commonplace in the business environment, and now there is an increasing emphasis on computer communications. This communication can occur exclusively between two computers or among a group of computers in a communications network.

In addition to the direct benefit of improved business information flow, the growth in computer communications has been fueled further by the equipment sharing possibilities provided through computer communications. For example, a high speed printer can be easily shared among several computer users joined in a communications network. This sharing provides for more efficient usage of the printer and reduces the required investment in printer hardware.

Model 50/60/80 computers represent a powerful communications tool. They support a new family of improved communications adapters and communications software. Understanding how to apply these adapters and their software in useful communications configurations can be confusing. This chapter provides sample configurations of these adapters and supporting software that allow Model 50/60/80 computers to participate in Terminal Emulation and various Local Area Networks.

All of the adapters used in these sample configurations were discussed in Chapter 2. You are encouraged to refer to that chapter for further information on the adapters as necessary.

TERMINAL EMULATION

Mainframe and minicomputers can offer substantial computing resources above and beyond those of Model 50/60/80 computers in terms of processing speed, storage capacity, communications networks, and peripherals. Model 50/60/80 computers, on the other hand, are less expensive, easier to use, and sometimes provide for higher productivity than larger computer systems. Clearly, both Model 50/60/80 computers and larger computers have their place in the business environment. Further, many businesses have found that they can best enjoy both the convenience and economy of Model 50/60/80 computers along with the resources of larger computers by linking the two together. One of the methods used to effect this communication link is to have the Model 50/60/80 computer "act like" or emulate the classical terminals commonly used to interact with the larger computers. This allows the Model 50/60/80 computer to exchange information with the host computer. The Model 50/60/80 computer is said to be performing **terminal emulation.** Since a Model 50/60/80 computer has more capabilities than a terminal, it is often called an **intelligent workstation.**

The reasons behind the advent of terminal emulation are easy to trace. Before PCs, terminals existed for the sole purpose of interacting with mini- and mainframe computers, called conducting a **host computer session.** Then PCs penetrated the business environment and grew to be important tools in their own right. Thus, many computer users needed both a terminal attached to a host and a stand-alone PC to do their job. The computing capability of a PC made it possible to develop hardware adapters and software to allow a PC to emulate and thus replace the classical terminals. While other ways of linking larger computers and PCs exist, terminal emulation is commonplace in the business environment.

When your Model 50/60/80 computer becomes your terminal, three things happen. First, you no longer need a dedicated terminal to interact with the larger computers. The Model 50/60/80 computer can now fill this role in addition to performing its normal Model 50/60/80 computer functions. Second, the host computer and its peripheral equipment become an extension of your Model 50/60/80 computer. For example, the fixed disk space provided by the host can be used as an extension of your Model 50/60/80 computer's local disk storage. You can also print Model 50/60/80 computer documents on the host's printers. The third thing that happens is your Model 50/60/80 computer becomes an extension of the host computer. This means you can transfer information from the host computer to your Model 50/60/80 computer, capture the information on a local disk, and then modify, print, or otherwise manipulate that information with Model 50/60/80 computer application programs unassisted by the host. Manipulating the captured data locally allows you to use your favorite Model 50/60/80 computer application program and enjoy the instant response time associated with a single user computer system. Once the data has been manipulated locally, it can be sent back to the host for storage or other processing.

There are many different types of host computers, each with different types of terminals. Adapter cards and software available for Model 50/60/80 computers support the emulation of many different terminals. Configuring a Model 50/60/80 for terminal emulation for a given host computer environment requires detailed knowledge of the host computer's configuration. The specific device that must be emulated depends on the host computer type, available host interface equipment, host software, and the wiring installed in the building. These factors, along with performance and cost requirements, typically go into selecting the particular terminal to be emulated. We will cover three commonly used host terminals Model 50/60/80 computers can emulate:

- **Asynchronous terminals** are widely used to interact with computers of all sizes.
- **System/3X workstations** are used for IBM System/36 and System/38 interaction.
- **System/370 workstations** are used with the larger IBM System/370 computers.

Asynchronous Terminal Emulation

Asynchronous terminals are relatively simple, low-cost devices consisting of a display and a keyboard. They are used to interact with a wide variety of computers in use today and are called asynchronous after the asynchronous communications method they use to exchange information with the host computer. When a key on the terminal is depressed, an ASCII (American Standard Code for Information Interchange) code is sent to the host computer, representing the key pressed. Each ASCII code, which is one byte in length, is sent across the communications link one at a time and asynchronously, or with no fixed time relationship between them. This

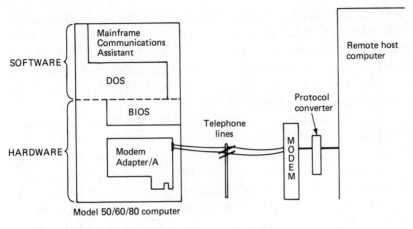

(a) Internal Modem Configuration

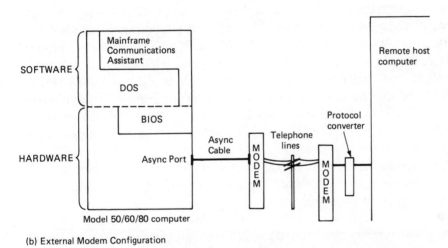

(b) External Modem Configuration

Figure 99. Asynchronous terminal emulation configuration. (a) Configuration with 300/1200 Internal Model/A. (b) Configuration requiring no feature cards and using an external modem. These configurations are useful for interacting with many different types of computer systems including other Model 50/60/80 computers.

one-at-a-time communication method is one of the reasons that asynchronous terminals often transfer information at a rate that is slower overall than the other terminals we cover.

Two Model 50/60/80 configurations for asynchronous terminal emulation are shown in Figure 99. In configuration (a), the Model 50/60/80 has been equipped with 300/1200 Internal Modem/A. This modem is attached directly to the telephone line jack and converts the information inside Model 50/60/80 into a form suitable for telephone line transmission. The computer at the other end of the line must also have a compatible modem that will convert the transmitted information into its original form. Often, the host will also need a protocol converter to change the information from the asynchronous format used by Model 50/60/80 to its "native tongue."

Another alternative is shown in configuration (b). In this implementation, the Model 50/60/80 computer requires no adapter card options, but does require an external modem. The standard Async Port that is provided on the System Board is cabled to an external modem via an external cable. If the standard Async Port is used for, say, a printer, the Dual Async Adapter/A or the Multi-Protocol Adapter/A could be used for this communications link.

The IBM Mainframe Communications Assistant program is one program that can make Model 50/60/80 appear to be the asynchronous terminal being emulated. This means that it must respond to special commands from the host supported by the terminal being emulated. For example, a host computer can send a special command to an IBM 3101 Asynchronous Terminal that will cause the terminal to display information in reverse video. When the Mainframe Communications Assistant is emulating the 3101, it must respond similarly to the same command when received from the host.

Although our sample configurations show a Model 50/60/80 computer communicating with a larger host computer, Model 50/60/80 computers can also communicate with other small computers (such as PCs, PC/XTs, Personal Computer ATs, IBM Convertible, and other Model 50/60/80 computers) through asynchronous terminal emulation. Small computer to small computer configurations can be used as a small-scale document delivery system for transferring computer files between distant Model 50/60/80 computers. Files can contain, for example, a memo, the daily cash register receipts of a retail store, or the orders taken by outbound salespeople sent from a portable computer.

The PC's emulating asynchronous terminals are also widely supported by many service companies that offer access to their host computers for the purpose of **information retrieval** and **electronic mail.**

Information retrieval services offer access to an overwhelming amount of information. These services provide general information such as UPI news stories and stock market quotes as well as highly specialized information. For example, if you are a lawyer, there are services available that allow you to look up information quickly on any and every legal decision in recent times faster than you can say "habeas corpus." Further, you can do patent and trademark searches in a fraction of the normal time. For doctors, there are services that provide information on virtually every subject of bio-medicine from over 3,000 international journals and publications. Virtually any topic you wish to research is covered extensively by one service company or another.

Electronic mail services are also available to Model 50/60/80 computers emulating asynchronous terminals. These services allow you to send computer generated documents electronically, resulting in very fast delivery. Here is basically how they work. Your Model 50/60/80 computer dials the host computer belonging to the service company over the modem link to establish the communications link. You are then prompted by the host to enter your ID and password. Once you have complied with these requests, you can send electronic mail to any other subscriber of the service. Later, when the addressee dials up the company's computer, he will be informed that he has mail in his electronic mailbox. What if you wish to send mail to someone who doesn't own a computer or doesn't subscribe to that particular service? In that case, you would still send your letter via your modem to the service company's host. They would then send your letter to one of their branch offices located near the addressee, print the letter, and hand deliver it.

System/3X Workstation Emulation

The IBM System/3X is a family of midrange computers commonly used as a primary processor in small businesses, or as departmental processors in larger companies (e.g., System/36). The 5250 family of workstations (terminals and printers) is used to interact with System/3X computers. The IBM System 36/38 Workstation Emulation Convenience Kit allows Model 50/60/80 computers to emulate the 5250 devices. The kit comes with the System 36/38 Workstation Emulation Adapter, the Workstation Emulation program, and a cable used to connect to System/3X computers. Figure 100 shows a Model 50/60/80 computer equipped for System/3X Workstation Emulation. Installed in the Model 50/60/80 computers is the System 36/38 Workstation Emulation Adapter. The adapter is attached to the twinaxial cable used in System/3X environments. Our figure shows the Model 50/60/80 locally attached to the System/3X. The same link could also be established over great distances through the 5294 Remote Control Unit.

The Emulation program allows Model 50/60/80 to emulate either a 5250 Workstation Display (e.g., 5292 Model 2) or a 5250 Printer (e.g., 5219). As a workstation display, the Workstation Emulation program gives the user access to the application programs on the System/3X as if he or she were at a 5250 Workstation. As a printer, the program allows the user to print the output of System/3X application programs on a printer attached to Model 50/60/80.

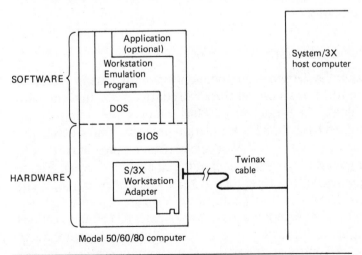

Figure 100. Configuration used for 5250 terminal/printer emulation. This set of hardware and software allows Model 50/60/80 computers to communicate with a System/3X minicomputer.

The Workstation Emulation program's multi-application capabilities allow the Model 50/60/80 computer to interact with the System/3X as if it were four separate terminals or printers. That is, the user can easily switch between up to four different System/3X sessions as well as one DOS program.

System/370 Workstation Emulation

At the high end of IBM's product line lies the IBM System/370 mainframe computers. This size computer system can be the single main processor for large businesses or part of a large computer network that may span the world. The 3270 family of products is a set of display terminals, printers, and control units specifically designed to work with System/370 mainframe computers. Display Terminals consist of a display and a keyboard and allow the user to interact with a System/370 host computer. The printers are used to produce paper copies of the information stored in the mainframe. Control units provide the essential communications links between the System 370 computer and these other devices. Through the proper combination of these devices, many useful System/370 configurations are possible.

Model 50/60/80 computers, equipped with the proper hardware and features, can emulate 3270 display terminals, control units, and printers designed for interaction with System/370 mainframe computers. This allows the user to combine the flexibility of personal computers with the power of System/370 computers. The family of 3270 Emulation programs available for Model 50/60/80 computers allows the user to choose among several levels of capability based on his or her particular needs. We will examine two sample configurations of Model 50/60/80 computers hardware and software that emulate 3270 devices:

- □ Display Terminal Emulation
- □ Control Unit Emulation

3270 Display Terminal Emulation

The IBM 3278 and 3279 Display Terminals are commonly used for System/370 mainframe interaction. Figure 101 shows a Model 50/60/80 configuration that emulates a 3278/79 Display Terminal. The Model 50/60/80 computers are equipped with the 3270 Connection and the IBM PC 3270 Emulation program, Entry Level. (We could also have used the more powerful 3270 Workstation Control program discussed in Chapter 5 in this configuration.) The remainder of the equipment shown in Figure 101 is the same equipment needed to support a real 3278/79 Display Terminal. The control unit, attached to Model 50/60/80 computers via a coaxial cable, supports the attachment of multiple 3278/79 terminals and consolidates all communications traffic for efficient exchanges with the host computer. It is attached, via a modem link, to a Communications Controller that manages the communications link for the System/370 host computer. If the control unit and the System/370 host computer are close to each other (e.g., in the same room), it is possible to attach the

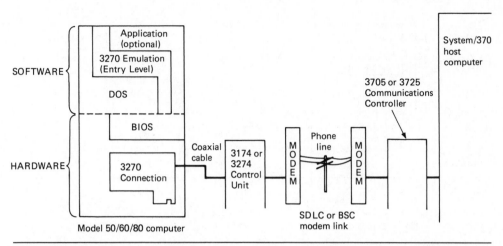

Figure 101. Configuration used for emulating a 3270 terminal. This set of hardware and software allows Model 50/60/80 computers to communicate with System/370 mainframe computers.

control unit directly to the System/370, bypassing the modem link and the Communications Controller. The appropriate features must also be installed on the control unit, Communications Controller, and System/370 computer.

The IBM PC 3270 Emulation program, Entry Level, will allow the Model 50/60/80 user to interact with the host computer as if he or she were at a 3278/79 Display Terminal. The user can execute host application programs, transfer files between Model 50/60/80 computers and the host in both directions, and use host disk space and printers.

The Application Program Interfaces (API) provided by the 3270 Emulation program, Entry Level, allows specially written DOS application programs to work more closely with System/370 programs. Further, an application program completely unrelated to the 3270 Emulation program can be loaded and used while the Emulation program's operation is suspended. This provides a program switching capability between the Emulation program and one other application program.

Control Unit Emulation

With a different configuration, Model 50/60/80 computers can emulate the 3270 terminal, printer, and the control unit, eliminating the need for an external control unit. Figure 102 shows this Model 50/60/80 configuration. The Model 50/60/80 computer is equipped with the Multi-Protocol Adapter/A and the IBM PC 3270 Emulation program (Version 3.0). The Multi-Protocol Communications Adapter in this configuration allows Model 50/60/80 computers to communicate using the Synchronous Data Link Control (SDLC) methods of computer communication. The "Synchronous" in SDLC refers to the fact that information is transmitted in blocks with a fixed relationship between each byte in the block. SDLC is basic to IBM's overall communications network strategy for large computers, called the **System Network Architecture (SNA).** The remainder of the equipment shown in Figure 102 is the same equipment discussed in the previous configuration except

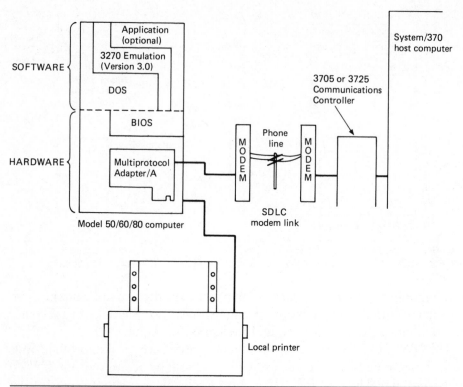

Figure 102. Configuration used for emulating a 3270 Terminal and printer as well as a 3274 Control Unit.

that no control unit is needed, since the Model 50/60/80 computer is now emulating that device as well as a terminal and/or printer. The modems used in the link must be capable of supporting SDLC communications and be compatible with the telephone lines used. There are two types of telephone lines that can be used:

Switched phone lines are those where the user must dial a telephone number to establish the proper connection with the host computer.

Dedicated phone lines, often called "leased lines," are dedicated to a particular connection with a host computer. Dedicated lines can transmit information at higher rates, but also cost more than switched phone lines.

(*Note:* These are the same phone line types used for the configuration in the previous section, 3270 Display Terminal Emulation.)

If Model 50/60/80 computers and the Communications Controller are close to each other (e.g., in the same building), the modem link is not needed. The Communications Controller, however, is needed in this configuration regardless of the distance between Model 50/60/80 computers and the host.

The IBM PC 3270 Emulation program supports all the functions provided by the Entry Level version used in the previous configuration as well as additional functions such as control unit and 3287 printer emulation. With this configuration, the user can execute host application programs, transfer files between Model 50/60/80 computers, and send messages to the host as with the earlier configuration. This configuration can also emulate a 3287 printer so that information in the System/370 mainframe can be printed on the local printer attached to the Model 50/60/80 computer.

LOCAL AREA NETWORKS AND MODEL 50/60/80 COMPUTERS

Just as there is a need for office personnel at any one location to talk frequently with each other, there is value to allowing the computers at a given location to communicate with each other efficiently and easily. We've seen some hardware and software configurations that allow various computers to communicate through terminal emulation. Local Area Networks (LANs) are another way of attaching computer systems together for the purposes of communication. LANs allow the user to electrically attach a group of local computers that might be found in a department, building, or campus. Each computer attached to the LAN is called a network **node** and can share information, programs, and computer equipment with other nodes in the network.

Model 50/60/80 computers, equipped with the proper adapter and software, can participate in any of three LANs:

- □ Baseband IBM PC Network
- □ Broadband IBM PC Network
- □ IBM Token-Ring Network

The IBM PC LAN program can be used with all three types of LANs to provide basic LAN functions. Before we get into the differences between these three networks, let's examine the basic functions provided by the PC LAN program on any LAN.

Basic LAN Functions

The IBM PC Local Area Network (LAN) Program is an extension to the DOS operating system that works with all three networks listed above and provides the basic LAN functions. This program can perform LAN communication directly under control of the user or directly under control of an application program. The user interacts with the PC LAN Program through either commands or the set of menus provided by the program. Through these menus, the user can conduct useful network communications. Application programs can also invoke the network functions provided by the PC LAN Program through the provided Application Program Interface (API). The Application Program Interface that comes with the PC LAN Program allows specially written DOS application programs to conduct network communications without user intervention. An application program completely unrelated to the PC LAN Program can also be used while the PC LAN Program is waiting in the background. When network communications are desired, the application program can be suspended and control given to the PC LAN Program. Again, this provides program swapping between the PC LAN Program and one other application program.

When you first install the PC LAN Program on Model 50/60/80 computers, you can choose to configure the system as either a **workstation node** or a **server node.**

> **A workstation node** can operate as any normal stand-alone Model 50/60/80 computer and can also participate in LAN communications. Any shared resources on the network are accessible by a workstation node, but the workstation node itself offers no resource for other nodes to use.

> **A server node** can do everything a workstation node can do and can also offer resources, such as fixed disk space or a printer, for use by the other nodes in the network.

The user can configure his or her Model 50/60/80 computer to be either a workstation or a server through the menus provided in the PC LAN Program. After the node has been configured, the PC LAN Program allows Model 50/60/80 computers to perform the following functions:

  □ Data sharing
  □ Program sharing
  □ Equipment sharing
  □ Electronic messaging

Data Sharing

Data sharing is often a good reason to connect Model 50/60/80 computers to a LAN. Often, multiple office workers need access to the same body of information, e.g., accounts payable information, a telephone directory, inventory information, and so forth. With a LAN and the proper programs, multiple users can simultaneously access a single body of information. This data sharing can easily be illustrated through an example using the LAN, as shown in Figure 103.

Let's say you are the user of Node 1 (the Model 50) and you wish to share your data with Node 3 (the PC/XT). Let's further say that you are currently configured as a server node. (Remember, to provide anything to other nodes, you must be configured as a server.) To allow other nodes to access your data, you would first step through some PC LAN Program menus where you will be requested to give a name to the shared section of your fixed disk. This is the name that the other

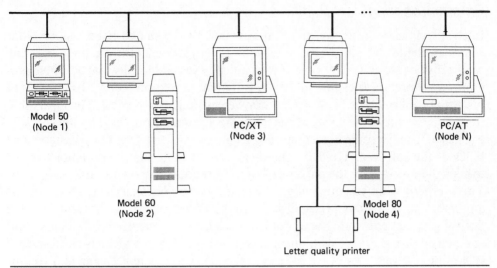

Figure 103. Example of a small Local Area Network.

nodes will use to access your data. You can also define a password to prevent unauthorized access and put restrictions such as **read only** to prevent others from altering your data. Now you can save this network setup, and the file will be shared automatically every time you power up. Any data you place in the shared section of the fixed disk can be accessed by any other node or server on the network, provided you give them the password.

Now if the user of Node 3 wants to use the data on your fixed disk, he steps through some PC LAN Program menus on his computer and accesses the shared disk on your node by the name and password you just defined. He assigns your shared directory an unused drive letter such as "E" or "F." He now saves this configuration so that he won't have to step through those menus the next time he wants to use Node 1's fixed disk. From this point on, the shared section of your fixed disk is just as available to Node 3 as it is to you. Anything he can do on his local drives, he can do on your shared drive, unless you as the server (Node 1) choose to impose limitations such as read only. Since this sharing occurs in the background, you can use your Model 50 undisturbed while the other nodes access your information.

More sophisticated data sharing can be implemented by application programs that are specially written to take advantage of the PC LAN Program's capabilities. For example, an accounting department may use Model 50/60/80 computers to do financial analysis of its company's sales. As sales are occurring every day (at least one would hope so), this information is constantly changing. The entire accounting department may need access to this information—perhaps for many different reasons. All accounting data can be stored on one of the server nodes on the network. With an accounting application program written to take advantage of PC LAN Program functions, the accounting data files can be simultaneously available to all network users without interfering with or even being aware of the other users.

Program Sharing

In the previous example, we said that any data on the shared fixed disk of Node 1 is as available to Node 3 as it is to Node 1. Can Node 3 also execute a program on the disk of Node 1? The answer is technically yes and legally maybe. Since programs are stored in files just like data, programs stored on Node 1's shared fixed disk can be executed by Node 3 as if they were installed on Node 3. The legal question centers around the terms of the licensing agreement provided by the software publisher. The licensing agreement is a legal contract between the purchaser and seller of the software. Typically, these agreements state that you are not allowed to copy the software for the purpose of running the software on multiple computers. This is exactly what you are doing if you allow other nodes on the LAN to execute a program on your shared fixed disk. Until the advent of LANs, the terms of these licensing agreements were not a problem because PCs were used as "islands," not components in a sharing environment. The growing popularity of LAN environments is causing software vendors to offer other terms such as site licensing and volume purchase contracts for their program products. These types of agreements allow the program to reside on a single network server and to be shared by all on the network. This is becoming more and more common, especially with versions of software specifically written for data sharing in LAN environments.

Equipment Sharing

We have just seen how part of a fixed disk can be shared among several users. The PC LAN Program also allows network nodes to share hardware such as printers. This can provide for more efficient usage of printing equipment, which is especially nice with the more expensive letter quality or high speed printers. Returning to our sample network in Figure 103, let's say that each of the users in this network occasionally has a need to produce letter quality documents. Since this need only arises occasionally for each node, it would be a wasteful investment to equip each individual node with its own letter quality printer.

The PC LAN Program provides an alternate approach to filling the needs of these users by allowing all nodes to share one letter quality printer attached to Node 4. Each node can print letters just as if each node had its own dedicated printer. The printer can be shared in the same way as a fixed disk can be shared. To allow the other nodes to access the printer, Node 4's user would step through some PC LAN Program menus where she would be requested to give a name to her printer. This is the name that the other nodes will use to access the printer. Here again, a password can be defined to prevent unauthorized access. Once the printer is shared, any other node can send files to the printer. The files to be printed are temporarily stored on Node 4's disk and automatically printed when the printer is available. Since this printing activity occurs in the background, all this occurs without interfering with the activities performed by the user of Node 4.

Besides fixed disks and printers, other computer hardware can be shared as you will see later in the chapter.

Electronic Messaging

Another function provided by the PC LAN Program is electronic messaging. This is a capability that allows the user or an application program to send text messages to any other network nodes. The addressee of the message will be notified that someone has sent him a message . . . even if he is in the middle of some application program not associated with the network. The message can be meeting notices, requests for appointments, or anything you might normally leave as a note on someone's desk. The electronic messaging feature can be a convenient time saver.

Broadband IBM PC Network

The broadband PC Network provides a means of attaching PCs together for the purpose of communications. The network can consist of a mixture of different types of PCs and Personal System/2s. The PC Network allows the various computers to share information, programs, and computer equipment with the other nodes in the LAN.

Figure 104 shows a configuration that allows Model 50/60/80 computers to become nodes in a broadband PC Network. The Model 50/60/80 computer is equipped with the PC Network Adapter II/A, the Network Support Program, and the PC LAN Program.

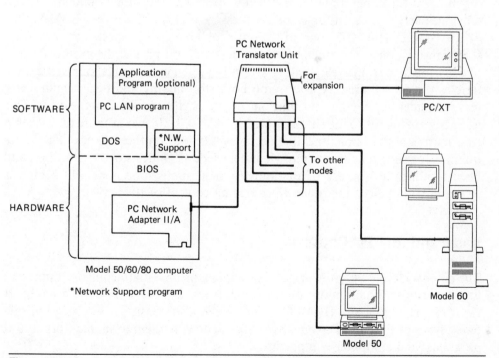

Figure 104. Configuration for attaching Model 50/60/80 computers to a broadband IBM PC Network.

The PC Network Adapter II/A performs the detailed electrical communications tasks necessary to send information to other nodes in the network. The adapter is attached to the required **Translator Unit.** The Translator Unit listens for messages transmitted from any node in the network, translates the message to a higher frequency, and then retransmits the message to all nodes in the network. Each message contains the address or **network ID** of the node for which it is intended. Only the addressed node will accept the message retransmitted from the Translator Unit. A single Translator Unit can accommodate up to eight nodes, each 200 feet away or less. A PC Network of up to 72 nodes within a 1,000-foot radius can be constructed by adding the appropriate IBM Cable System components. With the addition of commercially available cable television equipment, much larger networks are possible. Further, multiple networks can be linked together by a properly configured computer, known as a **bridge,** allowing for still further expansion.

Information is transferred over the PC Network at a rate of 2 million bits/second. While only one network node at a time may transmit a message over the network, the same coaxial cable can be used simultaneously for other communications besides the PC Network (e.g., cable television, voice, etc.) without interfering with the network's operation. To ensure that only one network node transmits at a time, there is a protocol that each node follows, unbeknownst to the user, when transmitting messages. This protocol is called Carrier Sense Multiple Access/Collision Detect (CSMA/CD). It's a mouthful but is really quite simple. In fact, we follow this protocol in our everyday telephone conversations. Here, too, only one person can speak at a time or neither is clearly understood. One party waits for the other to finish before he or she begins speaking. Thus the phone line carries only one party's voice at a time and the message is clear. This is the "CSMA" part of CSMA/CD. The "CD" part of the protocol handles the times when two nodes start transmissions simultaneously. To understand this part of the protocol, think of what you do during a telephone conversation when you begin talking at the same time as the other party. Typically, you both stop talking and begin again a few moments later hoping that this time one of you begins sooner than the other. This is exactly analogous to the situation with CSMA/CD. If two or more nodes begin transmitting at the same time, the messages "collide" on the network. The nodes monitor for such a collision and when detected, all nodes stop transmitting and begin again after a pause of random length. Usually, one node will begin his retransmission before the other, thus gaining control of the network.

Baseband IBM PC Network

The baseband IBM PC Network also provides a means of attaching PCs together for the purpose of communications, which is less expensive than the broadband Network. The baseband IBM PC Network can also consist of a mixture of different types of PCs and Personal System/2s, allowing them to share information, programs, and computer equipment.

Figure 105 shows a configuration that allows Model 50/60/80 computers to become nodes in a baseband IBM PC Network. The Model 50/60/80 computers

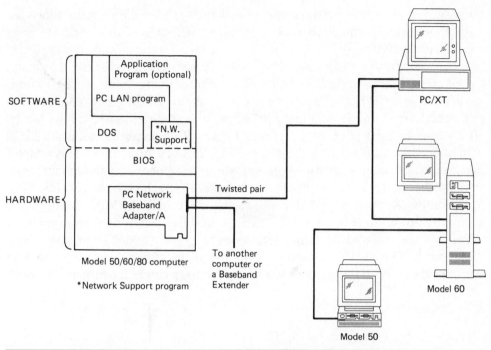

Figure 105. Configuration for attaching Model 50/60/80 computers to a baseband IBM PC Network.

are equipped with the PC Network Baseband Adapter/A, the Network Support Program, and the PC LAN Program. As in a broadband PC Network, information is transferred over the baseband PC Network at a rate of 2 million bits/second. The same CSMA/CD communications protocol discussed previously is employed on this network.

The main advantage of the baseband PC Network is cost. First of all, the twisted-pair cable used in the baseband Network is less expensive than the coaxial cable used in a broadband PC Network. Further, no Translator Unit is required with the baseband Network. The PC Network Baseband Adapters can be joined directly together in a daisy-chain fashion over a distance of up to 200 feet. For larger baseband PC Networks, the **IBM PC Network Baseband Extender** provides for the attachment of up to 80 computers over a distance of 800 feet.

One disadvantage of the baseband PC Network is that the less expensive cable used with this network cannot be simultaneously used for other communications than the PC Network (e.g., cable television, voice, etc.) without interfering with the network's operation. Further, larger networks can be constructed with the broadband PC Network than with the baseband PC Network.

IBM Token-Ring Network

The Token-Ring Network is another baseband Local Area Network in which Model 50/60/80 computers can participate. This network is designed to support larger computer systems as normal network nodes in addition to PCs. This feature allows the information and equipment sharing environment offered by LANs to include larger computers as well.

An example of a small Token-Ring Network is shown in Figure 106. The nodes of the network are arranged in a ring pattern, thus giving the network its name. As you can see, the network can consist of a mixture of different types of computers both small and large. Figure 107 shows a configuration that allows Model 50/60/80 computers to become nodes in a Token-Ring network. Model 50/60/80 computers are equipped with the Token-Ring Network Adapter/A. This adapter performs the detailed electrical communications tasks necessary to send information to other nodes in the network. The adapter is attached to the required **8228 Multi-station Access Unit (MAU)** via the network cable. The MAU supports the attachment of up to eight network nodes. A modular jack is used to attach each network node to the MAU, which lets nodes be quickly added or removed from the network. The MAU can automatically bypass any failing nodes by detecting their inactivity. With the proper cable components, a single Token-Ring Network

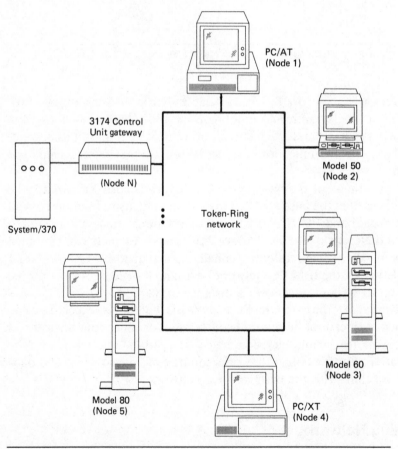

Figure 106. Example of a small Token-Ring Network. This network can accommodate personal computers as well as larger computer systems.

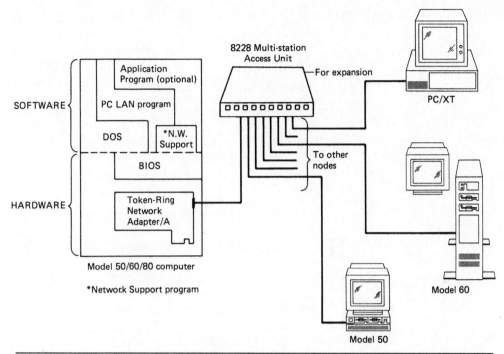

Figure 107. Configuration allowing Model 50/60/80 computers to be a node in a Token-Ring Network.

can contain from up to 260 nodes over several kilometers. Information is transmitted at 4 million bits/second (twice as fast as with the PC Network), which helps the overall performance of the network. As with the PC Network, multiple Token-Ring Networks can be linked together by a bridge.

The Token-Ring Network employs a communications protocol to control access to the shared cable. The protocol used by the Token-Ring Network is called the **Token Passing** protocol and is a simple concept. Basically, a single and unique network message called a **Token** is passed around the ring from node to node in a continuous circle. The Token is the "mailbag" of the network. It carries the network messages (one at a time) from the transmitting node to all other nodes in the network until the recipient is found and the message is delivered (see Figure 108). When a node receives the Token, it looks to see if it contains a message. If there is no message, it means that the network is idle and that that node can insert a message into the Token before passing it to the next node in the ring. If the Token already has a message when the node receives it, the network is busy and that node may not insert a message. The node will examine the address contained in the Token message to see if the message is intended for that node. If not, the Token will be passed to the next node in the ring unchanged.

The software used in our sample configuration is the same as that used with the PC Network. The Network Support Program interacts directly with the adapter hardware and allows the node to run most programs originally written for nodes of the PC Network. The PC LAN Program is the same program used in PC Net-

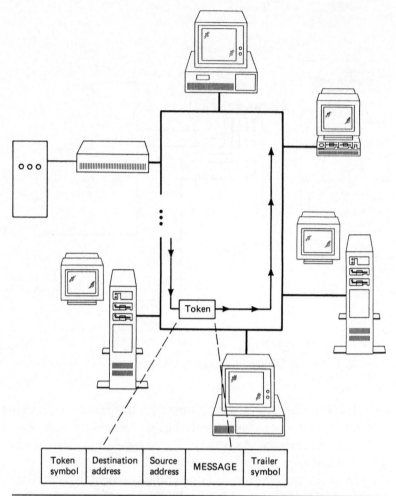

Token symbol	Destination address	Source address	MESSAGE	Trailer symbol

Figure 108. The Token-Ring Network uses a special Token message to deliver information over the network.

work nodes. It provides the same functions to a Token-Ring Network node as it does to the PC Network nodes:

▫ Data sharing

▫ Program sharing

▫ Equipment sharing

▫ Electronic messaging

GATEWAYS

We've seen one way that Model 50/60/80 computers can be directly attached to a host computer. We've also seen how personal computers can be attached together in a LAN for the purpose of sharing data, programs, and hardware. These two con-

figurations can be combined to form a network **gateway.** A network gateway is a
network server node that has a communications link with a computer not attached
to the LAN and that shares this communications link to other LAN nodes. That
is, a single terminal emulation link to a host computer can be shared by other users
on the LAN. Let's examine a sample gateway configuration.

A single Model 50/60/80 computer linked to a System/370 host through control
unit emulation and sharing this link with the nodes of a LAN is called a **3270 gateway.**
Figure 109 shows a Model 50/60/80 computer (Node 4) configured to be a 3270
gateway for the broadband PC Network. The PC Network Adapter II/A, the Network Support Program, and the PC LAN Program allow the Model 50/60/80 com-

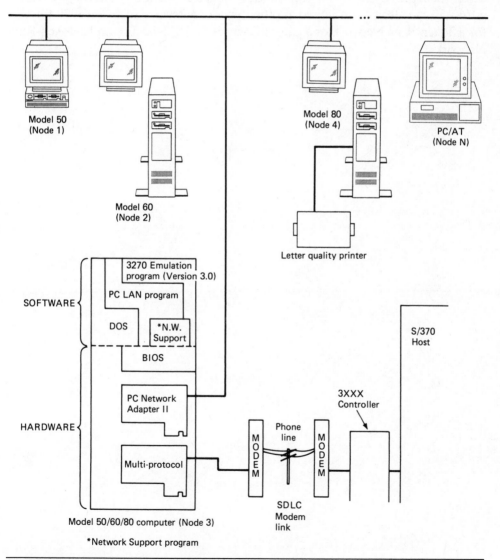

Figure 109. A configuration of Model 50/60/80 computers providing a broadband IBM PC Network
gateway to a System/370 mainframe computer.

puter to participate in the broadband PC Network as a server workstation. The Multi-Protocol Adapter/A attaches the Model 50/60/80 computer to the Communications Controller and finally to the host. The 3270 Emulation Program allows the Model 50/60/80 computer to emulate a 3274 Control Unit. If the Model 50/60/80 computer and the System/370 were close to each other, the modem link between them could be replaced with a direct attachment to the host via the 3270 Connection adapter or via a Token-Ring Network.

This Model 50/60/80 computer allows up to 32 other network nodes to communicate with the System/370 host computer as if they each had their own direct terminal emulation link with the host. These 32 nodes can perform the functions described in the "System/370 Workstation Emulation" section of this chapter. Model 50/60/80 can also be configured as other types of gateways, such as a 3270 gateway for a Token-Ring Network or a gateway between a PC Network and a Token-Ring Network.

Model 50/60/80 Computers and Your Business

An important first step in bringing a Model 50/60/80 or any computer into your business environment is planning. Largely depending on how well you plan, introducing new computer resources can be either like pouring water or pouring gasoline on a fire. Many of you will already have a significant number of computers in your business and will add Model 50/60/80 computers to your computer arsenal, while others will be bringing Model 50/60/80 computers in as their first business computer. In either case, the information in this chapter should help you understand how to introduce Model 50/60/80 computers into your particular environment. The chapter starts by discussing software selection and then offers specific Model 50/60/80 hardware configurations appropriate for small, medium, and large businesses. In addition, the following topics are discussed:

□ User training
□ Ergonomics
□ Security
□ Service
□ Migrating from PCs to Model 50/60/80 computers

This chapter is by no means a complete guide to introducing Model 50/60/80 computers into any business, but it gives you a starting point for developing a plan and discussing important issues.

CHOOSING THE SOFTWARE

Model 50/60/80 computers become a useful business tool only when they are executing the appropriate software. While there are many ways of generating a strategy for introducing computers, considering software needs before selecting detailed hardware configurations usually makes sense. The hardware requirements such as memory size and disk space will be based in part on the needs of the software selected.

The application programs you select must perform the tasks needed by your end users both today and in the foreseeable future. Chapter 4 already discussed some of the most common types of application programs used in business. Selecting the basic type of application program is often fairly simple. For example, an accounting department needs an accounting application program; a secretary needs a word processing application program. What is more difficult is identifying the specific application program that best fits your particular needs. Do you need a custom application program, or will a prewritten application program be acceptable? If you want a prewritten application program, exactly which one is best for your needs? If you prefer a custom application program, who should write it and what should it include? The answers to these questions depend largely on your specific business environment and are thus beyond the scope of this book. There are, however, a few basics that remain the same whether selecting a program for a multinational corporation or a corner fish market: first of all, you must understand precisely the tasks you are trying to computerize before pursuing any application program alternatives. A thorough knowledge of the task helps you to identify the specific requirements your application program must meet. After you obtain a detailed understanding of the tasks, you can begin the search through the sea of prewritten application programs. If you can find an appropriate prewritten application program that fits your needs, you can avoid the expense, delay, and effort associated with custom software development. However, since everyone has slightly different needs and methods even within a given business function, you can bet that any prewritten application will have features you don't need and won't have some features you will wish it did. This is the price you pay for acquiring a prewritten program. Don't forget to consider the more specialized type of prewritten application program—vertical market applications. Vertical market application programs address a highly specific segment of users such as lawyers, doctors, truckers, insurance salespeople, and so on.

There are many sources of information about the prewritten application programs on the market. Authorized dealers can help you select particular application programs to fit your needs. There are also many popular computer magazines that consistently conduct extensive reviews of prewritten application programs. Some have annual issues dedicated strictly to reviews of all types of software products. These can be excellent and timely sources of information. Independent consulting firms can also provide assistance for a price. Finally, don't overlook colleagues as potential sources of information. They may have had to evaluate application programs for needs similar to your own.

For specific or highly specialized needs, prewritten application programs may not be adequate. In this case, custom developed software may be desirable. While the development of custom software is typically more expensive, it may be less costly to pay for the development of custom software in the long run than to settle for a prewritten application program that doesn't do the job. If you do select the custom software route, an important step is to select the proper developer. Businesses that have their own programming staff can do their own custom program development. If you don't have your own programmers, you will have to seek outside help, that is, an outside software developer. In either case, it is the developer himself who will have the largest effect on the ultimate success or failure of the custom development activity. The developer's job is not an easy one. Besides programming expertise, he must become an expert in all aspects of your business right down to every step performed. He must be a good communicator to understand and discuss software requirements. He must understand human psychology when defining the user interface for the program. He must be a proficient teacher to train the end users on the new program. Finally, he must be dependable and reliable so that you know he will be there for technical support and any needed modifications.

You must also select an operating system. The operating system to be used depends on many factors. Chapter 5 covered the characteristics of operating systems for Model 50/60/80 computers. The one you choose depends on such things as:

Multi-application vs single-application: The operating system environment determines what level of multi-application capabilities you will have. While multi-application fits quite naturally into most business environments, not everyone will need multi-application. For example, a shipping clerk who uses only one inventory program day in and day out has no need for program switching or background processing.

Memory needs: Real mode operating systems generally have a 640 KB maximum memory limit. While the special memory management techniques discussed in Chapter 5, such as EMS and virtual disks, allow some Real Mode programs to use more than 640 KB, Protected Mode operating systems are required to make general use of memory above 640 KB.

Compatibility with PC application programs: Those with a significant investment in DOS application programs will want to be sure that this investment is retained by selecting a compatible operating system.

Communications: The specifics of the communications protocols and configurations used in your environment may affect your operating system choice. Some operating systems provide extensive built-in communications while others require additional communications application programs.

Understanding your needs in these areas and reading Chapter 5 will help you decide which operating system fits your needs best.

CHOOSING MODEL 50/60/80 HARDWARE

Selecting the proper Model 50/60/80 hardware components that will work together and fit your needs can be confusing. You must select among the Model 50/60/80 computers and their disk configurations, feature cards, and peripherals. While we can't possibly cover all needs for all environments in the limited scope of this book, we can examine some sample business environments and outfit them with the appropriate Model 50/60/80 configurations. We will examine a small business, a medium business, and a large business environment. With the insight provided by outfitting these hypothetical business environments, you will be better prepared to select the proper Model 50/60/80 components for your environment. Further assistance in selecting hardware components is also available from IBM or authorized dealers.

Small Business Environment—Bob's Appliances

Our hypothetical small business is an appliance store named Bob's Appliances. It is a sole proprietorship (owned by Bob, of course) and has thirteen employees. Bob has been in business for two years and has experienced a high growth rate. He currently conducts business by noncomputer methods but finds himself needing to streamline his operation as the business grows. The manual accounting methods he currently uses are proving to be laborious and time consuming. Bob wants to migrate the accounting function to Model 50/60/80.

Bob's service department has been receiving complaints about slow repair service. Bob discusses the problem with the service personnel and finds that the spare parts inventory is frequently out of certain parts needed for repair jobs. The time necessary to order and receive these parts has slowed repair services. Bob will therefore implement inventory control on a Model 50/60/80 to insure that necessary parts are kept in stock but that no more inventory than necessary is carried.

Bob's secretary has been using a typewriter for business correspondence and maintaining the customer mailing list. Bob decides to insure that word processing and mail list maintenance is a capability they will have.

Bob has basically three applications he will move to Model 50/60/80 computers: accounting, inventory control, and word processing. To keep tight control of his business, Bob will dedicate one Model 50/60/80 full time to the accounting and inventory control functions. One system should be able to handle both functions since the inventory control function requires only a few hours per week. Further, many prewritten accounting application programs also provide the inventory control function. The job of preparing business correspondence and customer mailings is a full-time job, so Bob will make sure that his secretary has her own system.

Should Bob buy a Local Area Network? One of the most important things that LANs offer is the ability to share data among different users. In Bob's case, no data will be shared between the accounting/inventory control and the word processing Model 50/60/80s. The data sharing need is nonexistent in Bob's operation today. Another important function provided by LANs is the ability to share fixed disks and printers among different users. While some benefit could be derived from this capability, Bob's small-scale needs don't warrant a LAN today. Bob will keep in mind that, as his business continues to grow, a LAN may become desirable.

Let's examine two Model 50/60/80 configurations suitable for Bob's Appliances.

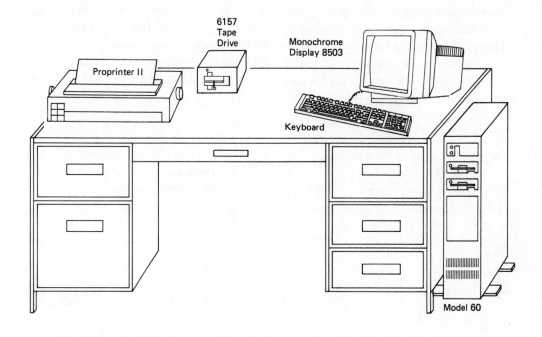

BASE SYSTEM	FEATURE CARDS	PERIPHERALS
44 MB Model 60	Slot 1: Tape Drive Feature	Monochrome Display 8503
*(1) 44 MB fixed disk	Slot 2: –	4201 Proprinter II
*(1) 1.44 MB diskette drive	Slot 3: –	6157 Streaming Tape Drive
*1 MB memory	Slot 4: –	
*Async/Parallel Port	Slot 5: –	
*VGA graphics	Slot 6: –	**SOFTWARE**
*(7) expansion slots	Slot 7: –	DOS 3.3
Second 1.44 MB diskette drive		Accounting/inventory control

*Denotes standard equipment

Figure 110. A 44 MB Model 60 configured as an accounting/inventory workstation for Bob's Appliances.

Accounting/Inventory Workstation

Bob finds an appropriate prewritten accounting application program that also supports inventory control. He selects the DOS operating system, since multi-application or large memory is not needed at this time. Based on the requirements of the software, Bob chooses the 44 MB Model 60 shown in Figure 110. Model 60 was selected for the fixed disk storage capacity and the flexibility provided by its seven expansion slots. This Model 60's standard 44 MB fixed disk should provide enough disk storage to contain the accounting/inventory control application program and data with room to spare. In an effort to keep expenses to a minimum, Bob selects the Monochrome Display 8503. Model 60's ability to support a second 44 MB fixed disk will allow for expansion as his business grows. The Proprinter II is chosen to produce accounting and inventory reports. The 6157 Streaming Tape Drive provides him with a way to back up data on the fixed disk, insuring that the important accounting/inventory information will not be accidentally lost. To support this device, the Model 60 must have a Tape Drive Feature card installed in one of the seven expansion slots. The remaining six slots will be empty, providing Bob with significant growth potential.

Secretarial Workstation

A prewritten word processing program with the ability to handle mailing lists will be installed on Bob's secretarial workstation. Bob will again use DOS since multi-application is not yet needed. Bob selects the Model 50 shown in Figure 111. Model 50 was selected for its small form factor and economy (the Model 30 described in

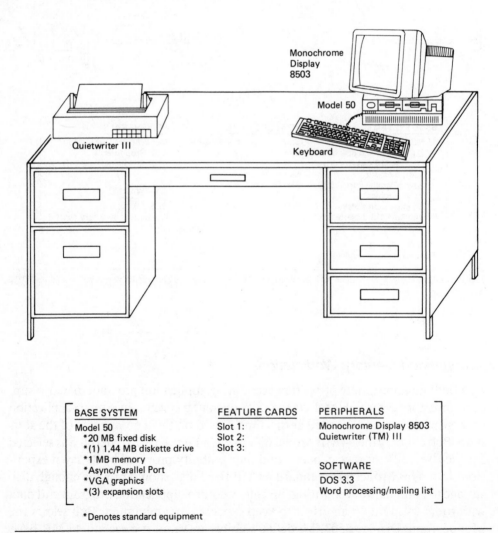

BASE SYSTEM	FEATURE CARDS	PERIPHERALS
Model 50	Slot 1:	Monochrome Display 8503
*20 MB fixed disk	Slot 2:	Quietwriter (TM) III
*(1) 1.44 MB diskette drive	Slot 3:	
*1 MB memory		
*Async/Parallel Port		SOFTWARE
*VGA graphics		DOS 3.3
*(3) expansion slots		Word processing/mailing list

*Denotes standard equipment

Figure 111. A Model 50 configured as a secretarial workstation for Bob's Appliances.

Chapter 1 would also be a good choice and would reduce costs even further). For the same reason, Bob again selects the Monochrome Display 8503. Model 50's standard 20 MB fixed disk should provide adequate storage for the word processing/mail list program and data. Bob chooses to back up the smaller 20 MB fixed disk with diskettes, eliminating the need for an external backup device. The Quietwriter III letter quality printer will provide documents for external correspondence and customer mailings. With this configuration, all three of the expansion slots are available for future use.

Medium Business Environment—Johnson and Thornbush

Our hypothetical medium business is an advertising agency named Johnson and Thornbush. This company has been in business for twelve years. It started with one major account and today boasts seventeen active clients. Susan Johnson and Perry Thornbush are both still active in managing the business. They currently use dedicated word processors and about 30 PCs in their business. The company has 148 employees. Susan has a strong interest in expanding the business's use of computers to improve productivity and communications. She intends to phase out the dedicated word processors and install a broadband PC Network consisting of existing PCs and new Model 50/60/80s. This will foster better office communications and provide for efficient sharing of peripheral equipment. Susan will use Model 50/60/80s as both network servers and network workstations.

PC Network Server

Susan will purchase a network version of a spreadsheet, a data base, and a word processing application program to be shared by other network nodes. She decides that DOS will be used on the server as well as all other network nodes for now. This will allow her to preserve her current investment in DOS application programs while providing a migration path to Operating System/2 as more Operating System/2 application programs become available. The PC LAN Program and the Network Support Program perform the server functions.

Figure 112 shows a 70 MB Model 60 configured to be a network server appropriate for Susan's environment. The 70 MB Model 60 was selected for the fixed disk storage capacity and the flexibility provided by its seven expansion slots.

Although this server could be in someone's office and used as a normal workstation, Susan will place it in a common area to allow all users physical access to the peripheral devices. Since this Model 60 will not be used as someone's primary workstation, the Monochrome Display 8503 is selected for its economy. Model 60's standard 70 MB fixed disk and ability to add either a second 70 MB fixed disk provides her with adequate future growth. The Quietwriter III letter quality printer can also be shared among the network users, eliminating the need for individual letter quality printers for every node. Depending on the expected usage, a higher speed printer such as the 3812 page printer could be used here. Model 60's seven expansion slots allow it to support an array of peripheral devices. The 6157 Streaming

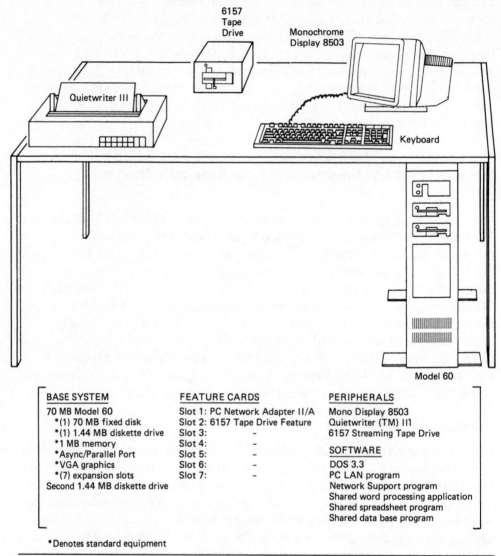

Figure 112. A 70 MB Model 60 configured as a broadband PC Network server for Johnson and Thornbush.

Tape Drive provides a way to back up the server's fixed disk as well as the fixed disks of other network nodes. To support this device, the Model 60 must also have a 6157 Tape Drive Feature installed in one of the expansion slots. The PC Network Adapter II/A provides the connection to the network. Since there are many PCs on the network, there is no need for a 5.25-inch External Diskette Drive on this server. The 5.25-inch diskette drives in the PCs on the network will be used to transfer information and programs between 5.25-inch diskettes and Model 50/60/80's 3.5-inch diskettes and fixed disks. As the network grows, additional servers can be attached to the network to support the users as needed.

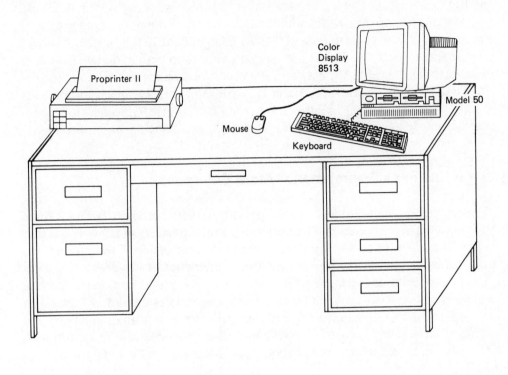

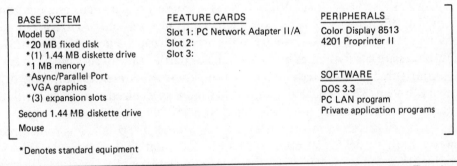

BASE SYSTEM

Model 50
  *20 MB fixed disk
  *(1) 1.44 MB diskette drive
  *1 MB menory
  *Async/Parallel Port
  *VGA graphics
  *(3) expansion slots

Second 1.44 MB diskette drive

Mouse

FEATURE CARDS

Slot 1: PC Network Adapter II/A
Slot 2:
Slot 3:

PERIPHERALS

Color Display 8513
4201 Proprinter II

SOFTWARE

DOS 3.3
PC LAN program
Private application programs

*Denotes standard equipment

Figure 113. Model 50 configured as a general purpose workstation for Johnson and Thornbush.

General Purpose Workstation

In addition to the server, Susan will provide most of her employees with individual workstations. The users of these workstations can use programs and data on the server as well as their own private application programs and data. The PC LAN Program will provide electronic messaging and allow the Model 50s to share the server's application programs, data, letter quality printer, and tape drive. Figure 113 shows the Model 50 configuration Susan will use as general purpose workstations. Model 50 was selected for its size and economy. To allow for maximum ease of use and user comfort, the Color Display 8513 and a Mouse will be provided. A second 1.44 MB diskette drive provides additional convenience when installing programs and copying from diskette to diskette. Model 50's standard 20 MB fixed disk should provide adequate storage for the user's private application programs and data. The Proprinter II printer fills the user's printer needs for documents that don't require letter quality. A PC Network Adapter II/A consumes one of the expansion slots and allows the Model 50 to be attached to the PC Network. The other two expansion slots are left available for future growth (e.g., host attachment, modem, etc.).

Large Business Environment—Atole Enterprises

The hypothetical large business that will be outfitted with Model 50/60/80s is Atole Enterprises. This multinational corporation is a manufacturer of paper goods that enjoys financial prowess worthy of its Fortune 500 membership. The many benefits afforded by computers are no news to Atole Enterprises. It has been using computers in its day-to-day operations for many years. Atole has at least one mainframe computer at every major Atole facility. These mainframes are linked together in a computer network, enabling the electronic transfer of information all over the world. It has developed many custom application programs for the mainframes. We will look more closely at the hypothetical Atole site on the outskirts of Pensacola, Florida.

Atole-Pensacola is a large manufacturing and process research facility. The company has installed a Token-Ring Network. A variety of personal computers are attached to this network as is a System/370 mainframe. PC and S/370 custom application programs take full advantage of the network's capabilities. Two other S/370 mainframes are configured as hosts and are not part of the Token-Ring Network. PCs, configured for 3270 terminal emulation, are used to interact with these off-network System/370s. There are many other more specialized computers used by Atole-Pensacola, but they are not of interest here.

Atole will begin to migrate from PCs to Model 50/60/80s. For some time, however, both Model 50/60/80s and PCs will coexist at Atole-Pensacola. We will examine three Model 50/60/80 configurations of interest.

- □ Token-Ring Network Server/Gateway
- □ Workstation
- □ Advanced Workstation

Token-Ring Network Server/Gateway

This server will participate in the Token-Ring Network in order to provide both hardware and software to be shared by other network nodes. Atole's custom application programs will also be installed on this server and shared by other network nodes. The Operating System/2 (Extended Edition) is selected for its built-in communications capabilities although the Standard Edition along with the proper communications application programs could also have been used.

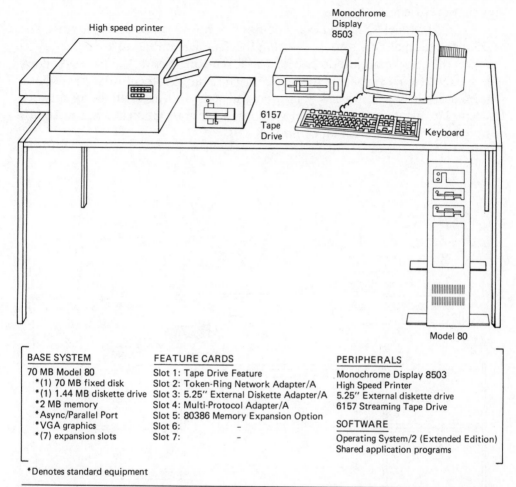

High speed printer

Monochrome
Display
8503

6157
Tape
Drive

Keyboard

Model 80

BASE SYSTEM	FEATURE CARDS	PERIPHERALS
70 MB Model 80	Slot 1: Tape Drive Feature	Monochrome Display 8503
*(1) 70 MB fixed disk	Slot 2: Token-Ring Network Adapter/A	High Speed Printer
*(1) 1.44 MB diskette drive	Slot 3: 5.25″ External Diskette Adapter/A	5.25″ External diskette drive
*2 MB memory	Slot 4: Multi-Protocol Adapter/A	6157 Streaming Tape Drive
*Async/Parallel Port	Slot 5: 80386 Memory Expansion Option	
*VGA graphics	Slot 6: –	SOFTWARE
*(7) expansion slots	Slot 7: –	Operating System/2 (Extended Edition)
		Shared application programs

*Denotes standard equipment

Figure 114. A 70 MB Model 80 configured as a Token-Ring Network server/gateway for Atole-Pensacola.

Figure 114 shows a 70 MB Model 80 configured to be a network server for Atole-Pensacola's Token-Ring Network. Atole-Pensacola will have several of these servers on the network. The Model 80 was selected for its superior performance and the flexibility provided by its seven expansion slots. The server is equipped with a Monochrome Display 8503 and is located in a common area to allow the users of other nodes physical access to the peripheral devices. Model 80's standard 70 MB fixed disk augments the disk storage available on the network, but the primary disk storage is provided by the System/370 workstation server. The 3812 page printer can produce up to twelve letter quality pages per minute. It will be attached to the server and shared with other network nodes. The Streaming Tape Drive is used to back up information on the server as well as on other network nodes. Both Model 50/60/80s and PCs will coexist for some time at Atole-Pensacola. The 5.25-inch External Diskette Drive will be available to help users migrate programs and data from 5.25-inch diskettes to 3.5-inch diskettes and visa versa. While there are 5.25-inch based PCs on the network, the external 5.25-inch diskette drive is centrally located for network users.

Five of Model 80's seven expansion slots are used in this configuration. The 5.25-inch External Drive Adapter/A and the Tape Drive Feature are necessary to support the peripherals just described. The Token-Ring Network Adapter/A allows the Model 80 to participate in the network. The Multi-Protocol Adapter/A allows the Model 80 to be a 3270 gateway, providing all nodes with access to the off-network System/370 mainframes. The 80386 Memory Expansion Option and kits add 6 MB of memory for a system total of up to 8 MB.

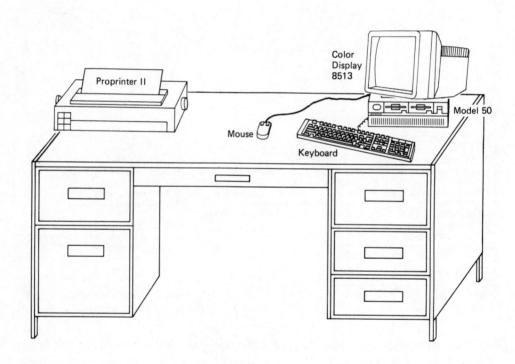

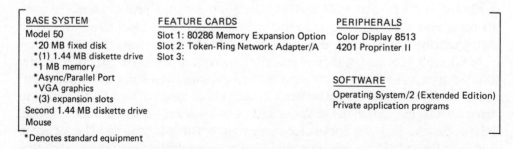

BASE SYSTEM	FEATURE CARDS	PERIPHERALS
Model 50	Slot 1: 80286 Memory Expansion Option	Color Display 8513
*20 MB fixed disk	Slot 2: Token-Ring Network Adapter/A	4201 Proprinter II
*(1) 1.44 MB diskette drive	Slot 3:	
*1 MB memory		
*Async/Parallel Port		SOFTWARE
*VGA graphics		Operating System/2 (Extended Edition)
*(3) expansion slots		Private application programs
Second 1.44 MB diskette drive		
Mouse		

*Denotes standard equipment

Figure 115. Model 50 configured as a general purpose workstation for Atole-Pensacola.

General Purpose Workstation

The Operating System/2 (Extended Edition) operating system is used by all of Atole's general purpose workstations because of the multi-application, extended memory, and communications support. Figure 115 shows a Model 50 configuration appropriate for Atole's general purpose workstations. Model 50 was selected for its size and economy. Model 50's standard 20 MB fixed disk should provide adequate storage for private application programs and data. The second 1.44 MB diskette drive makes installing programs or copying information convenient. To allow for maximum ease of use and user comfort, the Mouse and the Color Display 8513 are selected. The Proprinter II will be used to print draft quality documents. The Token-Ring Network Adapter/A allows the Model 50 to participate in the Token-Ring Network. The 80286 Memory Expansion Option and kits add 2 MB of memory, bringing the system total up to 3 MB. Note that two of the three expansion slots are consumed by this configuration. If more expansion capability is desired, a similarly configured 44 MB Model 60 could be used as these general purpose workstations.

Advanced Workstation

The advanced workstation is used by the process research personnel at Atole-Pensacola. Operating System/2 (Extended Edition) is the operating system, chosen for its multi-application, extended memory, and communications capabilities. Operating System/2 (Extended Edition)'s data base features will also come in handy for logging the data collected by experiments.

Figure 116 shows a 115 MB Model 80 configured to be an advanced workstation. The 115 MB fixed disk contains many custom scientific applications and their data as well as other normal application programs. The Internal Optical Disk Drive is used to back up the fixed disk. The optical disk is also used to archive the large quantities of scientific data resulting from the experiments conducted by this department. The complex custom application programs and large data files used by this department justify a large memory. The 20 MHz 80386 System Board Memory Expansion Kit brings the amount of memory on the System Board up to 4 MB. Two 80386 Memory Expansion Options (each adding 6 MB) bring the total system memory to 16 MB. The 80387 Math Co-processor is added to speed up the many complex mathematical calculations.

The research activity is highly intensive in the graphics area, requiring high resolution and many colors. The Color Display 8514 and Display Adapter 8514/A are therefore used to extend the standard VGA capabilities. The Quietwriter III is used to produce high quality reports with graphics.

Six of the seven expansion slots are consumed in this configuration. The Optical Disk Adapter/A is needed to support the corresponding peripherals. The Display Adapter 8514/A accommodates the Color Display 8514. The Token-Ring Network Adapter/A allows the Model 80 to participate in the network. There is also an IBM System/38 dedicated to the research department. The System 36/38 Workstation Emulation Adapter allows Model 80 to communicate with the System/38 through terminal emulation.

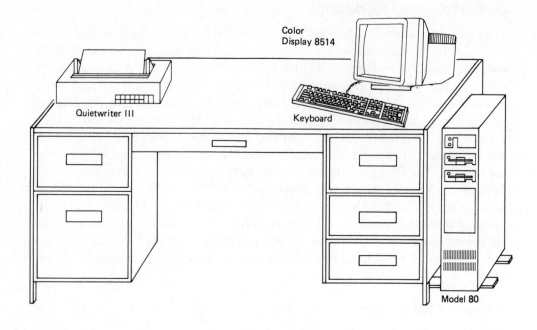

BASE SYSTEM

115 MB Model 80
 *(1) 115 MB fixed disk
 *(1) 1.44 MB diskette drive
 *2 MB memory
 *Async/Parallel Port
 *VGA graphics
 *(7) expansion slots
Second 1.44 MB diskette drive
Internal Optical Disk
80386 System Board Memory Expansion Kit
80387 Math Co-processor

*Denotes standard equipment

FEATURE CARDS

Slot 1: Optical Disk Adapter/A
Slot 2: System 36/38 W.S. Adapter/A
Slot 3: Token-Ring Network Adapter/A
Slot 4: Display Adapter 8514/A
Slot 5: 80386 Memory Expansion Option
Slot 6: 80386 Memory Expansion Option
Slot 7:   −

PERIPHERALS

Color Display 8514
Quietwriter III

SOFTWARE

Operating System/2
(Extended Edition)
Private applications

Figure 116. A 115 MB Model 80 configured as an advanced workstation for Atole-Pensacola.

USER TRAINING

The discussions in the chapter so far should assist you in selecting the appropriate software and hardware to fit your needs. However, no matter what computer hardware and software you select, they will require people to operate them. In order to maximize efficiency, these people must be provided with training in the use of the computer hardware and software. The goal of this training is to make the users proficient at using the computer hardware and software and to make their interaction with the computer system enjoyable. If using the computer is enjoyable, the user will be more highly motivated. If using the computer represents a frustrating struggle, the user will be less productive or perhaps avoid the computer altogether.

The training should cover both Model 50/60/80 hardware and the software that will be used. Model 50/60/80's hardware has been designed with close attention to making the hardware elements as easy to use as possible. Further, a detailed tutorial is provided on the Reference Diskette supplied with all Model 50/60/80 systems. This tutorial provides a method for an inexperienced user to take a self-guided tour of the basic Model 50/60/80 elements. The procedures discussed in Chapter 3 should be used to teach the first-time user how to run the tutorial program as well as the other programs on the Reference Diskette. This should provide adequate training on the use of Model 50/60/80 hardware in most cases.

After the user is familiar with the hardware, he or she should be trained in the use of the operating system and application programs. The amount of training needed on the operating system will depend on the tasks being performed, but many times the operating system can be hidden from the user, minimizing training needs in this area. Training in the use of the application program is usually the most important thing. The content of this training is dependent on the particular application program selected. Typically, manuals provided with the application program will contain a step-by-step tutorial designed to train the user. Depending on the complexity of the application program, the experience of the user, and the quality of the tutorial, this training method achieves varying levels of success. There are other alternatives to application program training. Many companies offer special classes tailored to teaching how to use the more popular application programs. These classes are typically held by software publishers or consulting firms. Many times businesses will send one person to a class of this type and then have him teach other users upon his return. Books and videotapes are also available for the more popular application programs. There are even programs written specifically to train users how to use other programs. These can be very helpful training aids.

Any authorized dealer should be able to provide information about various training classes, books, videotapes, and so on. Computer magazines and consultants can also be a source of such information.

ERGONOMICS

No plan would be complete without addressing the human needs that directly affect the day-to-day productivity of computer users—**ergonomics.** Ergonomics is a science dedicated to investigating the designs for effective interaction between devices and human beings. Human beings have many physiological and psychological characteristics that should be considered when designing computers, software, desks, lighting, chairs, and so forth. Attention to ergonomics will increase efficiency, work quality, health and safety, and job satisfaction.

Model 50/60/80's hardware has been designed with careful attention to ergonomics. Everything from the power switch location to the length of the Mouse cable was scrutinized. Much effort was also expended fine-tuning the ergonomics of the application programs. Organizations such as the American Optometric Association (AOA), and the New York Committee for Occupational Safety and Health (NYCOSH), as well as IBM, have probed deeply into the relationship between the computer and the user. Desks, chairs, lighting, noise, and the like are important to productivity. Some of these steps are inexpensive and easily accomplished. Others may be expensive and accomplished over time. Let's explore some specific steps you can do to help improve the ergonomics in your environment.

Comfort for the Eyes

The eyes, like any other part of the human body, can get tired as a result of intensive use. This fatigue, called eyestrain, is nothing new to people who spend long hours reading. Although it is only a temporary condition, eyestrain can cause a user to feel tired and irritated, especially if he or she continues to work due to the pressures of deadlines.

The eyes function most naturally at distances greater than or equal to arm's length. After all, throughout the majority of human history, a person's vision needs were to pick fruit, not to read contracts. When the eyes focus on anything closer than arm's reach, be it a computer display or newspaper, they are forced to look inward toward one's nose. This is extra work for the muscles that move the eye within its socket, thus causing fatigue. To reduce this fatigue, the computer user should take breaks and go to an area where he or she tends to focus on more distant objects.

Another factor contributing to eye fatigue results from the work done by a muscle in the eye that reforms the lens of your eye to maintain sharp focus. If you are frequently changing from looking at objects at different distances, such as looking from a computer display to a paper on your desk, the focusing muscles effectively do "push-ups." This also leads to tired eyes. To help prevent these eye "push-ups," it is desirable to put any paper that is frequently referenced during a computer session at the same distance and orientation as the computer screen. A clip-type holder used by secretaries to hold documents as they are typing works well for this.

Poor image quality can cause the eyes to constantly change focus in a futile attempt to correct the image. Model 50/60/80's VGA and associated displays are capable of providing better image quality than those of earlier PCs. Eyestrain caused by low quality images should be reduced.

As if this isn't enough, there is still another contributor to eye fatigue commonly found in offices, namely, improper lighting. Your eye adjusts to all of the light in the field of vision. Unwanted light reflections, or glare, can appear in the user's field of vision, causing nonuniform light intensities. If the light intensity varies widely, the iris in your eye will continuously expand and contract to adjust for the light level variance. To reduce the glare in the user's environment, Model 50/60/80 computer displays have antiglare glass. Likewise, the workstation (desk, table, etc.) surface should have antiglare or nonreflective surfaces. Windows are big culprits as far as causing glare, but most everyone likes windows. You can reduce the amount of glare caused by windows by positioning your computer display screen at right angles to any window. You can also use curtains or preferably horizontal blinds to direct the light away from the screen. Diffused office lighting will provide fewer "hot spots" and tend to provide the most uniform light and soften harsh shadows. For using computer displays, 30- to 50-foot candles of ambient light is optimum. The goal is to have the screen brightness three or four times the ambient light. Since most offices were originally designed for work to be done with paper, not video displays, there is usually too much light in the office. This may be difficult to change, depending on the type of lighting used. Using fewer or lower-intensity bulbs or fluorescent tubes may help. Another possibility is to install dimmer switches.

Workstation Comfort

The workstation furniture shared by the computer and the user can also affect productivity. For this reason, you should give attention to the chair and desk/table to be used.

A properly designed chair can help reduce back problems and make the user more comfortable and more productive. An improperly designed chair can lead to reduced alertness and shorter concentration spans. A user may not even realize he is uncomfortable as he unconsciously but constantly seeks a more comfortable position.

What makes a chair a good chair? First, since a chair will typically be used by many sitters during its life with a company, it is important for a chair to be adjustable. The seat pan height should be adjustable from around 16 to 22 inches and should allow the feet to rest flat on the floor. Weight should be distributed through the buttocks, not the thighs. The front of the seat pan should roll off smoothly, as in the **water fall** design, to provide for proper blood flow to the legs. A 20 mm compression is about firm enough.

Backrests should adjust up and down over a two-inch range and backward and forward between 80 and 120 degrees for good support. Both the seat pans and backrests should be upholstered and covered in a material that absorbs perspiration.

If mobility is required, wheels or casters are recommended unless the floor is slippery, which makes the chair unstable. Hard casters should be used for soft floors and visa versa. A five-legged chair will provide stability to prevent tipping. Seats should swivel if lateral movement is required.

Once the user is seated, his or her relationship with the computer display and keyboard will directly affect comfort and therefore productivity. The computer display should be positioned properly. The computer's display should be positioned such that the center of the display is about 15 degrees below eye level and about 28 inches away. A tilt-swivel stand under the display will allow the user to adjust the display angle as desired. The user should avoid using bifocal lenses, since they make the user tip his or her head back while reading the screen. This can lead to discomfort in the back and shoulder.

The keyboard should also be in a comfortable position. Model 50/60/80's separate keyboard is attached by a flexible cable that allows the user to position the keyboard as desired. The keyboard height should be such that the elbow is bent at about 90 degrees when typing. Finally, sufficient desk space for documents used during the computer session should always be provided.

What About Noise?

Noise is not conducive to efficiency. Irregular noise is more distracting than constant noise. Unfortunately, irregular noise is commonplace in the office environment and results from nearby conversations, telephones, printers, copy machines, and many other things. If possible, isolate noise sources such as impact printers and copy machines by placing them in isolated areas or separate rooms. Noise can also be reduced by installing doors, carpets, and other sound-insulating materials.

SECURITY

There are two issues to consider that fall under the security heading:

- □ Loss prevention
- □ Theft prevention

Loss Prevention

One of the hazards in dealing with information is the possibility that it will be lost. This is an important issue in computer environments. Storage media such as a diskette or a fixed disk are not immune to failure. Further, human error can cause data to be accidentally corrupted, resulting in lost information.

One way to deal with the risk of losing computer information is to make multiple copies of information on a regular basis. This way, if information is lost, it can be easily recovered from a backup copy. Information stored on Model 50/60/80 computers can be backed up through different methods. When the information you wish to protect is stored on diskettes, a simple precaution is to maintain backup copies of the information on other diskettes and store them separately. When protecting information on a Model 50/60/80 fixed disk, you can still choose to back up the information to diskettes. This will be fine for smaller disk systems, but it can quickly become cumbersome with larger fixed disks due to the many diskettes required. For example, it takes over 48 1.44 MB diskettes to back up a full 70 MB fixed disk.

Other alternatives include copying the fixed disk information to the 6157 Streaming Tape Drive or the Optical Disk Drive discussed in Chapter 2. No matter what method you use to back up information on Model 50/60/80, back up your fixed disks regularly.

Theft Prevention

Theft prevention deals with protecting sensitive information from nonauthorized disclosure. These security requirements vary widely from environment to environment. Consider your particular needs early in your planning.

Model 50/60/80 provides both **physical** and **operational** security features. Physical security features include a key-lock that secures the cover to the chassis. This discourages unauthorized disassembly of Model 50/60/80 computers and makes the theft of a fixed disk more difficult.

The operational security provided by Model 50/60/80 is implemented through permanent software contained inside Model 50/60/80's Read Only Memory (ROM) chips. When security is enabled and the computer is switched on, the user must enter a password before normal operation can commence. Further, during normal operation, the user can choose to invoke a software lock that requires a password before normal keyboard or Mouse interaction may continue. Finally, if Model 50/60/80 is operating unattended (as with a Local Area Network server, for example), the keyboard can be locked in a fashion that allows the system to restart normal operation after a power failure without user assistance while maintaining keyboard security. These operational security features can be optionally enabled or disabled by the user after access to the system has been granted.

For highly sensitive environments, you may wish to consider restricting access to areas where the Model 50/60/80s are stored or locking up diskettes containing sensitive information.

SERVICE

While Model 50/60/80 computers are two to three times more reliable than PCs, some computers will fail. If yours does, you must have a way of getting it fixed. Your Model 50/60/80 system comes with a one-year warranty that provides free repairs from any IBM Service Exchange Center or authorized IBM dealer. You must, however, deliver the system to the repair center and pick it up when repairs are complete. This is known as **carry-in service.** For a nominal fee, you can upgrade your warranty to provide **on-site service.** This means that if your computer fails, IBM will send someone to your site to effect repairs free of charge.

After the warranty period, you become responsible for the maintenance of your system. The more convenience you want, the more you will have to pay. IBM offers a service agreement that provides post-warranty, on-site service. Alternately, you can purchase a dealer service option for a fixed fee from any authorized IBM dealer. This provides post-warranty, carry-in service. Dealers may also offer their own service contracts.

If your system fails and you don't have any type of service contract, you will have to bring the system to a service center and pay for parts and labor, which can quickly become expensive.

The particular service approach you choose depends on the amount of convenience you desire and the level of risk you are willing to accept.

MIGRATING FROM PCs TO MODEL 50/60/80 COMPUTERS

Some businesses may be completely replacing their PCs with Model 50/60/80 computers. In the majority of businesses, however, PCs and Model 50/60/80s will probably coexist for some period of time. In either case, you will have to manage some logistical details when introducing Model 50/60/80 into your business environment. These include:

- Existing PC hardware
- Disk logistics

Existing PC Hardware

Model 50/60/80 will not accept feature cards designed for PCs. This is because the Micro Channel slots in the Model 50/60/80 are a new design providing additional capabilities beyond PC expansion slots. Further, the displays used with PCs cannot be used with Model 50/60/80 computers. Model 50/60/80's standard graphics circuitry has been designed to provide capabilities beyond most of the PC graphics adapters and must be used with Model 50/60/80 displays. Therefore, the feature cards and displays used with PCs should stay with the PC system being replaced whether it is sold, redistributed, or otherwise disposed of.

Most peripheral devices such as printers, plotters, and external modems designed for use with PCs will probably work with Model 50/60/80. This is due to the fact that Model 50/60/80's Async Port and Parallel Port are software and hardware compatible with those of the PC system. Most peripherals attach to one of these two ports. Appendix E contains a list of peripheral devices that have been tested for compatibility with Model 50/60/80. Devices not listed may also work and were simply not included in the testing.

Disk Logistics

Up until 1986, PCs used 5.25-inch diskettes exclusively. Naturally, the 5.25-inch diskettes are widely used to distribute programs and store information. Model 50/60/80 computers use the 3.5-inch diskette media to enjoy the increased capacity, reliability, and convenience afforded by this storage media. As a result, the user must adapt to this change in a way that is nondisruptive to his or her present environment, depending on the particular situation.

In some cases, Model 50/60/80 computers will be the first computers introduced into the business and there will be no transition to be managed. More often, however, Model 50/60/80 computers will be introduced to augment or replace existing PCs. If you are replacing a PC with a Model 50/60/80 computer, you will need a way to **migrate** your programs and information from your PC's diskettes and fixed disk to Model 50/60/80 diskettes and fixed disks. If Model 50/60/80 is introduced in an environment where 5.25-inch diskette PCs will be used for some time, you will need a way to **coexist** in a "two-diskette size" world. Depending on whether you need to migrate or coexist, you can exploit the following tools to help manage the situation:

- ▫ Existing Communications
- ▫ Data Migration Facility
- ▫ 5.25-inch Diskette Drive for Model 50/60/80
- ▫ 3.5-inch Diskette Drive for PCs
- ▫ Backup devices

One word of caution: before copying your programs to 3.5-inch diskettes through any of these methods, check with the program supplier for any copy restrictions that may prohibit copying the program for any reason.

Exploiting Existing Communications

If your computers participate in either Local Area Networks (LAN) or terminal emulation communications, these capabilities can be used to manage the 3.5-inch/5.25-inch diskette difference. In LAN environments, it is common practice to transfer programs and data between computer systems. The information can then be copied onto the Model 50/60/80's disk via a few simple network commands.

In situations where PCs are connected to a host computer, programs and data can be transferred between the 5.25-inch disks and the 3.5-inch diskettes using the host computer as the middle man. For example, the information could be transferred from the earlier PC family members to the host computer's disk. Then the Model 50/60/80 performing terminal emulation could retrieve the program or data from the host's disk and save it on a Model 50/60/80 disk.

Although it wouldn't make sense to install a LAN or terminal emulation just to manage the disk logistics, if they are available they can be used for this. Copy protected programs may not be transferable by these methods.

Data Migration Facility

If you don't have the LAN or terminal emulation capability, the Data Migration Facility is an alternative designed specifically to manage information migration from PCs to Model 50/60/80 computers. This tool, mentioned in Chapter 2, allows you to transfer information from a PC to a Model 50/60/80 but not in the other direction. That is, programs and data can only be transferred from the PC to the Model 50/60/80 but not from the Model 50/60/80 to a PC. The transfer can be from diskette to diskette, fixed disk to fixed disk, diskette to fixed disk, or fixed disk to diskette. IBM has granted permission to copy IBM licensed programs, using this Data Migration Facility, to a new medium. For non-IBM programs, the user should consult the applicable license agreement that governs its use or contact the program supplier to determine copying restrictions.

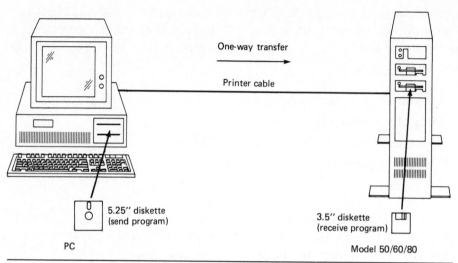

Figure 117. The Data Migration Facility allows the user to transfer information from a PC to a Model 50/60/80 computer.

The Data Migration Facility comes with a Cable Adapter, a 5.25-inch diskette, and instructions. Figure 117 shows how the systems are attached. To transfer information using this facility, you attach a standard printer cable between the ports using the Cable Adapter on the Model 50/60/80 end of the cable. The Cable Adapter allows a standard printer cable to connect the PC's printer port to the Model 50/60/80 printer port (System Unit's Parallel Port). The 5.25-inch diskette provided contains a Send program that is loaded into the PC. A Receive program was provided on the 3.5-inch Reference Diskette provided with every Model 50/60/80 computer. The user initiates the Send program on the PC and then the Receive program on the Model 50/60/80. A simple DOS-like COPY command allows the user to transfer the information from the PC to the Model 50/60/80. File names can include the "*"wild card to copy multiple files with similar names. Copy protected programs may not be transferable using this facility.

The rate of information transfer via the Data Migration Facility varies largely depending on whether the transfers involve fixed disks or diskettes as well as the performance of the computers involved. As a reference point, transferring 5 MB from a PC/XT's fixed disk to a Model 50's 3.5-inch fixed disk takes about twenty-five minutes.

5.25-inch Diskette Drive for Model 50/60/80 Computers

In environments where PCs and Model 50/60/80 computers will coexist, the 5.25-inch External Diskette Drive may be desirable. When this option is installed, it becomes the "B" drive and allows Model 50/60/80 computers to read or write the PC's 5.25-inch diskettes. The user can then easily copy programs and data between 5.25-inch and 3.5-inch diskettes. Alternately, the user can choose to use 5.25-inch diskettes with Model 50/60/80 computers exclusively. This may be desirable when using copy protected programs not transferable to 3.5-inch diskettes. However, if the program requires that the 5.25-inch program diskette reside in drive "A," it may not work with this option since it can only be used as drive "B."

3.5-inch Diskette Drives for PCs

There are both internal and external versions of 3.5-inch diskette drives for PCs. These drives allow you to read and write 3.5-inch diskettes used by Model 50/60/80 computers. They are, however, limited to the 720 KB format. The Model 50/60/80 diskette drives can read both the 720 KB diskettes and the high density 1.44 MB diskettes.

With this option you can easily copy programs and data between 3.5-inch diskettes and 5.25-inch diskettes. Alternately, you may want your PC to use 3.5-inch diskettes directly if, for example, you have a PC at home and a Model 50/60/80 at the office. In this case, the 3.5-inch diskette drive for your PC would allow you to use the same 720 KB diskettes at home and at the office.

Backup Devices

Devices designed to back up information from fixed disks can be used to migrate diskette or fixed disk information between a PC and a Model 50/60/80. The 6157 Streaming Tape Drive or Optical Disk Drive can be used for this purpose. The information to be migrated can first be stored to the tape or optical disk cartridge and then restored to the destination computer in the normal fashion. In the case of the Tape Drive, both the PC and the Model 50/60/80 computer must have the Tape Drive Adapter/A. Then a single Tape Drive can be shared by both computers. In the case of the Optical Disk Drive, each computer must have a complete Optical Disk System since the Optical Disk Adapter/A is not sold separately. It would not make sense from a cost standpoint to purchase either the 6157 Tape Drive or the Optical Disk Drive just for this purpose. However, if the devices are available for other reasons (e.g., fixed disk backup), they can also serve as migration tools.

Performance Testing*

*Reprinted courtesy of the International Business Machines Corp.

IBM PERSONAL SYSTEM/2 GUIDE PREFACE

ABOUT THIS GUIDE.

This guide is an aid to persons who want to understand how the new IBM Personal System/2 performs relative to each other, and relative to previously installed IBM Personal Computers.

A total of 15 application programs were subdivided into seven categories:

> Word Processing
> Spreadsheets
> Graphics
> Databases
> Engineering/Scientific
> Accouting
> Compilers

These applications were run on four previous models and four IBM Personal System/2 models. The results are expressed as an index relative to the IBM PC XT ™ 089.

The testing was performed for IBM by an independent software testing organization, National Software Testing Laboratory, Inc. (NSTL), One Winding Drive, Philadelphia, Pa. 19131. NSTL is an independent testing laboratory specializing in microprocessor performance evaluation.

PERFORMANCE MEASUREMENT.

The applications used to measure performance span a range from processor-intensive, making heavy use of math coprocessors (CAD/CAM), to fixed disk intensive (database).

The execution time on the IBM PC XT 089 (which in all cases was the longest time) is established as an index of 1.0. The execution times of all the other systems are divided into the execution time of the IBM PC XT 089. The shorter the execution time of another system, the faster it is, and hence the larger its index of relative performance.

An example: the programs in the spreadsheet category took 318 seconds to execute on the IBM PC XT 089, the same programs took 39 seconds to execute on the IBM Personal System/2 Model 80. This produced an index of 8.2 for the Model 80. In other words, the Model 80 ran the spreadsheet application programs 8.2 times as fast as the IBM PC XT 089. Category execution times on the IBM PC XT 089 ranged from five minutes and 18 seconds (spreadsheets) to 24 minutes and 29 seconds (word processing).

GROUNDRULES.

All the systems tested use fixed disk. The following IBM PC Disk Operating System (DOS) options were set in the CONFIG.SYS file:

> BUFFERS = 25
> FILES = 20
> BREAK = OFF

Each test was set up to execute without intervention, so the only factor being measured was system performance, not operator response time. All the tests are self-timing using the system internal timer. The optional coprocessor was used for all applications.

Some applications produce printed reports. To exclude variations that would be introduced by printer time, a null printer was used. A null printer is a wrap plug on the parallel channel that allows the system to transfer data at the channel's maximum capacity.

The IBM Personal System/2 Models 50, 60, and 80 are distributed with a fixed disk caching program included on the Reference Diskette. These models are tested with that caching program active (more about caching in the appendix).

IBM Personal System/2 Guide Preface

1

SYSTEMS TESTED.

Figure 1 on page 2 and Figure 2 on page 2 describe the systems tested. In general, each model was tested using its standard hardware configuration. In the case of previous models, an IBM Enhanced Graphics Adapter (EGA) and IBM Enhanced Color Display were used. In the case of the IBM Personal System/2 models, an IBM Personal System/2 Color Display 8513 was used with the integrated graphics function of the particular IBM Personal System/2 model.

Each system operated under DOS Version 3.3.

Performance data for the IBM Personal System/2 Model 8580-111 is not included.

System	Model 30	Model 50	Model 60	Model 80
Memory	640Kb	1Mb	1Mb	2Mb
Coprocessor	8087 (8MHz)	80287 (10MHz)	80287 (10MHz)	80387 (16MHz)
Fixed Disk	20Mb	20Mb	44Mb	70Mb

Figure 1. Table of IBM Personal System/2 Feature/Option Configurations Tested.

System	XT 089	AT 239	XT 286	AT 339
Memory	512Kb	512Kb	640Kb	512Kb
Coprocessor	8087 (4.8MHz)	80287 (4.0MHz)	80287 (5.3MHz)	80287 (5.3MHz)
Fixed Disk	20Mb	30Mb	20Mb	30Mb

Figure 2. Table of Previous System Feature/Options Configurations Tested.

OVERALL CONCLUSIONS.

Figure 3 on page 3 details overall performance conclusions. The range shown portrays the slowest and the fastest of the seven application categories. The average performance is the unweighted average of all seven categories shown in Figures 4-10.

An example: The IBM Personal System/2 Model 80 bar has three values: 5.4, 7.6, and 12.2. The Model 80 was 5.4 times as fast as an IBM PC XT 089 for graphics. (The low end of the application range.) Similarly, the application area that was fastest for the Model 80, relative to the XT, was

database. Here the average performance of the Model 80 was 12.2 times that of the IBM PC XT 089. For all seven categories, the Model 80 ran 7.6 times as fast as the IBM PC XT 089.

Figures 4-10 that follow depict a range of application indices per category. The vertical line within the bar is an average index, obtained by using the total application category time for the IBM PC XT 089 and dividing by the total application category time for the comparison model.

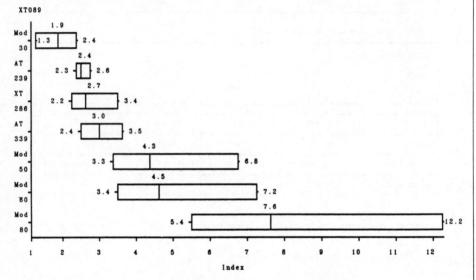

Figure 3. Overall IBM Personal System/2 Performance (IBM PC XT 089 = 1.0)

Overall Conclusions.   3

WORD PROCESSING

The following programs were used for the word processing test:

PROGRAM NAME	VERSION	PUBLISHER
IBM DisplayWrite ™ 4	1.00	IBM Corporation
Microsoft Word (R)	3.00	Microsoft Corporation
Wordstar (R) Professional	3.31	MicroPro International

Test Description:

Perform the following editing and printing functions on a word processing file consisting of 90 paragraphs of 13 lines each (15,364 words):

1. Replace all occurrences of "tomorrow" with "today".

2. Copy a block of text (one paragraph) from the beginning to the end of the document.
3. Spell check the entire document. (The document contains no errors to prevent the program from stopping for corrections.)

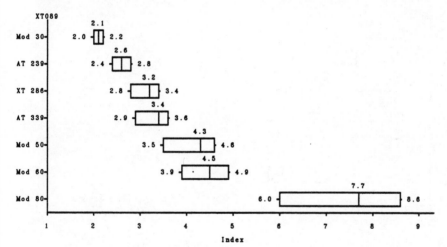

Figure 4. Word Processing Performance Comparison (IBM PC XT 089 = 1.0)

<u>SPREADSHEETS</u>

The following programs were used for the spreadsheet test:

PROGRAM NAME	VERSION	PUBLISHER
Lotus 1-2-3 (R)	2.01	Lotus Development Corporation
SuperCalc (R) 4	1.00	Computer Associates International

Test Description:

The applicaton for both programs is functionally the same, but written in the macro language of the individual product. First, enter a number and define a formula which performs a calculation using a value in an adjacent cell. Copy the formula to a 50 by 50 cell matrix. Recalculate the spreadsheet three times, using a different value each time. Repeat, using five different formulas, focusing on: addition, subtraction, multiplication, division, and exponentiation. Execute a block move; and finally, blank the entire 50 by 50 cell matrix.

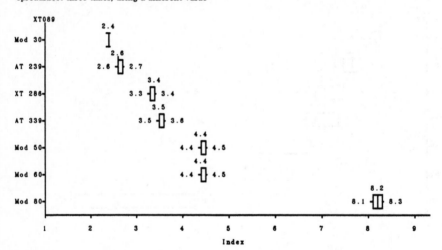

Figure 5. Spreadsheet Performance Comparison (IBM PC XT 089 = 1.0)

GRAPHICS

The following programs were used for the graphics test:

PROGRAM NAME	VERSION	PUBLISHER
Freelance (R)	1.00	Lotus Development Corporation
IBM PC Storyboard ™		IBM Corporation

Test Descriptions:

Freelance

A rectangle is drawn in the upper left quadrant of the screen. It is replicated clockwise 63 times to form a large rectangle. This large rectangle is replicated to the right and joins the first rectangle. Now this larger rectangle is replicated below and joins the large rectangle to form one rectangle composed of 256 smaller rectangles. This last rectangle is redrawn, flipped horizontally and vertically and filled with an "XX" pattern.

IBM PC Storyboard

Three consecutive demo stories are run. The delays between pictures were removed. The three stories were run from a batch file.

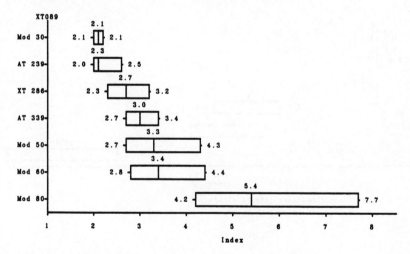

Figure 6. Graphics Performance Comparison (IBM PC XT 089 = 1.0)

Graphics

6

DATABASE

The following programs were used for the database test:

PROGRAM NAME	VERSION	PUBLISHER
dBASE III (R) Plus	1.10	Ashton-Tate
Rbase (R) System V	1.00	Microrim Corporation

Test Description:

Produce a report based on a three-file join, select, and sort. The report includes calculated fields and subtotals.

Use three existing files (customer, invoice, and item files). The files contain the following: Customer File - 500 - 8 field records; Invoice File - 1000 - 8 field records; Item File - 1000 - 4 field records.

Produce a report of companies delinquent in payment for merchandise shipped before a specified date and for which the payment status is "N". The report contains the company name, part number, quantity, price, and total cost (a calculated field, quantity times price). The report is sorted by state, with quantity and total cost subtotaled for each state and totaled for the entire report.

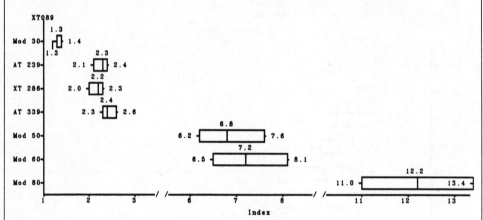

Figure 7. Database Performance Comparison (IBM PC XT 089 = 1.0)

ENGINEERING/SCIENTIFIC

The following program was used for the engineering/scientific test:

PROGRAM NAME	VERSION	PUBLISHER
AutoCAD ™	2.52	AutoDesk, Inc.

Test Description:

Load a three-dimensional drawing of an office (provided with the AutoCAD package). Execute a script (or macro) to display the drawing as it was saved, zoom in to show the detail of a phone, zoom out to display the entire drawing on the screen. Print the drawing as it appears on the screen. Next display six two-dimensional and seven three-dimensional predefined views. These views show the detail of each section of the office.

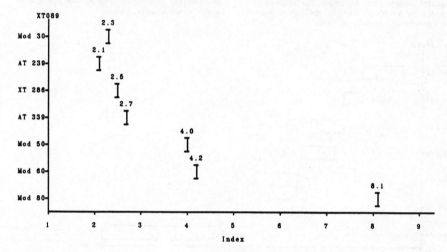

Figure 8. Engineering/Scientific Performance Comparison (IBM PC XT 089 = 1.0)

Engineering/Scientific

8

<u>ACCOUNTING</u>

The following programs were used for the accounting test:

PROGRAM NAME	VERSION	PUBLISHER
Back to Basics	1.02	Peachtree
IBM Accounting Assistant ™	1.01	IBM Corporation
IBM Business Management Series(BMS)	1.00	IBM Corporation

Test Descriptions:

<u>Back to Basics</u>

<u>IBM Acct. Assist. and BMS</u>

Perform a month-end closing procedure with 200 journal entries. First make a back up then close the ledger for the month. This updates the General Ledger records, prints the journal and creates an archive. End by making a second backup after the month-end close.

Perform a General Ledger posting procedure consisting of 100 journal entries. After the Chart of Account was set up and the journals entered, the General Journal is printed and the entries posted to the General Ledger.

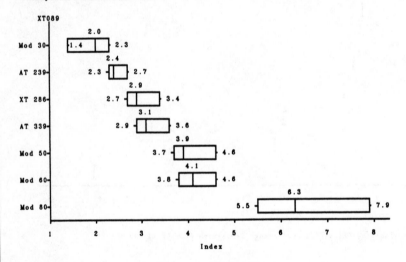

Figure 9. Accounting Performance Comparison (IBM PC XT 089 = 1.0)

COMPILERS

The following programs were used for the compiler test:

PROGRAM NAME	VERSION	PUBLISHER
Lattice (R) C Compiler	3.10	Lattice Inc.
Turbo Pascal TM		Borland International

Test Descriptions:

Lattice C Compiler

Compile and link two 1000 line programs.

Turbo Pascal

Compile the FIRST.ED program found in the Turbo Editor's toolbox.

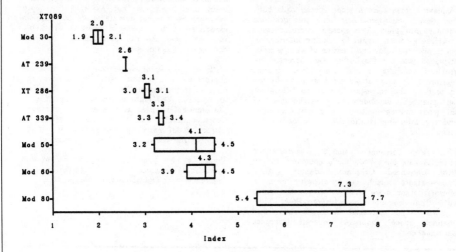

Figure 10. Compiler Performance Comparison (IBM PC XT 089 = 1.0)

APPENDIX A: IMPROVED SYSTEM THROUGHPUT

Improved system throughput is the ability of the IBM Personal System/2 to execute applications in less time. The new IBM Personal System/2 offers several performance enhancements discussed in more detail in this appendix. In particular, the new integrated graphic function, coprocessors, fixed disk caching and interleaving are discussed.

GRAPHICS PERFORMANCE

Displaying images on a video screen calls both the system microprocessor and the graphics adapter into play. The system microprocessor describes a screen layout by loading information concerning the color and location of what is to be displayed into a video buffer. Concurrently the graphics adapter reads the video buffer, interprets the information and directs the display to produce the corresponding image. Graphics performance is dependent both on the speed of the main microprocessor, the graphics adapter and the interplay of the two in accessing the video buffer.

With IBM Personal System/2 , performance improvements have been made compared to the IBM Enhanced Graphics Adapter (EGA). Improvements are achieved by allowing the main microprocessor more time to access the video buffer than was the case with the EGA. This, coupled with increased microprocessor and channel speed, improves overall graphics performance.

COPROCESSOR

A math coprocessor can deliver significant performance improvements for applications that are numerically intensive, i.e., make frequent use of complex functions, such as floating point and trigonometric operations. It does this by expanding the microprocessor's hardware instruction repertoire that would require software subroutines without a coprocessor.

In previous systems coprocessors often operated at speeds that were slower than the speed of the main microprocessor. For example the main microprocessor might operate at 8MHz, while its associated math coprocessor operated at 4MHz. In such cases the full potential of the math coprocessor was not realized.

With IBM Personal System/2, the speed of the coprocessor is consistent with the speed of the main microprocessor. Thus, the Model 30 offers an optional 8087 math coprocessor operating at the same 8MHz speed as its 8086 microprocessor. Correspondingly the Model 80-071 offers an optional 80387 math coprocessor operating at the same 16MHz rate as its 80386 microprocessor.

Figure 11 on page 11 uses the SuperCalc4 Spreadsheet Benchmark to illustrate performance differences with and without the coprocessor.

Model	Without Coprocessor	With Coprocessor
30	2.2	3.4
50	4.8	6.3
60	8.7	11.7
80	10.6	14.6

Figure 11. Coprocessor – SuperCalc4 Performance Comparisons (IBM PC XT 089, No Coprocessor = 1.0)

FIXED DISK CACHING - MODELS 50, 60, & 80

Fixed disk caching is a technique that has been used by larger systems to improve fixed disk performance. A caching device driver is included on the Reference Diskette with Models 50, 60, and 80. It requires user setup by means of an accompanying installation program. The caching program runs in memory below 640Kb.

It works through a set of sector buffers which may be in main memory (below 640Kb) or in extended memory (above 1Mb). On the Models 50, 60 and 80 at least 384Kb of extended memory is standard on the system plannar. The tests were run using a portion of this memory as cache sector buffers.

Whenever a fixed disk sector read is requested, the buffers are searched for that sector. If the sector is found, the data is passed via a memory to memory data transfer without performing a physical fixed disk read, which substantially improves performance. If the sector is not found in the buffer, then the requested sector is physically read along with adjacent sectors. These sectors are stored in the cache buffer. The number of sectors read at the same time is called

the page size and can be either 2, 4, or 8. Caching differs from the normal DOS buffers option in that when a single sector read request is executed, multiple sectors are actually read. Most of the time taken in reading a fixed disk consists of waiting for the head to move to the proper cylinder and waiting for the first sector of the data to rotate under the head. Therefore, reading multiple sectors in the same rotation normally does not materially increase the time over reading one sector.

The cache device driver uses a write-through approach. This means that whenever a fixed disk write is requested, the data will be physically written to the disk. This protects against loss of data in the event of a power failure.

The following graphs show the effect of caching using DisplayWrite 4 and Rbase System V. Other programs were tested with results between these two. Performance without a cache is the reference point, with execution time set to equal 1.0. Figure 12 on page 12 illustrates that with a 192Kb cache, the Rbase System V Benchmark executed 4.4 times faster than it did on the same system without a cache. See the application performance section for a description of the tests.

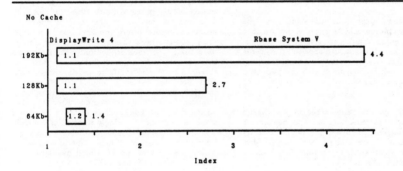

Figure 12. Cache Size Performance Index (Page Size = 4)

No Cache

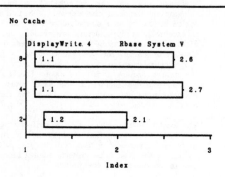

Figure 13. Page Size Performance Index (Cache Size = 128Kb)

Figure 13 on page 13 illustrates that for the selected applications, performance peaked at four sectors per read. Programs which do not do heavy fixed disk I/O or do mainly sequential reads may not show any improvement. Programs, such as database applications, which do frequent random I/O operations, may show a greater improvement. Any increase in size of the cache beyond the file size may not show improvement.

The optimum page size depends on the application. Measurements show a performance increase in going from a page size of two to four. Going from four to eight also showed an increase except in the Rbase System V Test. Individual applications can be fine tuned with the page size, but overall performance will be affected more by the cache size.

The size of the file being accessed also has a definite affect on performance. The benchmark files are relatively small and are not necessarily representative of performance with larger files. Larger files would generally require larger cache sizes for similar effects.

FIXED DISK INTERLEAVE FACTOR

The IBM Personal System/2 offers improved fixed disk performance over previous systems. This is achieved partially through a different fixed disk interleave factor.

Because of differences in the rate at which the fixed disk can read or write data, and the microprocessor/channel can produce or accept it, previous systems did not write sectors on the physical fixed disk track one after the other. Rather, logically sequential fixed disk sectors were written on the physical fixed disk track after skipping two or more (interleaving) physical sectors. This provided more time for the fixed disk adapter/channel or the microprocessor to process a record before the next one was under the read/write head. Thus to read all the sectors on a fixed disk track sequentially, the fixed disk had to rotate from three (interleave factor of three) to six (interleave factor of six) times. With IBM Personal System/2 Models 50, 60 and 80 interleaving has been eliminated and logically sequential sectors are written one after the other on the fixed disk track. Thus all the sectors on a track can be read in a single rotation of the disk. The IBM Personal System/2 Model 30 uses an interleave factor of three. This contrasts to previous models of the PC which had interleave factors of three (AT) to six (XT).

There is a relationship between fixed disk interleaving and fixed disk caching. Some application programs may use the fixed disk rotation time between sectors to process data and be ready to read the next sector prior to the time it appears under the fixed disk read/write head. Such programs are time-dependent and may miss

Appendix A: Improved System Throughput

this precise timing, requiring another fixed disk rotation if the interleave factor is reduced -- this will vary depending on fixed disk adapter, channel and microprocessor speed. Fixed disk caching insulates such programs from their time-dependency by reading as many as eight adjacent sectors from the disk. If, for example, the next seven sectors are read, they can be in the buffer and can be transferred with no fixed disk rotational delay. The fixed disk interleave factor determines how many rotations must occur to read a full track of data.

System	Model 30	Model 50	Model 60	Model 80
Fixed Disk Interleave	3:1	1:1	1:1	1:1
Sectors/Track	17	17	17/35	17/35

Figure 14. Table IBM Personal System/2 Fixed Disk Interleave Factors.

System	XT 089	AT 239	XT 286	AT 339
Fixed Disk Interleave	6:1	3:1	3:1	3:1
Sectors/Track	17	17	17	17

Figure 15. Table of Previous System Fixed Disk Interleave Factors.

<u>APPENDIX B: TRADE MARKS</u>

The following lists contain the registered trade marks and trade marks used in this publication.

<u>IBM CORPORATION</u>

Personal System/2	Trade Mark of IBM Corporation
XT	Trade Mark of IBM Corporation
DisplayWrite	Trade Mark of IBM Corporation
Storyboard	Trade Mark of IBM Corporation
Accounting Assistant	Trade Mark of IBM Corporation
AT	Registered Trade Mark of IBM Corporation
IBM PC	Registered Trade Mark of IBM Corporation

<u>OTHER</u>

AutoCAD	Trade Mark of Autodesk, Inc.
dBASE III	Registered Trade Mark of Ashton-Tate
Freelance	Registered Trade Mark of Lotus Development Corp.
Lattice	Registered Trade Mark of Lattice, Inc.
Lotus 1-2-3	Registered Trade Mark of Lotus Development Corp.
Microsoft Word	Registered Trade Mark of Microsoft Corp.
Rbase	Registered Trade Mark of MicroRim Corp.
SuperCalc	Registered Trade Mark of Computer Associates
Turbo Pascal	Registered Trade Mark of Borland International, Inc.

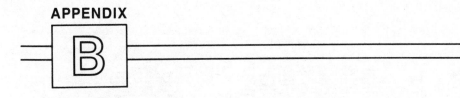

Under the Model 50 Covers

Figure 118 shows a Model 50 with the cover off. Many key elements are plainly visible. The three Micro Channel expansion slots are located in the lower left of the photo. Notice that the third slot from the bottom is a little longer than the rest. This slot contains the extra electrical signals (auxiliary video connector) that allow a feature card to control or monitor the display circuitry on the System Board as discussed in Chapter 1. These 16-bit Micro Channel expansion slots have 112 pins (not counting the 20 pins in the auxiliary video connector). In order to accommodate this many pins, the spacing of the pins in the Micro Channel expansion slots (50 mills) has been cut in half as compared to the PC and Personal Computer AT (100 mills).

The 20 MB fixed disk can be seen beside the Fixed Disk Adapter card that is installed in a fourth specialized Micro Channel expansion slot. This specialized slot allows Model 50 to support the 20 MB fixed disk without consuming any of the three general purpose Micro Channel expansion slots. The fixed disk plugs directly onto the Fixed Disk Adapter card, removing the need for any flex cable. While electrically identical to the other slots, this fourth slot cannot mechanically accommodate a standard Model 50 feature card.

The single 1.44 diskette drive standard with Model 2 is shown. The flex cables that were used to connect the diskette drives to the diskette drive controller card in earlier PC family members have been replaced by an interposer card. This card is effectively a "hard cable" between the diskette drive and the diskette drive controller circuits on the System Board. The optional second diskette drive can be installed in the space next to the first diskette drive.

The socket for the optional 80287 Math Co-processor is visible next to the 80286 microprocessor. The 3-inch speaker gives Model 50 the ability to produce sounds. This speaker can be driven by electronics on the System Board or by feature cards. The battery installed on the speaker assembly is used to sustain the functions of the Clock/Calendar Chip when Model 50 is turned off.

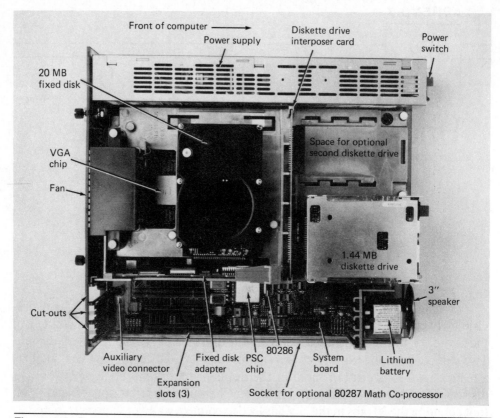

Front of computer ⟶

Power supply

Diskette drive
interposer card

Power
switch

20 MB
fixed disk

Space for optional
second diskette drive

VGA
chip

Fan

1.44 MB
diskette drive

3″
speaker

Cut-outs

Auxiliary
video connector

Fixed disk
adapter

PSC
chip

80286

System
board

Lithium
battery

Expansion
slots (3)

Socket for optional 80287 Math Co-processor

Figure 118. Personal System/2 Model 50 with cover removed.

Two of the IBM-designed chips used in Model 50 are visible: the Video Graphics Array, which generates computer images, and the Processor Support Chip (PSC), which provides some support functions for the 80286 and the Micro Channel.

The power supply was designed to accept the voltages used in the United States and many foreign countries. It provides all of Model 50's electrical power. Next to it is the fan that draws air through the Model 50 System Unit. This air flow is necessary to cool Model 50's internal components.

C

Guide to Other Personal System/2 Publications

The following documents concerning the Personal System/2 products are published by IBM:

Quick Reference Manuals. Each Model 50/60/80 comes with a Quick Reference Manual. These manuals provide introductory information about the Personal System/2 computer. Instructions for unpacking and performing the initial setup are provided. It also guides the user through the power-up sequence of the system and introduces the Reference Diskette. Option installation instructions and trouble-shooting procedures are provided.

Technical Reference Manuals. The Technical Reference Manuals discuss the detailed characteristics and specifications of the computer system. These manuals are not included with your Model 50/60/80 computer and must be purchased separately. The information in these manuals is provided to assist an engineer or programmer in the development of programs, options, and peripherals for use with Model 50/60/80 computers. There are Technical Reference Manuals that cover each Personal System/2 Model, the BIOS programming interfaces, and all of the options.

Hardware Maintenance Library. Model 50/60/80 computers each have their own Hardware Maintenance library, each of which consists of a Hardware Maintenance Reference Manual and a Hardware Maintenance Service Manual. These are not included with the Model 50/60/80 computers and must be purchased separately. The manuals, along with the Reference Diskette, provide the information necessary to diagnose and repair Model 50/60/80 failures. They are designed for service personnel and include step-by-step procedures and parts lists.

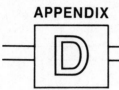

Application Program Compatibility Guide*

To insure compatibility with software originally written for PCs, IBM conducted software compatibility testing on Personal System/2 computers with various operating systems. This appendix contains a copy of the compatibility statement issued by IBM on the day the Personal System/2 computers were announced. Programs not listed in this section are not necessarily incompatible with Personal System/2 computers. Their absence may only mean that they were not part of the compatibility test. At the time of this writing, compatibility testing information for the 70 MB Model 60 and the Model 80 was not available.

*Reprinted courtesy of International Business Machines Corp.

INTRODUCTION

IBM Personal System/2™ and Personal Computer Software Compatibility Guide presents an extensive array of software products compatible with various combinations of IBM Personal System/2 Model 30, IBM Personal System/2 Model 50 and IBM Personal System/2 Model 60 (8560-041), IBM Operating System/2™ Standard Edition and IBM Personal Computer Disk Operating System (DOS) Version 3.30.

This guide is organized in the following sections:

- IBM Software Compatible with IBM Personal System/2 Model 30
- Independent Publishers' Software on IBM Personal System/2 Model 30
- IBM Software Compatible with IBM Personal System/2 Model 50 and Model 60 (8560-041)
- Independent Publishers' Software on IBM Personal System/2 Model 50 and Model 60 (8560-041)
- IBM Software Compatible with IBM PC DOS Version 3.30

- IBM Software Compatible with IBM Local Area Networks
- IBM Software Compatible with PC Local Area Network Program 1.20
- IBM Software Compatible with IBM 3270 Workstation Program
- IBM Operating System/2 Applications
- Independent Publishers' Applications on Operating System/2
- IBM PC DOS Applications on IBM Operating System/2
- Independent Publishers' PC DOS Applications on IBM Operating System/2

Each section lists the software compatible with each of the preceding products, and serves as a quick reference to the software that is supported for these products. The appropriate program version, diskette media on which the product was tested, part numbers and special requirements are also listed for each software product.

IBM SOFTWARE COMPATIBLE WITH IBM PERSONAL SYSTEM/2 MODEL 30

The following IBM licensed software products are compatible with IBM Personal System/2 Model 30 and PC DOS 3.30, and will operate substantially as described in their program documentation.

Numbers that appear in the 3.5-inch diskette and/or 5.25-inch diskette product number columns indicate the diskette media on which the product was tested. The absence of a product number does not necessarily imply that the product is not available on that medium.

Refer to the product documentation for individual software program descriptions for any additional system requirements.

PRODUCT	VERSION	3.5" PART NO.	5.25" PART NO.
COMMUNICATION PRODUCTS			
3270 Workstation Program	1.00	74X9921	
3270 Workstation Program	1.10	75X1088	
3278 Emulation via IBM Personal Computer (5360/5362)[1]	5.1		

PRODUCT	VERSION	3.5" PART NO.	5.25" PART NO.
COMMUNICATION PRODUCTS			
3278 Emulation via IBM Personal Computer (5364)[1]	5.1		
4700 Personal Computer Application Services[2]	1.10		6934406
5364 System Support Program[3,4]	5.1		59X3637
Advanced Program-to-Program Communication for the IBM Personal Computer[5]	1.11	75X1047	
Asynchronous Communications Server Program	1.00		1642003
Distributed Data Management/PC	1.00	59X3653	59X3653
Enhanced 5250 Emulation Program[4]	2.12	74X8402	
Local Area Network Support Program	1.00	83X7873	
Mainframe Communications Assistant	1.05	6024452	
Network Protocol Driver[5]	1.00	6280061	
PC 3270 Emulation Local Area Network Management Program	1.00	83X8873	
PC 3270 Emulation Program[4]	3.00	59X9969	
PC 3270 Emulation Program, Entry Level[4]	1.10	75X1037	
PC 3270 Emulation Program, Entry Level[4]	1.20	75X1085	
PC/Host File Transfer and Terminal Emulator Program	1.00	6476052	
PC Local Area Network Program	1.20	75X1081	
PC Network Analysis Program [6]	1.01		6489762
PC Support/36 (5360/5362) [1,7]	5.1		
PC Support/36 (5364) [1,7]	5.1		
PC Support/36 Expansion Feature (5360/5362)[1]	5.1		
PC Support/36 Expansion Feature (5364)[1]	5.1		
PC Support/36 Workstation Feature (5360/5362) [4,8]	5.1		
PC Support/36 Workstation Feature (5364) [4,8]	5.1		
PC Support/38[9]	8.0		
PC Support/38 Expansion Feature[9]	8.0		
Remote NETBIOS Access Facility	1.00	69X7771	69X7771
Token-Ring Network NETBIOS Program	1.10	6476039	
PROGRAMMER TOOLS AND LANGUAGES			
3270 PC High Level Language Application Program Interface	3.00		59X9959
3270 PC High Level Language Application Program Interface	3.10	75X1087	75X1087
BASIC Compiler[10]	2.00	6280078	
BASIC Compiler/2	1.00	6280179	
BASIC Interpreter	3.30	6280060	
C/2	1.00	6280187	
C Compiler[10]	1.00	6280081	

PRODUCT	VERSION	3.5" PART NO.	5.25" PART NO.
COBOL/2	1.00	6280207	
COBOL Compiler	2.00	6280177	
EZ-PREP (Cross System Product/ Application Generation)	1.00		6317011
EZ-RUN(Cross System Product/ Application Execution)	1.00		6317010
FORTRAN/2	1.00	6280185	
Graphics Development Toolkit [10,11,12,13]	1.20	6280203	
Image Support Facility 2	1.10	6457821	
Interactive System Productivity Facility for the IBM Personal Computer (ISPF/PC II) Version 2 (EZ-VU II Development Facility)	2.00		6317026
Interactive System Productivity Facility for the IBM Personal Computer (ISPF/PC II) Version 2 (EZ-VU II Runtime Facility)	2.00		6317025
Interactive System Productivity Facility/Program Development Facility Editor for the IBM Personal Computer (EZ-VU Editor)	1.00		6466974
Macro Assembler [10]	2.00	6280077	
Macro Assembler/2	1.00	6280181	
Pascal Compiler [10]	2.02	6280166	
Pascal Compiler/2	1.00	6280183	
Professional FORTRAN Compiler [10]	1.30	6280127	

BUSINESS/PRODUCTIVITY APPLICATIONS

PRODUCT	VERSION	3.5" PART NO.	5.25" PART NO.
DisplayWrite™ 4	1.00	74X9913	
ImagEdit Licensed Program [12,13]	1.00	6476113	
PC Storyboard	1.20		6316998
Personal Editor II	1.01	6276701	
Personal Services/PC	1.20	6476054	
Personal Services/PC	1.30	6476148	
PROFS PC Support Feature of PROFS (5664-309) [16,17]	2.00		
Storyboard Plus [11,12]	1.00	6024401	
Word Proof II	1.01	6276700	

Assistant Series

PRODUCT	VERSION	3.5" PART NO.	5.25" PART NO.
DisplayWrite™ Assistant [14]	1.00	59X9958	
Filing Assistant®	2.00	6024457	
Graphing Assistant	2.00	6024458	
Mainframe Communications Assistant	1.05	6024452	
Planning Assistant	2.00	6024461	
Project Assistant	1.00	6024462	
Reporting Assistant	2.00	6024459	
Writing Assistant	2.00	6024460	

PRODUCT	VERSION	3.5" PART NO.	5.25" PART NO.
BUSINESS/PRODUCTIVITY APPLICATIONS			
Accounting Assistant Series			
Accounts Payable Edition	1.00	6467004	
Accounts Receivable and Billing Edition	1.00	6467005	
General Accounting Edition	1.00	6467003	
Inventory Control and Purchasing Edition	1.00	6467007	
Job Cost Edition	1.00	6467008	
Payroll Edition	1.00	6467006	
Business Adviser			
Accounts Payable Edition	1.20	6476056	
Accounts Receivable Edition	1.20	6476057	
General Accounting Edition	1.20	6476055	
Information Management Edition	1.20	6476069	
Inventory Control Edition	1.20	6476067	
Network Extension Edition[15]	1.20	6476059	
Order Entry Edition	1.20	6476068	
Payroll Edition	1.20	6476058	
Personal Decision Series			
Data Edition	2.00	6476085	
English Access Edition	1.00	6476079	
Network+ Edition	1.00	6476077	
Plans+ Edition	2.00	6476076	
Reports+ Edition	2.00	6476075	
ENGINEERING/SCIENTIFIC APPLICATIONS			
CADwrite [11,18]	1.00	5472415	
Data Acquisition and Control Adapter Support[19]	1.00		6024202
General Purpose Interface Bus (GPIB) Adapter Support[19]	1.00		6024201
OTHER APPLICATIONS			
Doctor's Office Manager II*[20]	1.00		6467035
Infowindow Pilot Authoring System	1.00	6476094	
Infowindow Pilot Presentation System	1.00	6476095	
PC/Colorview	1.10		6410982
PC/VTXACCESS	1.00	6476071	
TopView® [10,11,21]	1.12	6024475	
Video Passage Authoring	1.00	6403822	6403822
Video Passage Presentation	1.00	6403823	6403823
EDUCATION PRODUCTS			
Adventures in Math	1.00		6024112
Bouncy Bee Learns Letters	1.00/1.01	6024511	6024137
Bouncy Bee Learns Words	1.00/1.01	6024510	6024139
Classroom LAN Administration System	1.00		6024159
Comma Cat™	1.00		6024093
Dictionary Dog™	1.00		6024067
Electric Poet®	1.00		6024172
Get Set For Writing To Read[22]	1.00/1.01		6024468

PRODUCT	VERSION	3.5" PART NO.	5.25" PART NO.
Listen to Learn	1.00/1.01	6024506	6024165
Logo	1.00	6024731	6024076
Logo Learner	1.00/1.01	6024515	6024136
Missing Letters	1.00/1.01	6024507	6024104
Monster Math	1.00		6024072
Primary Editor[23]	1.00/1.01		6024294
Teacher's Quiz Designer	1.00/1.01	6024509	6024075
Typing Tutor	1.00		6024013
Writing to Read Program Kit[22]	3.00	6024513	6024447
Basic Skills Series			
Combining Sentences: Level II	1.01	6024689	6024482
Combining Sentences: Level III	1.01	6024690	6024483
Combining Sentences: Level IV	1.01	6024691	6024884
Geometry One: Foundations	1.01	6024707	6024485
Geometry Two: Proofs & Extensions	1.01	6024728	6024486
Math Concepts: Level P	1.01	6024721	6024356
Math Concepts: Level I	1.01	6024722	6024355
Math Concepts: Level II	1.01	6024723	6024357
Math Concepts: Level III	1.01	6024724	6024427
Math Concepts: Level IV	1.01	6024716	6024429
Math Practice: Level I	1.01	6024663	6024353
Math Practice: Level II	1.01	6024664	6024354
Math Practice: Level III	1.01	6024665	6024431
Math Practice: Level IV	1.01	6024666	6024432
Parts of Speech: Level II	1.01	6024679	6024333
Parts of Speech: Level III	1.01	6024680	6024334
Punctuation: Level II	1.01	6024695	6024487
Punctuation: Level III	1.01	6024696	6024488
Punctuation: Level IV	1.01	6024697	6024489
Reading for Information: Level II	1.01	6024683	6024358
Reading for Information: Level III	1.01	6024684	6024359
Reading for Information: Level IV	1.01	6024685	6024360
Reading for Meaning: Level I	1.01	6024671	6024330
Reading for Meaning: Level II	1.01	6024672	6024336
Reading for Meaning: Level III	1.01	6024673	6024337
Reading for Meaning: Level IV	1.01	6024674	6024338
Spelling: Level I	1.01	6024720	6024347
Spelling: Level II	1.01	6024708	6024348
Spelling: Level III	1.01	6024709	6024349
Touch Typing for Beginners	1.01	6024698	6024339
Vocabulary: Level II	1.01	6024701	6024350
Vocabulary: Level III	1.01	6024702	6024351
Vocabulary: Level IV	1.01	6024703	6024352

PRODUCT	VERSION	3.5" PART NO.	5.25" PART NO.
EDUCATION PRODUCTS			
Private Tutor Series			
Basic Number Concepts	1.00		6024297
Capitalization Skills	1.00		6024085
Computers and Communications	1.00		6024069
Language Skills	1.00		6024084
Learning DOS	1.00		6024063
Learning to Program in BASIC	1.00		6024081
Math Computation Skills	1.00		6024305
Preparing for Geometry and Algebra	1.00		6024307
Private Tutor[24]	2.00/2.01	6024508	6024113
Punctuation Skills	1.00		6024083
Reading Comprehension Skills	1.00		6024325
Solving Math Word Problems	1.00		6024308
Spelling Skills	1.00		6024086
Vocabulary Building Skills	1.00		6024326
Word Knowledge Skills	1.00		6024327
Biology Series (1–20)			
Cell Functions: Growth & Mitosis	1.00/1.01	6024635	6024316
Chemicals of Life I: The Structure of Matter	1.00/1.01	6024636	6024317
Chemicals of Life II: Water, Carbohydrates, & Lipids	1.00/1.01	6024647	6024344
Chemicals of Life III: Proteins & Nucleic Acids	1.00/1.01	6024614	6024409
Cytology & Histology: Cells & Tissues	1.00/1.01	6024612	6024407
Human Life Processes I: Cellular Physiology	1.00/1.01	6024649	6024346
Human Life Processes II: Systems Level	1.00/1.01	6024616	6024411
Human Life Processes III: Development & Differentiation	1.00/1.01	6024657	6024414
Leaf: Structure & Physiology	1.00/1.01	6024637	6024318
Light, Plants, and Photosynthesis: Energy in Conversion	1.00/1.01	6024638	6024319
Mendelian Genetics: The Science of Inheritance	1.00/1.01	6024613	6024408
Modern Genetics: Chromosomes & Coding	1.00/1.01	6024648	6024345
Passive Transport: Diffusion and Osmosis	1.00/1.01	6024639	6024320
Pathology: Diseases & Defenses	1.00/1.01	6024646	6024343
Plants: Growth and Specialization	1.00/1.01	6024645	6024321
Pollination & Fertilization: Seeds, Fruits, and Embryos	1.00/1.01	6024633	6024415
Regulation & Homeostatis: Systems in Balance	1.00/1.01	6024615	6024410
Taxonomy: Classification & Organization	1.00/1.01	6024655	6024416
The Environment I: Habitats & Ecosystems	1.00/1.01	6024658	6024412
The Environment II: Cycles & Interactions	1.00/1.01	6024656	6024413

PRODUCT	VERSION	3.5" PART NO.	5.25" PART NO.
Scientific Reasoning Series (1-5)			
Concept Development: Heat & Temperature, & Graphs	1.00	6024632	
Measurement Process: Distance & Area	1.00	6024730	
Ratio Reasoning: Crystals & Speed	1.00	6024631	
Scientific Models: Batteries and Bulbs, & Families	1.00	6024630	
Theory Formation: Reflections & Patterns	1.00	6024729	
Physics Discovery Series (1-8)			
Investigating Acceleration	1.01	6024624	6024403
Investigating Atomic Models	1.00	6024523	6024118
Investigating Conservation of Energy	1.01	6024625	6024406
Investigating Electric Fields	1.01	6024627	6024464
Investigating Gravitational Force	1.01	6024622	6024404
Investigating Models of Light	1.01	6024626	6024465
Investigating Thermal Energy	1.01	6024623	6024405
Investigating Wave Interference	1.01	6024628	6024466
Earth Science Series (1-8)			
Earthquakes	1.00/1.01	6024517	6024322
Glacial Landforms	1.00	6024514	6024117
Ground Water	1.00/1.01	6024516	6024122
Hydrologic Cycle	1.00/1.01	6024518	6024121
Landslides	1.01	6024522	6024324
Moisture in the Atmosphere	1.00/1.01	6024520	6024124
Surface Water	1.00/1.01	6024519	6024123
Volcanoes	1.00/1.01	6024521	6024323

[1]*Product is downloaded from System/36.*

[2]*Requires current level of maintenance to be applied.*

[3]*5364 PC attachment programs support IBM Personal System/2 Model 30 at the availability of Release 5.1 of System/36.*

[4]*Hot-key to MultiColor Graphics Array and Video Graphics Array modes not supported.*

[5]*Compatible with IBM PC Network Adapter II.*

[6]*Compatible with IBM PC Network Adapter.*

[7]*Includes 3.5-inch and 5.25-inch PC compatible installation diskettes in addition to System/36 installation diskette at the availability of Release 5.1 of System/36.*

[8]*Product runs from virtual disk on attached System/36 or can be downloaded from System/36.*

[9]*Product is downloaded from System/38.*

[10]*Compatibility with IBM Personal System/2 Display Adapter has been verified.*

[11]*Supports IBM Personal System/2 Mouse.*

[12]*Supports graphics mode 320X200-256 colors.*

[13]*Supports graphics mode 640X480-2 colors.*

[14]*If DISPLAY.SYS is present on the target diskette or fixed disk, it must be renamed to some other name before the install program is executed. It must later be renamed back to DISPLAY.SYS after the install program completes.*

[15]*Update required for installation; dedicated server required.*

[16]*Product is downloaded from the host.*

[17]*PC 3720 Emulation Program 3.0 is not supported.*

[18]*Requires IBM Personal System/2 Display Adapter; supports 640X480-16 mode.*

[19]*Tested with code written in BASIC only.*

[20]*Can be used as a remote PC on a Local Area Network. Cannot be used as the server or in a single user mode.*

[21]*TopView 1.12 is the required version of TopView for IBM Personal System/2 Model 30.*

[22]*Requires IBM Personal System/2 Speech Adapter.*

[23]*Version 1.00 requires IBM Personal System/2 Speech Adapter.*

[24]*Screen alignment function in Version 2.00 neither required nor supported.*

INDEPENDENT PUBLISHERS' SOFTWARE ON IBM PERSONAL SYSTEM/2 MODEL 30

The following independent software publishers have informed IBM that they have tested the following products on 3.5-inch media on IBM Personal System/2 Model 30 with PC DOS 3.30 and have determined that these programs operate substantially as described in their program documentation.

Products marked with an asterisk (*) will be available in a new release from the independent software publisher. Contact the appropriate independent software publisher directly for more information.

SOFTWARE PUBLISHER	PRODUCT	VERSION
Alpha® Software Corporation	Alpha®/Three	1.0
	DataBase Manager II™ The Integrator	2.02
	Electric Desk™	1.1
Ashton-Tate®	CHART-MASTER™	
	dBase III™ Plus	*
	Framework II™[1]	*
	MultiMate™ Advantage	*
	SIGN-MASTER™	*
BORLAND INTERNATIONAL INC.	Reflex®[1]	*
	Turbo Pascal®[1]	*
Computer Associates International, Inc.	SuperCalc® 4	1.0
	SuperCalc 4[1,2]	*
	SuperProject® Plus™	2.00F
Digital Research®, Inc.	GEM Graph™[1]	*
	GEM Word Chart™[1]	*
	GEM Write™[1]	*
Fifth Generation Systems, Inc.	FASTBACK	5.14
Lifetree Software, Inc.	VOLKSWRITER® 3	1.0
	VOLKSWRITER®DeluxePlus	1.0
Living Videotext, Inc.	Ready!™[3]	*
	ThinkTank™	2.30NP
Lotus™ Development Corporation	1-2-3™[1]	*
	Symphony™[1]	*
Media Cybernetics, Inc.	DR. HALO™ II™[1,2]	*
Micro-Integration Corporation	BIS-3270®	*
MicroPro International Corporation	Easy™ Extra	1.5
	WordStar® 2000 Plus	2.0
	WordStar® Professional	4.0
Microrim®, Inc.	R: BASE® 5000	1.01
	R: BASE® CLOUT®	*
	R: BASE® Extended ReportWriter	*
	R: BASE® System V	1.1
Microsoft®, Corporation	Microsoft® MultiPlan®	*
	Microsoft® Word	*
Software Products International, Inc.	O-P-E-N Access II[1,2]	*

SOFTWARE PUBLISHER	PRODUCT	VERSION
Software Publishing Corporation	Harvard™ Total Project Manager II	*
	pfs: Professional Write	*
	pfs: Professional File/Report	*
	pfs: Professional Plan	*
TCS Software, Inc.	TCS Client Ledger System	3.36
Timberline Systems, Inc. Medallion® Collection	Architect/Engineer I	3.0
	Estimating	2.0
	General Ledger	2.2
	Job Cost	5.1
	Starter Set	2.2
WordPerfect® Corporation	WordPerfect®	4.2
	WordPerfect® Math Plan	3.0
	WordPerfect® Library	1.0
Z-SOFT CORPORATION	PC Paintbrush®+[1,2]	*

[1]*Modified to support graphics mode 640X480-2 colors.*
[2]*Modified to support graphics mode 320X200-256 colors.*
[3]*Requires EGASAVE program from Living Videotext, Inc.*

INDEPENDENT PUBLISHERS' SOFTWARE ON IBM PERSONAL SYSTEM/2 MODEL 30

The following independent software publishers have stated that they intend to make the following products available for IBM Personal System/2 Model 30 on 3.5-inch media. Contact the appropriate independent software publisher directly for more information.

SOFTWARE PUBLISHER	PRODUCT
Autodesk, Inc.	AutoCAD®[1]
BORLAND INTERNATIONAL INC.	SideKick® Turbo Lightning™
Digital Research®, Inc.	GEM Draw™ Plus[1]
Enertronics Research, Inc.	ENERGRAPHICS™[1,2]
Lotus™ Development Corporation	FREELANCE® Plus[1]
Microsoft®, Corporation	Microsoft® Chart[1] Microsoft® Flight Simulator[1,2] Microsoft® Project Microsoft® Windows[1] Microsoft® Word[1]
Novell Incorporated	Advanced NetWare®/286[3] Advanced NetWare®/86 NetWare® Bridge
WordPerfect® Corporation	WordPerfect® Math Plan[1,2] WordPerfect® Library[1,2]

[1]*Modified to support graphics mode 640X480-2 colors.*
[2]*Modified to support graphics mode 320X200-256 colors.*
[3]*The IBM Personal System/2 Model 30 can be a workstation on the network.*

IBM SOFTWARE COMPATIBLE WITH IBM PERSONAL SYSTEM/2 MODEL 50 AND MODEL 60 (8560-041)

The following IBM licensed software products are compatible with IBM Personal System/2 Model 50 and Model 60 (8560-041) and PC DOS 3.30, and will operate substantially as described in their program documentation.

Software on IBM Personal System/2 Model 50 or Model 60 (8560-041) that is designed to run in CGA, EGA or Video Graphics Array modes should not be effected when using IBM Personal System/2 Color Display 8514 attached to

an IBM Personal System/2 Display Adapter 8514/A.

Numbers that appear in the 3.5-inch diskette and/or 5.25-inch diskette product number columns indicate the diskette media on which the software was tested. The absence of a product number does not necessarily imply that the product is not available on that medium.

Refer to the product documentation for individual software program descriptions for any additional system requirements.

PRODUCT	VERSION	3.5" PART NO.	5.25" PART NO.
COMMUNICATION PRODUCTS			
3270 Workstation Program	1.00	74X9921	74X9921
3270 Workstation Program	1.10	75X1088	75X1088
3278 Emulation via IBM Personal Computer (5360/5362)[1]	5.1		
3278 Emulation via IBM Personal Computer (5364)[1]	5.1		
Advanced Program-to-Program Communication for the IBM Personal Computer[2]	1.11	75X1047	75X1047
Asynchronous Communications Server Program	1.00		1642003
Distributed Data Management/PC	1.00	59X3653	59X3653
Local Area Network Manager	1.00	83X9100	83X9100
Local Area Network Support Program[3]	1.00	83X7873	83X7873
Mainframe Communications Assistant[4]	1.05	6024452	
PC 3270 Emulation Local Area Network Management Program	1.00	83X8873	83X8873
PC 3270 Emulation Program[4,5]	3.00	59X9969	59X9969
PC 3270 Emulation Program, Entry Level[4,6]	1.20	75X1085	75X1085
PC/Host File Transfer & Emulator Program[7]	1.00	6476052	6476052
PC Local Area Network Program[8]	1.20	75X1081	75X1081
PC Network Protocol Driver	1.00	6280061	6280061
PC Support/36 (5360/5362)[1,9]	5.1		
PC Support/36 (5364)[1,9]	5.1		
PC Support/36 Expansion Feature (5360/5362)[1]	5.1		
PC Support/36 Expansion Feature (5364)[1]	5.1		
PC Support/36 Workstation Feature (5360/5362)[6,10]	5.1		
PC Support/36 Workstation Feature (5364)[6,10]	5.1		
PC Support/38[11]	8.0		
PC Support/38 Expansion Feature[11]	8.0		
Remote NETBIOS Access Facility	1.00	69X7771	69X7771
System 36/38 Work Station Emulation Program for the IBM Personal System/2/A	1.00	69X6286	
Token-Ring Network Bridge Program	1.10	83X7860	83X7860
Token-Ring Network Manager Program	1.10	6476107	6476107

PRODUCT	VERSION	3.5" PART NO.	5.25" PART NO.
PROGRAMMER TOOLS AND LANGUAGES			
3270 PC High Level Language Application Program Interface	3.10	75X1087	75X1087
BASIC Compiler[12]	2.00	6280078	
BASIC Compiler/2	1.00	6280179	
C/2	1.00	6280187	
C Compiler[12]	1.00	6280081	
COBOL/2	1.00	6280207	
COBOL Compiler[13]	2.00	6280177	
EZ-PREP (Cross System Product/ Application Generation)	1.00		6317011
EZ-RUN (Cross System Product/ Application Execution)	1.00		6317010
FORTRAN/2	1.00	6280185	
Graphics Development Toolkit[14]	1.20	6280203	
Image Support Facility 2	1.10	6457821	6457821

Interactive System Productivity Facility
  for the IBM Personal Computer
  (ISPF/PC II) Version 2
  (EZ-VU II Development Facility)[15]
	2.00		6317026

Interactive System Productivity Facility
  for the IBM Personal Computer
  (ISPF/PC II) Version 2
  (EZ-VU II Runtime Facility)[15]
	2.00		6317025

Interactive System Productivity Facility/
  Program Development Facility Editor
  for the IBM Personal Computer
  (EZ-VU Editor)
	1.00		6466974

Macro Assembler[12]	2.00	6280077	
Macro Assembler/2	1.00	6280181	
Pascal Compiler[12]	2.02	6280166	
Pascal Compiler/2	1.00	6280183	
Professional FORTRAN Compiler[12]	1.30	6280127	
BUSINESS/PRODUCTIVITY APPLICATIONS			
DisplayWrite™ 4[4,8,16,17,18]	1.00	74X9913	
ImagEdit Licensed Program[14,19]	1.00	6476113	
Personal Editor II	1.01	6276701	
Personal Services/PC	1.20	6476054	
Personal Services/PC	1.30	6476148	
PROFS PC Support Feature of PROFS (5664-309)[20,21]	2.00		
Storyboard Plus[14,22,23]	1.00	6024401	6024401
Word Proof II	1.01	6276700	

PRODUCT	VERSION	3.5" PART NO.	5.25" PART NO.
Assistant Series			
DisplayWrite™ Assistant[8,18,24]	1.00	59X9958	
Document Retrieval Assistant	1.00		6024306
Drawing Assistant[25]	1.00		6024089
Filing Assistant®	2.00	6024457	6024457
Graphing Assistant[26]	2.00	6024458	6024458
Mainframe Communications Assistant[4]	1.05	6024452	
Planning Assistant	2.00	6024461	6024461
Project Assistant	1.01	6024462	6024462
Reporting Assistant	2.00	6024459	6024459
Writing Assistant	2.00	6024460	6024460
Accounting Assistant Series			
Accounts Payable Edition	1.00	6467004	
Accounts Receivable and Billing Edition	1.00	6467005	
General Accounting Edition	1.00	6467003	
Inventory Control and Purchasing Edition	1.00	6467007	
Job Cost Edition	1.00	6467008	
Payroll Edition	1.00	6467006	
Business Adviser			
Accounts Payable Edition	1.20	6476056	
Accounts Receivable Edition	1.20	6476057	
General Accounting Edition	1.20	6476055	
Information Management Edition	1.20	6476069	
Inventory Control Edition	1.20	6476067	
Network Extension Edition[27]	1.20	6476059	
Order Entry Edition	1.20	6476068	
Payroll Edition	1.20	6476058	
Personal Decision Series			
Data Edition	2.00	6476085	
English Access Edition	1.00	6476079	
Network+ Edition	1.00	6476077	
Plans+ Edition	2.00	6476076	
Reports+ Edition	2.00	6476075	
ENGINEERING/SCIENTIFIC APPLICATIONS			
CADwrite[14,23,28]	1.00	5472415	
Computer Integrated Electrical Design Series (CIEDS)™/Design Capture for PC/AT (5669-191)[29,30]	1.1.1		
OTHER APPLICATIONS			
Doctor's Office Manager II*[31]	1.00		6467035
PC/Colorview	1.10		6410982
TopView®[13,14,32]	1.12	6024475	

PRODUCT	VERSION	3.5" PART NO.	5.25" PART NO.
EDUCATION PRODUCTS			
Bouncy Bee Learns Letters	1.00/1.01	6024511	6024137
Bouncy Bee Learns Words	1.00/1.01	6024510	6024139
Missing Letters	1.00/1.01	6024507	6024104
Primary Editor	1.00/1.01		6024294
Teacher's Quiz Designer	1.00/1.01	6024509	6024075
Basic Skills Series			
Combining Sentences: Level II	1.01	6024689	6024482
Combining Sentences: Level III	1.01	6024690	6024483
Combining Sentences: Level IV	1.01	6024691	6024484
Geometry One: Foundations	1.01	6024707	6024485
Geometry Two: Proofs and Extensions	1.01	6024728	6024486
Math Concepts: Level P	1.01	6024721	6024356
Math Concepts: Level I	1.01	6024722	6024355
Math Concepts: Level II	1.01	6024723	6024357
Math Concepts: Level III	1.01	6024724	6024427
Math Concepts: Level IV	1.01	6024716	6024429
Math Practice: Level I	1.01	6024663	6024353
Math Practice: Level II	1.01	6024664	6024354
Math Practice: Level III	1.01	6024665	6024431
Math Practice: Level IV	1.01	6024666	6024432
Parts of Speech: Level II	1.01	6024679	6024333
Parts of Speech: Level III	1.01	6024680	6024334
Punctuation: Level II	1.01	6024695	6024487
Punctuation: Level III	1.01	6024696	6024488
Punctuation: Level IV	1.01	6024697	6024489
Reading for Information: Level II	1.01	6024683	6024358
Reading for Information: Level III	1.01	6024684	6024359
Reading for Information: Level IV	1.01	6024685	6024360
Reading for Meaning: Level I	1.01	6024671	6024330
Reading for Meaning: Level II	1.01	6024672	6024336
Reading for Meaning: Level III	1.01	6024673	6024337
Reading for Meaning: Level IV	1.01	6024674	6024338
Spelling: Level I	1.01	6024720	6024347
Spelling: Level II	1.01	6024708	6024348
Spelling: Level III	1.01	6024709	6024349
Touch Typing for Beginners	1.01	6024698	6024339
Vocabulary: Level II	1.01	6024701	6024350
Vocabulary: Level III	1.01	6024702	6024351
Vocabulary: Level IV	1.01	6024703	6024352
Biology Series (1-20)			
Cell Functions: Growth and Mitosis	1.00/1.01	6024635	6024316
Chemicals of Life I: The Structure of Matter	1.00/1.01	6024636	6024317
Chemicals of Life II: Water, Carbohydrates, and Lipids	1.00/1.01	6024647	6024344
Chemicals of Life III: Proteins and Nucleic Acids	1.00/1.01	6024614	6024409
Cytology & Histology: Cells and Tissues	1.00/1.01	6024612	6024407
Human Life Processes I: Cellular Physiology	1.00/1.01	6024649	6024346

PRODUCT	VERSION	3.5" PART NO.	5.25" PART NO.
Human Life Processes II: Systems Level	1.00/1.01	6024616	6024411
Human Life Processes III: Development and Differentiation	1.00/1.01	6024657	6024414
Leaf: Structure and Physiology	1.00/1.01	6024637	6024318
Light, Plants, and Photosynthesis: Energy in Conversion	1.00/1.01	6024638	6024319
Mendelian Genetics: The Science of Inheritance	1.00/1.01	6024613	6024408
Modern Genetics: Chromosomes and Coding	1.00/1.01	6024648	6024345
Passive Transport: Diffusion and Osmosis	1.00/1.01	6024639	6024320
Pathology: Diseases and Defenses	1.00/1.01	6024646	6024343
Plants: Growth & Specialization	1.00/1.01	6024645	6024321
Pollination and Fertilization: Seeds, Fruits, and Embryos	1.00/1.01	6024633	6024415
Regulation & Homeostatis: Systems in Balance	1.00/1.01	6024615	6024410
Taxonomy: Classification and Organization	1.00/1.01	6024655	6024416
The Environment I: Habitats and Ecosystems	1.00/1.01	6024658	6024412
The Environment II: Cycles and Interactions	1.00/1.01	6024656	6024413
Earth Science Series (1-8)			
Earthquakes	1.00/1.01	6024517	6024322
Glacial Landforms	1.00	6024514	6024117
Ground Water	1.01	6024516	6024122
Hydrologic Cycle	1.01	6024518	6024121
Landslides	1.00/1.01	6024522	6024324
Moisture in the Atmosphere	1.00	6024520	6024124
Surface Water	1.01	6024519	6024123
Volcanoes	1.00/1.01	6024521	6024323
Physics Discovery Series (1-8)			
Investigating Acceleration[33]	1.00/1.01	6024624	6024403
Investigating Atomic Models[33]	1.00	6024523	6024118
Investigating Conservation of Energy[33]	1.00/1.01	6024625	6024406
Investigating Electric Fields[33]	1.00/1.01	6024627	6024464
Investigating Gravitational Force[33]	1.00/1.01	6024622	6024404
Investigating Models of Light[33]	1.00/1.01	6024626	6024465
Investigating Thermal Energy[33]	1.00/1.01	6024623	6024405
Investigating Wave Interference[33]	1.00/1.01	6024628	6024466
Scientific Reasoning Series (1-5)			
Concept Development: Heat and Temperature, and Graphs	1.00	6024632	
Measurement Process: Distance and Area	1.00	6024730	
Ratio Reasoning: Crystals & Speed	1.00	6024631	
Scientific Models: Batteries and Bulbs, and Families	1.00	6024630	
Theory Formation: Reflections and Patterns	1.00	6024729	

¹*Product is downloaded from System/36.*

²*Coexists with the Redirector configuration of PC Local Area Network Program Version 1.20.*

³*Required for IBM Token-Ring Network support.*

⁴*Coexists with PC Local Area Network Program Version 1.20.*

⁵*Compatible with IBM Personal System/2 Multiprotocol Adapter/A for communications up to 19.2K BPS.*

⁶*Hot-key to MultiColor Graphics Array and Video Graphics Array modes not supported.*

⁷*Requires EC 6476152 to support 19.2K BPS.*

⁸*Coexists with PC 3270 Emulation Program Version 3.00.*

⁹*Includes 3.5-inch and 5.25-inch PC compatible installation diskettes in addition to System/36 installation diskette at the availability of Release 5.1 of System/36.*

¹⁰*Product runs from virtual disk on attached System/36 or can be downloaded from System/36.*

¹¹*Product is downloaded from System/38.*

¹²*Coexists with PC 3270 Emulation Program Version 3.00 and/or PC Local Area Network Program Version 1.20.*

¹³*Coexists with PC 3270 Emulation Program Version 3.00 or PC Local Area Network Program Version 1.20 but not both.*

¹⁴*Supports IBM Personal System/2 Mouse.*

¹⁵*"NumLock" state does not function correctly.*

¹⁶*Supports Microsoft® Serial Mouse, PC Mouse, or Visi-On Mouse only.*

¹⁷*Voice Note function is not supported.*

¹⁸*Product supports the following programs: PROFS PC Support Feature of PROFS Version 2.00; Personal Services/PC Version 1.20; TopView® Version 1.12.*

¹⁹*Supports 640X480-2 mode.*

²⁰*Product is downloaded from the host.*

²¹*PC 3720 Emulation Program Version 3.00 and PC 3270 Emulation Program, Entry Level Version 1.20 are not supported.*

²²*Supports 320X200-256 mode.*

²³*Supports 640X480-16 mode.*

²⁴*If DISPLAY.SYS is present on the target diskette or fixed disk, it must be renamed to some other name before the install program is executed. It must later be renamed back to DISPLAY.SYS after the install program completes.*

²⁵*Supports IBM Personal System/2 Mouse with its supplied mouse driver when configured under the category "OTHER."*

²⁶*Pie charts may not appear round on IBM Personal System/2 Color Displays 8512 and 8513 and IBM Personal System/2 Monochrome Display.*

²⁷*Update required for installation; dedicated server required.*

²⁸*Supports 1024X768-256 mode on IBM Personal System/2 Color Display 8514 attached to an installed IBM Personal System/2 Display Adapter 8514/A.*

²⁹*Specify Feature Code 5855 for 3.5-inch media.*

³⁰*Host transfer has not been tested.*

³¹*No message displays when screen output is sent to a file.*

³²*Version 1.12 is REQUIRED for IBM Personal System/2 Model 50 and Model 60 (8560-041).*

³³*Supports IBM Personal System/2 Color Display 8514 only if the DOS command "MODE CO80" is issued first.*

INDEPENDENT PUBLISHERS' SOFTWARE ON IBM PERSONAL SYSTEM/2 MODEL 50 AND MODEL 60 (8560-041)

The following independent software publishers have informed IBM that they have tested the following software programs on 3.5-inch media on IBM Personal System/2 Model 50 and Model 60 (8560-041) with PC DOS 3.30 and have determined that these programs operate substantially as described in their program documentation.

Software on IBM Personal System/2 Model 50 or Model 60 (8560-041) that is

designed to run in CGA, EGA or Video Graphics Array modes should not be effected when using IBM Personal System/2 Color Display 8514 attached to an IBM Personal System/2 Display Adapter 8514/A.

Products marked with an asterisk (*) will be available in a new release from the independent software publisher. Contact the appropriate independent software publisher directly for more information.

SOFTWARE PUBLISHER	PRODUCT	VERSION
Alpha® Software	Alpha®/Three	1.0
	DataBase Manager II™ The Integrator	2.02
	Electric Desk™	1.1
Ashton-Tate®	CHART-MASTER™[1]	*
	dBase III™ Plus	*
	Framework II™[2]	*
	Multimate™ Advantage	*
	SIGN-MASTER™[1]	*
Autodesk, Inc.	AutoCAD®[1,3]	*
BORLAND INTERNATIONAL INC.	Reflex®[2,3]	*
	SideKick®	*
	Turbo Lightning™	*
	Turbo Pascal®	*
Computer Associates International, Inc.	SuperCalc® 4[1,4]	*
	SuperProject® Plus™	*
Digital Research®, Inc.	GEM Draw™ Plus[1,2,3]	2.0
	GEM Graph™[1,2,3]	*
	GEM Word Chart™[1,2,3]	*
	GEM Write™[1,2,3]	*
Fifth Generation Systems, Inc.	FASTBACK	*
Lattice, Inc.	Lattice™ C Compiler	*
Lifetree Software, Inc.	VOLKSWRITER® 3	1.0
	VOLKSWRITER®DeluxePlus	1.0
Living Videotext, Inc.	Ready!™[5]	*
	ThinkTank™	2.30NP
Lotus™ Development Corporation	1-2-3™[1,2]	*
	Symphony™[1,2]	*
Media Cybernetics, Inc.	DR. HALO™ II™[1,2,3,4]	*
Micro-Integration Corporation	BIS-3270®	*
MicroPro International Corporation	Easy™ Extra	1.5
	Wordstar® Professional	4.0
	Wordstar® 2000 Plus	2.0

SOFTWARE PUBLISHER	PRODUCT	VERSION
Microrim®, Inc.	R: BASE® 5000	1.01
	R: BASE® CLOUT®	*
	R: BASE® Extended ReportWriter	*
	R: BASE® System V	1.1
Microsoft®, Corporation	Microsoft® Multiplan®[3]	*
	Microsoft® Word	*
Software Products International, Inc.	O-P-E-N Access II[2,4]	*
Software Publishing Corporation	Harvard™ Total Project Manager II	*
	pfs: Professional File/Report	*
	pfs: Professional Plan	*
	pfs: Professional Write	*
TCS Software, Inc.	TCS Client Ledger System	3.36
Timberline Systems, Inc. Medallion® Collection	Architect/Engineer I	3.0
	Estimating	2.0
	General Ledger	2.2
	Job Cost	5.1
	Starter Set	2.2
WordPerfect® Corporation	WordPerfect®	4.2
	WordPerfect® Library	1.0
	WordPerfect® Math Plan	3.0
Z-SOFT CORPORATION	PC Paintbrush®+[1,2,3,4]	*

[1]*Modified to support 640X480-16 mode.*
[2]*Modified to support 640X480-2 mode.*
[3]*Supports IBM Personal System/2 Mouse.*
[4]*Modified to support 320X200-256 mode.*
[5]*Requires EGASAVE program from Living Videotext, Inc.*

INDEPENDENT PUBLISHERS' SOFTWARE ON IBM PERSONAL SYSTEM/2 MODEL 50 AND MODEL 60 (8560-041)

The following independent software publishers have stated that they intend to make the following products available for IBM Personal System/2 Model 50 and Model 60 (8560-041) on 3.5-inch media.

Contact the appropriate independent software publisher directly for more information.

SOFTWARE PUBLISHER	PRODUCT
BORLAND INTERNATIONAL INC.	EMS Toolbox[1] Reflex® [1,2,3] SideKick® Plus[1] Turbo Pascal®[2,4,5]
Enertronics Research, Inc.	ENERGRAPHICS™[2,3,4,5,6]
Lotus™ Development Corporation	FREELANCE® Plus[2,3,5]
Microsoft®, Corporation	Microsoft® Access Microsoft® Chart[2,3,5] Microsoft® Flight Simulator[2,3,4,5] Microsoft® Project[3] Microsoft® Windows[2,3,5] Microsoft® Word[2,3,5]
Novell Incorporated	Advanced NetWare®/86 Advanced NetWare®/286 NetWare® Bridge
WordPerfect® Corporation	WordPerfect® Library[2,4,5] WordPerfect® Math Plan[2,5]
Z-SOFT CORPORATION	PC Paintbrush®+[6] Publisher's Paintbrush[1,2,3,4,5,6]

[1]*Supports Lotus™/Intel® /Microsoft® Expanded Memory Specification for IBM Personal System/2 Model 50 and Model 60 equipped with IBM Personal System/2 80286 Memory Expansion Option.*

[2]*Modified to support 640X480-2 mode.*

[3]*Supports IBM Personal System/2 Mouse.*

[4]*Modified to support 320X200-256 mode.*

[5]*Modified to support 640X480-16 mode.*

[6]*Modified to support 1024X768-256 mode on IBM Personal System/2 Color Display 8514 attached to an installed IBM Personal System/2 Display Adapter 8514/A.*

IBM SOFTWARE COMPATIBLE WITH IBM PC DOS VERSION 3.30

The following IBM licensed software products are compatible with IBM PC DOS Version 3.30 and will operate substantially as described in their program documentation.

The software programs listed below are compatible with IBM Personal System/2 Model 30, Model 50 or Model 60 (8560-041) only if they are listed under the compatibility sections for those systems.

Numbers that appear in the 3.5-inch and 5.25-inch columns indicate the diskette media on which the product was tested. The absence of a product number does not necessarily imply that the product is not available on that medium.

Refer to the product documentation for individual software program descriptions for any additional system requirements.

PRODUCT	VERSION	3.5" PART NO.	5.25" PART NO.
COMMUNICATION PRODUCTS			
3270 PC Graphics Control Program[1]	3.20		6243245
3270 PC Graphics Control Program[1]	3.21		6243245
3270 Workstation Program	1.00	74X9921	74X9921
3270 Workstation Program	1.10	75X1088	75X1088
3278 Emulation via IBM Personal Computer (5360/5362)[2]	5.1		
3278 Emulation via IBM Personal Computer (5364)[2]	5.1		
5364 LAN LPP[3]	5.1		
5364 System Support Program[4]	5.0		59X5042

Advanced Program-to-Program
    Communication for the IBM
    Personal Computer
	1.11	75X1047	75X1047

Asynchronous Communications Server	1.00		1642003
Communications SubSystem (CSS)	1.10		5669-179
Distributed Data Management/PC	1.00	59X3653	59X3653
Enhanced 5250 Emulation Program[4]	2.12	74X8402	74X8402
Local Area Network Manager	1.00	83X9100	83X9100
Local Area Network Printmanager	1.00		6317042
Local Area Network Support Program	1.00	83X7873	83X7873
Mainframe Communications Assistant	1.05	6024452	6024451
PC 3270 Emulation Local Area Network Management Program	1.00	83X8873	83X8873
PC 3270 Emulation Program	3.00	59X9969	59X9969
PC 3270 Emulation Program, Entry Level	1.10	75X1037	75X1037
PC 3270 Emulation Program, Entry Level	1.20	75X1085	75X1085
PC/Host File Transfer & Emulator Program	1.00	6476052	6476052
PC Local Area Network Program	1.20	75X1081	75X1081
PC Network Analysis Program	1.01		6489762
PC Network Protocol Driver	1.00	6280061	6280061
PC Support/36 (5360/5362)[2,5]	5.1		
PC Support/36 (5364)[2,5]	5.1		
PC Support/36 Expansion Feature (5360/5362)	5.1		

PRODUCT	VERSION	3.5" PART NO.	5.25" PART NO.
PC Support/36 Expansion Feature (5364)	5.1		
PC Support/36 Workstation Feature (5360/5362) [4,6]	5.1		
PC Support/36 Workstation Feature (5364) [4,6]	5.1		
PC Support/38 [7]	8.0		
PC Support/38 Expansion Feature [7]	8.0		
PC/VM Bond	2.10		6476128
Realtime Control Program DOS Support	1.02	85X2000	67X1250
Realtime Interface Co-Processor C Language Support	1.00	85X1996	85X2003
Realtime Interface Co-Processor Developer's Kit	1.00	85X2001	67X1251
Remote NETBIOS Access Facility	1.00	69X7771	69X7771
ROLM Juniper II (Model 46614)	2.10		
ROLM Juniper II (Model 46614)	2.20		
Token-Ring Network Bridge Program	1.00		6403831
Token-Ring Network Bridge Program	1.10	83X7860	83X7860
Token-Ring Network NETBIOS Program	1.10	6476039	6476039
Token-Ring Network Manager Program	1.10	6476107	6476107
Token-Ring Network/PC Network Interconnect Program	1.00		6467036
VM/PC Program	2.01		6467040
System 36/38 Work Station Emulation Program for the IBM Personal System/2 /A	1.00	69X6286	

PROGRAMMERS TOOLS AND LANGUAGES

PRODUCT	VERSION	3.5" PART NO.	5.25" PART NO.
3270 PC High Level Language Application Program Interface	3.00		59X9959
3270 PC High Level Language Application Program Interface	3.10	75X1087	75X1087
BASIC Compiler	2.00	6280078	6024216
BASIC Compiler/2	1.00	6280179	6280179
C/2	1.00	6280187	6280187
C Compiler	1.00	6280081	6280072
COBOL Compiler	1.00		6024011
COBOL Compiler	2.00	6280177	6280177
COBOL/2	1.00	6280207	6280207
EZ-PREP (Cross System Product/ Application Generation)	1.00		6317011
EZ-RUN (Cross System Product/ Application Execution)	1.00		6317010
FORTRAN Compiler	2.00		6024127
FORTRAN/2	1.00	6280185	6280185
Graphics Development Toolkit	1.20	6280203	6280203
Image Support Facility 2	1.10	6457821	6457821
Interactive System Productivity Facility for the IBM Personal Computer (ISPF/PC II) Version 2 (EZ-VU II Development Facility)	2.00		6317026

PRODUCT	VERSION	3.5" PART NO.	5.25" PART NO.
PROGRAMMERS TOOLS AND LANGUAGES			
Interactive System Productivity Facility for the IBM Personal Computer (ISPF/PC II) Version 2 (EZ-VU II Runtime Facility)	2.00		6317025
Interactive System Productivity Facility/Program Development Facility Editor for the IBM Personal Computer (EZ-VU Editor)	1.00		6466974
Macro Assembler	2.00	6280077	6024193
Macro Assembler/2	1.00	6280181	6280181
Pascal Compiler	2.02	6280166	6280166
Pascal Compiler/2	1.00	6280183	6280183
Professional FORTRAN Compiler	1.30	6280127	6280127
TopView® Programmer's ToolKit	1.10		6024454
BUSINESS/PRODUCTIVITY APPLICATIONS			
DisplayWrite™ 4	1.00	74X9913	74X9904
ImagEdit Licensed Program	1.00	6476113	
PC Storyboard	1.20		6316998
Personal Editor	1.00		6024051
Personal Editor II	1.01	6276701	
Personal Services/PC	1.20	6476054	6476054
Personal Services/PC	1.30	6476148	6476148
PROFS PC Support Feature (5664-309) [8]	2.00		
Professional Editor	1.00		6024048
Storyboard Plus	1.00	6024401	6024401
Word Proof II	1.01	6276700	
Assistant Series			
DisplayWrite™ Assistant [9]	1.00	59X9958	59X9958
Document Retrieval Assistant	1.00		6024306
Drawing Assistant	1.00		6024089
Filing Assistant®	2.00	6024457	6024457
Graphing Assistant	2.00	6024458	6024458
Mainframe Communications Assistant	1.05	6024452	6024451
Planning Assistant	2.00	6024461	6024461
Project Assistant	1.00	6024462	6024462
Reporting Assistant	2.00	6024459	6024459
Voice/Phone Assistant	1.10		6280741
Writing Assistant	2.00	6024460	6024460
Accounting Assistant Series			
Accounts Payable Edition	1.00	6467004	6317050
Accounts Receivable and Billing Edition	1.00	6467005	6317051
General Accounting Edition	1.00	6467003	6317049
Inventory Control and Purchasing Edition	1.00	6467007	6317053
Job Cost Edition	1.00	6467008	6317054
Payroll Edition	1.00	6467006	6317052
Business Adviser			
Accounts Payable Edition	1.20	6476056	6466989
Accounts Receivable Edition	1.20	6476057	6466990
General Accounting Edition	1.20	6476055	6466988
Information Management Edition	1.20	6476069	6466995

PRODUCT	VERSION	3.5" PART NO.	5.25" PART NO.
Inventory Control Edition	1.20	6476067	6466993
Network Extension Edition	1.20	6476059	6466992
Order Entry Edition	1.20	6476068	6466994
Payroll Edition	1.20	6476058	6466991
Business Management Series			
Accounts Payable Edition	1.00		6410951
Accounts Receivable Edition	1.00		6410952
General Ledger Edition	1.00		6410950
Inventory Accounting Edition	1.00		6410955
Order Entry and Invoicing Edition	1.00		6410954
Payroll Edition	1.00		6410953
Personal Decision Series			
Data Edition	2.00	6476085	6476060
English Access Edition	1.00	6476079	6476065
Network+ Edition	1.00	6476077	6476063
Plans+ Edition	2.00	6476076	6476062
Reports+ Edition	2.00	6476075	6476061
Voice Products			
Augmented Phone Services	1.00		6280740
Voice-Activated Keyboard Utility	1.00		6280742
Voice Communication Application Program Interface Reference Toolkit	1.10		74X9912
ENGINEERING/SCIENTIFIC APPLICATIONS			
CADwrite	1.00	5472415	6466997
Data Acquisition and Control Adapter Support	1.00		6024202
General Purpose Interface Bus (GPIB) Adapter Support	1.00		6024201
RT PC AT Co-Processor Services	1.10	5669-057	74X9982
RT PC Advanced Interactive Executive Operating System	1.10	5669-061	74X9995
RT PC Advanced Interactive Executive Operating System	2.10	5601-061	79X3850
OTHER APPLICATIONS			
Doctor's Office Manager II*	1.00		6467035
Fixed Disk Organizer	1.00	6024328	6024328
PC/Colorview	1.10		6410982
PC/Videotex	B1.10		6410985
PC/Videotex-Graphic Artists Facility VTXGRAF	1.00		6317012
PC/VTXACCESS	1.00	6476071	6476071
Slidewrite	1.00		6317034
TopView®	1.12	6024475	6024475
Video Passage Authoring	1.00	6403822	6403822
Video Passage Presentation	1.00	6403823	6403823

PRODUCT	VERSION	3.5" PART NO.	5.25" PART NO.
EDUCATION PRODUCTS			
Adventures in Math	1.00		6024112
Bouncy Bee Learns Letters	1.00/1.01	6024511	6024137
Bouncy Bee Learns Words　.	1.00/1.01	6024510	6024139
Bumble Games™	1.00		6024094
Bumble Plot™	1.00		6024096
Classroom LAN Administration System	1.00		6024159
Comma Cat™[10]	1.00		6024093
Dictionary Dog™[10]	1.00		6024067
Electric Poet®[10]	1.00		6024172
Gertrude's Puzzles™[11]	1.00		6024098
Gertrude's Secrets™[11]	1.00		6024097
Get Set For Writing To Read[12]	1.00/1.01		6024468
Juggles' Butterfly™	1.00		6024095
Listen to Learn[12]	1.00/1.01	6024506	6024165
Logo[12]	1.00	6024731	6024076
Logo Learner[10]	1.00/1.01	6024515	6024136
Missing Letters	1.00/1.01	6024507	6024104
Monster Math	1.00		6024072
Primary Editor	1.00/1.01		6024294
Rocky's Boots™[12]	1.00		6024099
Teacher's Quiz Designer[13]	1.00/1.01	6024509	6024075
Typing Tutor[13,14]	1.00		6024013
Writing to Read Program Kit[15]	3.00	6024513	6024447
Basic Skills Series[15]			
Combining Sentences: Level II	1.00/1.01	6024689	6024482
Combining Sentences: Level III	1.00/1.01	6024690	6024483
Combining Sentences: Level IV	1.00/1.01	6024691	6024484
Geometry One: Foundations	1.00/1.01	6024707	6024485
Geometry Two: Proofs & Extensions	1.00/1.01	6024728	6024486
Math Concepts: Level P	1.00/1.01	6024721	6024356
Math Concepts: Level I	1.00/1.01	6024722	6024355
Math Concepts: Level II	1.00/1.01	6024723	6024357
Math Concepts: Level III	1.00/1.01	6024724	6024427
Math Concepts: Level IV	1.00/1.01	6024716	6024429
Math Practice: Level I	1.00/1.01	6024663	6024353
Math Practice: Level II	1.00/1.01	6024664	6024354
Math Practice: Level III	1.00/1.01	6024665	6024431
Math Practice: Level IV	1.00/1.01	6024666	6024432
Parts of Speech: Level II	1.00/1.01	6024679	6024333
Parts of Speech: Level III	1.00/1.01	6024680	6024334
Punctuation: Level II	1.00/1.01	6024695	6024487
Punctuation: Level III	1.00/1.01	6024696	6024488
Punctuation: Level IV	1.00/1.01	6024697	6024489
Reading for Information: Level II	1.00/1.01	6024683	6024358
Reading for Information: Level III	1.00/1.01	6024684	6024359
Reading for Information: Level IV	1.00/1.01	6024685	6024360
Reading for Meaning: Level I	1.00/1.01	6024671	6024330
Reading for Meaning: Level II	1.00/1.01	6024672	6024336
Reading for Meaning: Level III	1.00/1.01	6024673	6034337
Reading for Meaning: Level IV	1.00/1.01	6024674	6024338
Spelling: Level I	1.00/1.01	6024720	6024347

PRODUCT	VERSION	3.5" PART NO.	5.25" PART NO.
Spelling: Level II	1.00/1.01	6024708	6024348
Spelling: Level III	1.00/1.01	6024709	6024349
Touch Typing for Beginners	1.00/1.01	6024698	6024339
Vocabulary: Level II	1.00/1.01	6024701	6024350
Vocabulary: Level III	1.00/1.01	6024702	6024351
Vocabulary: Level IV	1.00/1.01	6024703	6024352
Private Tutor Series			
Basic Number Concepts	1.00		6024297
Capitalization Skills	1.00		6024085
Computers and Communications[14]	1.00		6024069
Language Skills	1.00		6024084
Learning DOS	1.00		6024063
Learning to Program in BASIC[14]	1.00		6024081
Math Computation Skills	1.00		6024305
Preparing for Geometry and Algebra	1.00		6024307
Private Tutor[16]	2.00/2.01	6024508	6024113
Punctuation Skills	1.00		6024083
Reading Comprehension Skills	1.00		6024325
Solving Math Word Problems	1.00		6024308
Spelling Skills	1.00		6024086
Vocabulary Building Skills	1.00		6024326
Word Knowledge Skills	1.00		6024327
Biology Series (1-20)[10,13]			
Cell Functions: Growth and Mitosis	1.00/1.01	6024635	6024316
Chemicals of Life I: The Structure of Matter	1.00/1.01	6024636	6024317
Chemicals of Life II: Water, Carbohydrates, and Lipids	1.00/1.01	6024647	6024344
Chemicals of Life III: Proteins & Nucleic Acids	1.00/1.01	6024614	6024409
Cytology & Histology: Cells and Tissues	1.00/1.01	6024612	6024407
Human Life Processes I: Cellular Physiology	1.00/1.01	6024649	6024346
Human Life Processes II: Systems Level	1.00/1.01	6024616	6024411
Human Life Processes III: Development & Differentiation	1.00/1.01	6024657	6024414
Leaf: Structure & Physiology	1.00/1.01	6024637	6024318
Light, Plants, and Photosynthesis: Energy in Conversion	1.00/1.01	6024638	6024319
Mendelian Genetics: The Science of Inheritance	1.00/1.01	6024613	6024408
Modern Genetics: Chromosomes and Coding	1.00/1.01	6024648	6024345
Passive Transport: Diffusion and Osmosis	1.00/1.01	6024639	6024320
Pathology: Diseases & Defenses	1.00/1.01	6024646	6024343
Plants: Growth and Specialization	1.00/1.01	6024645	6024321
Pollination & Fertilization: Seeds, Fruits, & Embryos	1.00/1.01	6024633	6024415
Regulation & Homeostatis: Systems in Balance	1.00/1.01	6024615	6024410
Taxonomy: Classification & Organization	1.00/1.01	6024655	6024416
The Environment I: Habitats & Ecosystems	1.00/1.01	6024658	6024412
The Environment II: Cycles & Interactions	1.00/1.01	6024656	6024413

PRODUCT	VERSION	3.5" PART NO.	5.25" PART NO.
EDUCATION PRODUCTS			
Physics Discovery Series (1-8)[13]			
Investigating Acceleration	1.00/1.01	6024624	6024403
Investigating Atomic Models	1.00	6024523	6024118
Investigating Conservation of Energy	1.00/1.01	6024625	6024406
Investigating Electric Fields	1.00/1.01	6024627	6024464
Investigating Gravitational Force	1.00/1.01	6024622	6024404
Investigating Models of Light	1.00/1.01	6024626	6024465
Investigating Thermal Energy	1.00/1.01	6024623	6024405
Investigating Wave Interference	1.00/1.01	6024628	6024466
Earth Science Series (1-8)[10,13]			
Earthquakes	1.00/1.01	6024517	6024322
Glacial Landforms	1.00	6024514	6024117
Ground Water	1.00/1.01	6024516	6024122
Hydrologic Cycle	1.00/1.01	6024518	6024121
Landslides	1.00/1.01	6024522	6024324
Moisture in the Atmosphere	1.00/1.01	6024520	6024124
Surface Water	1.00/1.01	6024519	6024123
Volcanoes	1.00/1.01	6024521	6024323

[1]A required APAR can be retrieved from the Early Warning System after 05/01/87 by searching with the following keywords: 5669-017 DOS 3.3 R321.

[2]Product is downloaded from System/36.

[3]Requires a System/36.

[4]Hot-key to MultiColor Graphics Array and Video Graphics Array modes not supported.

[5]Includes 3.5-inch and 5.25-inch PC compatible installation diskettes in addition to System/36 installation diskette at the availability of Release 5.1 of System/36.

[6]Product runs from virtual disk on attached System/36 or can be downloaded from System/36.

[7]Product is downloaded from System/38.

[8]Product is downloaded from the host.

[9]If DISPLAY.SYS is present on the target diskette or fixed disk, it must be renamed to some other name before the install program is executed. It must later be renamed back to DISPLAY.SYS after the install program completes.

[10]Version 1.00 requires 192KB of memory with PC DOS 3.30.

[11]Cannot be used with PCjr™.

[12]Version 1.00 requires 256KB of memory with PC DOS 3.30.

[13]Disk Setup procedure in Version 1.00 product is not applicable.

[14]Version 1.00 requires 128KB of memory with PC DOS 3.30.

[15]These programs cannot be copied from a 5.25-inch diskette to a 3.5-inch diskette when formatted by PC DOS 3.30.

[16]Version 2.00 requires 256KB of memory with PC DOS 3.30.

IBM SOFTWARE COMPATIBLE WITH IBM LOCAL AREA NETWORKS

The following IBM licensed software products are compatible with the IBM Local Area Network Support Program and/or IBM Network Protocol Driver (except as noted) and IBM PC DOS 3.30. These software programs will operate substantially as described in their program documentation.

The software programs listed below are compatible with IBM Personal System/2 Model 30, Model 50 and Model 60 (8560-041) only if they are listed under the compatibility sections for those systems.

Refer to the product documentation for individual software program descriptions for any additional system requirements.

PRODUCT	VERSION	3.5" PART NO.	5.25" PART NO.
PC NETWORK BASEBAND[1]			
Advanced Program-to-Program Communication for the IBM Personal Computer	1.11	75X1047	75X1047
Asynchronous Communications Server	1.00		1642003
PC 3270 Emulation Local Area Network Management Program	1.00	83X8873	83X8873
PC 3270 Emulation Program	3.00	59X9969	59X9969
PC Local Area Network Program	1.20	75X1081	75X1081
Remote NETBIOS Access Facility	1.00		69X7771
PC NETWORK BROADBAND			
3270 Workstation Program[2,3]	1.00	74X9921	74X9921
3270 Workstation Program[2,3]	1.10	75X1088	75X1088
Advanced Program-to-Program Communication for the IBM Personal Computer[2]	1.11	75X1047	75X1047
Asynchronous Communications Server[2,4]	1.00		1642003
Local Area Network Manager[2]	1.00	83X9100	83X9100
PC 3270 Emulation Local Area Network Management Program[2]	1.00	83X8873	83X8873
PC 3270 Emulation Program[2,4,5]	3.00	59X9969	59X9969
PC 3270 Emulation Program, Entry Level[3,5]	1.10	75X1037	75X1037
PC 3270 Emulation Program, Entry Level[2,3,4,5]	1.20	75X1085	75X1085
PC Local Area Network Program[2,4]	1.20	75X1081	75X1081
PC Network Analysis Program[6]	1.00		6489762
Remote NETBIOS Access Facility[2,4]	1.00		69X7771
Token-Ring Network/PC Network Interconnect[7]	1.00		6467036

PRODUCT	VERSION	3.5" PART NO.	5.25" PART NO.
TOKEN-RING NETWORK			
3270 Workstation Program[8,10]	1.00	74X9921	74X9921
3270 Workstation Program[8]	1.10	75X1088	75X1088
3278 Emulation via IBM Personal Computer (5360/5362)[8,11]	5.1		

3278 Emulation via IBM Personal Computer (5364)[8,11]	5.1		
5364 LAN LPP[12]	5.1		
Advanced Program-to-Program Communication for the IBM Personal Computer[8]	1.11	75X1047	75X1047
Asynchronous Communications Server[8]	1.00		1642003
Distributed Data Management/PC[8]	1.00	59X3653	59X3653
Local Area Network Manager[9]	1.00	83X9100	83X9100
PC 3270 Emulation Local Area Network Management Program[8]	1.00	83X8873	83X8873
PC 3270 Emulation Program[8]	3.00	59X9969	59X9969
PC 3270 Emulation Program, Entry Level[10,13]	1.10	75X1037	75X1037
PC 3270 Emulation Program, Entry Level[8,14]	1.20	75X1085	75X1085
PC Local Area Network Program[8]	1.20	75X1081	75X1081
Remote NETBIOS Access Facility[8]	1.00		69X7771
Token-Ring Network Bridge Program[15]	1.10	83X7860	83X7860
Token-Ring Network Manager Program[9]	1.10		6476107
Token-Ring Network/PC Network Interconnect Program[14]	1.00		6467036
PC Support/36 (5360/5362)[8,11,16]	5.1		
PC Support/36 (5364)[8,11,16]	5.1		
PC Support/36 Expansion Feature (5360/5362)[8,11]	5.1		
PC Support/36 Expansion Feature (5364)[8,11]	5.1		
PC Support/36 Workstation Feature (5360/5362)[8,17,18]	5.1		
PC Support/36 Workstation Feature (5364)[8,17,18]	5.1		

[1]*These products are supported on PC Network Baseband Adapter, and Baseband Adapter/A with Local Area Network Support Program.*

[2]*Supported on PC Network Adapter II and Adapter II/A with Local Area Network Support Program.*

[3]*Compatible on PC Network.*

[4]*Supported on PC Network Adapter II and Adapter II/A with PC Network Protocol Driver Program.*

[5]*Supported on PC Network Adapter.*

[6]*Runs on PC Network Adapter only, but can monitor PC Network Adapter II and Adapter II/A in other PC's on the network.*

[7]*Supported on PC Network Adapter II with Local Area Network Support Program on IBM Personal Computer XT ™ system or IBM Personal Computer AT® system only.*

[8]*Supported on Token-Ring Network Adapter, Adapter II and Adapter/A with Local Area Network Support Program.*

[9]*Supported on Token-Ring Network Adapter, Adapter II and Adapter/A.*

[10]*Compatible with Token-Ring Network.*

[11]*Product downloaded from System/36.*

[12]*Requires a System/36 and Token-Ring Network Adapter II.*

[13]*Supported on Token-Ring Network Adapter and Adapter II.*

[14]*Supported on Token-Ring Network Adapter and Adapter II with Local Area Network Support Program.*

[15]*Supported on Token-Ring Network Adapter II and Adapter/A.*

[16]*Includes 3.5-inch and 5.25-inch PC compatible installation diskettes in addition to System/36 installation diskette at the availability of Release 5.1 of System/36.*

[17]*Product runs from virtual disk on attached System/36 or can be downloaded.*

[18]*Hot-key to MultiColor Graphics Array and Video Graphics Array modes are not supported.*

IBM SOFTWARE COMPATIBLE WITH PC LOCAL AREA NETWORK PROGRAM 1.20

The following IBM licensed software products are compatible with one or more of the indicated Local Area Network environments with the IBM PC Local Area Network Program 1.20 and IBM PC DOS 3.30, and will operate substantially as described in their program documentation.

The software programs listed below are compatible with IBM Personal System/2

Model 30, Model 50 and Model 60 (8560-041) only if they are listed under the compatibility sections for those systems.

Refer to the product documentation for individual software program descriptions for any additional system requirements.

PRODUCT	VERSION	3.5" PART NO.	5.25" PART NO.
COMMUNICATION PRODUCTS			
3270 Workstation Program[1]	1.00	74X9921	74X9921
Advanced Program-to-Program Communication for the IBM Personal Computer[1,2]	1.11	75X1047	75X1047
Asynchronous Communications Server[3,4]	1.00		1642003
Local Area Network Printmanager[5,6]	1.00		6317042
Mainframe Communications Assistant[5,7]	1.05	6024452	6024451
PC 3270 Emulation Program[1,2,3,5,7]	3.00	59X9969	59X9969
PC 3270 Emulation Program, Entry Level[1,5,7]	1.10	75X1037	75X1037
PC 3270 Emulation Program, Entry Level[1,5,7]	1.20	75X1085	75X1085
Remote NETBIOS Access Facility[3,4]	1.00		69X7771
VM/PC Program[3,4]	2.01		6467040
BASIC Compiler[1,5,7]	2.00	6280078	6024216
BASIC Interpreter[1,5,7]	3.30	6280060	6280060
PROGRAMMER TOOLS AND LANGUAGES			
C Compiler[1,5,7]	1.00	6280081	6280072
COBOL Compiler[1,5,7]	1.00		6024011
EZ-PREP (Cross System Product/ Application Generation)[3,4]	1.00		6317011
EZ-RUN (Cross System Product/ Application Execution)[3,4]	1.00		6317010
FORTRAN Compiler[1,5,7]	2.00		6024127
Graphics Development Toolkit[5,7]	1.10		6280076
Graphics Development Toolkit[5,7]	1.20	6280203	6280203
Image Support Facility 2[3]	1.10	6457821	6457821
Interactive System Productivity Facility for the IBM Personal Computer (ISPF/PC) Version 2 (EZ-VU II Development Facility)[3,4]	2.00		6317026

PRODUCT	VERSION	3.5" PART NO.	5.25" PART NO.
PROGRAMMER TOOLS AND LANGUAGES			
Interactive System Productivity Facility for the IBM Personal Computer (ISPF/PC) Version 2 (EZ-VU II Runtime Facility) [3,4]	2.00		6317025
Macro Assembler [1,5,7]	2.00	6280077	6024193
Pascal Compiler [1,5,7]	2.02	6280166	6280166
Professional FORTRAN [1,5,7]	1.30	6280127	6280127
BUSINESS/PRODUCTIVITY APPLICATIONS			
DisplayWrite™ 4 [1,5,7]	1.00		74X9904
DisplayWrite™ Legal Support [1,5,7]	1.00		6024190
DisplayWrite™ Medical Support [1,5,7]	1.00		6024197
Personal Editor [1,5,7]	1.00		6024051
Personal Services/PC [1,2,3,5,7]	1.20	6476054	6476054
Personal Services/PC [1,2,3,5,7]	1.30	6476148	6476148
Professional Editor [1,5,7]	1.00		6024048
TopView® [1,5,7]	1.12	6024475	6024475
Accounting Assistant Series [3,5]			
Accounts Payable Edition	1.00	6467004	6317050
Accounts Receivable and Billing Edition	1.00	6467005	6317051
General Accounting Edition	1.00	6467003	6317049
Inventory Control and Purchasing Edition	1.00	6467007	6317053
Job Cost Edition	1.00	6467008	6317054
Payroll Edition	1.00	6467006	6317052
Assistant Series			
Document Retrieval Assistant [3]	1.00		6024306
Drawing Assistant [3]	1.00		6024089
Filing Assistant™ [3]	2.00	6024457	6024457
Graphing Assistant [3]	2.00	6024458	6024458
Mainframe Communications Assistant [5,7]	1.05	6024452	6024451
Planning Assistant [3]	2.00	6024461	6024461
Project Assistant [3]	1.00	6024462	6024462
Reporting Assistant [3]	2.00	6024459	6024459
Writing Assistant [3]	2.00	6024460	6024460
Business Adviser [3,5,8]			
Accounts Payable Edition	1.20	6476056	6466989
Accounts Receivable Edition	1.20	6476057	6466990
General Accounting Edition	1.20	6476055	6466988
Information Management Edition	1.20	6476069	6466995
Inventory Control Edition	1.20	6476067	6466993
Network Extension Edition	1.20	6476059	6466992
Order Entry Edition	1.20	6476068	6466994
Payroll Edition	1.20	6476058	6466991

PRODUCT	VERSION	3.5" PART NO.	5.25" PART NO.
Personal Decision Series[5]			
Data Edition	2.00	6476085	6476060
English Access Edition	1.00	6476079	6476065
Network+ Edition	1.00	6476077	6476063
Plans+ Edition	2.00	6476076	6476062
Reports+ Edition	2.00	6476075	6476061

[1] *Token-Ring Network Adapter, Adapter II and/or Adapter/A with Local Area Network Support Program.*

[2] *PC Network Adapter II, Adapter II/A, Baseband Adapter, and/or Baseband Adapter/A with Local Area Network Support Program.*

[3] *PC Network Adapter.*

[4] *Token-Ring Network Adapter and/or Adapter II with NETBIOS 1.1.*

[5] *PC Network Adapter II with PC Network Protocol Driver Program.*

[6] *Token-Ring Network Adapter and/or Adapter II with Local Area Network Support Program.*

[7] *PC Network Adapter II/A with PC Network Protocol Driver Program.*

[8] *Update to Network Extension Edition required for installation on the network; a dedicated server with 640K of memory is required.*

IBM SOFTWARE COMPATIBLE WITH IBM 3270 WORKSTATION PROGRAM

The following IBM licensed software products are compatible with the IBM 3270 Workstation Program Version 1.00 when used in a CUT or DFT mode, attached via an IBM 3278/79 Emulation Adapter, and will operate substantially as described in their program documentation.

The software programs listed below are compatible with IBM Personal System/2 Model 30, Model 50 and Model 60 (8560-041) only if they are listed under the compatibility sections for those systems.

Numbers that appear in the 3.5-inch and 5.25-inch columns indicate the diskette media on which the product was tested. The absence of a product number does not necessarily imply that the product is not available in that medium.

Refer to the product documentation for individual software program descriptions for any additional system requirements.

PRODUCT	VERSION	3.5" PART NO.	5.25" PART NO.
COMMUNICATION PRODUCTS			
Local Area Network Support Program	1.00		83X7873
PC Local Area Network Program[1]	1.20		75X1081
PROGRAMMER TOOLS AND LANGUAGES			
3270 PC High Level Language Application Program Interface	3.00		59X9959
Graphics Development Toolkit	1.00		6024196
BUSINESS/PRODUCTIVITY APPLICATIONS			
DisplayWrite™ 4	1.00		74X9904
Personal Editor	1.00		6024051
Personal Editor II	1.00		6276560
Professional Editor	1.00		6024048
ENGINEERING/SCIENTIFIC APPLICATIONS			
Graphical Kernel System	1.00		6024203
Graphics Plotting System	1.00		6024204
Voice Products			
Voice/Phone Assistant	1.01		6280741
Voice Communications Operating Subsystem	1.10		74X9910

[1] Token-Ring Network Adapter, Adapter II and/or Adapter/A with Local Area Network Support Program.

IBM OPERATING SYSTEM/2 APPLICATIONS

The following Operating System/2 software programs will aid in developing applications.

Refer to the product documentation for individual software program descriptions for any additional system requirements.

PRODUCT	VERSION	3.5" PART NO.	5.25" PART NO.
BASIC Compiler/2[1]	1.00	6280179	6280179
C/2[1]	1.00	6280187	6280187
COBOL/2[1]	1.00	6280207	6280207
FORTRAN/2[1]	1.00	6280185	6280185
Macro Assembler/2[1]	1.00	6280181	6280181
Operating System/2 Programmer Toolkit	1.00	6280200	6280200
Operating System/2 Graphics Development Toolkit	1.00	6280202	6280202
Pascal Compiler/2[1]	1.00	6280183	6280183

The following Operating System/2 application is for Operating System/2 Standard Edition.

DisplayWrite™ 4 /2	1.00	75X1121	75X1122

[1]*Also runs in the PC DOS environment of Operating System/2.*

INDEPENDENT PUBLISHERS' APPLICATIONS ON IBM OPERATING SYSTEM/2

The following independent software publishers have stated that they intend to make the following products available for the Operating System/2 Standard Edition Version 1.00 environment.

Contact the appropriate independent software publisher directly for more information.

IBM does not warrant that this work will be performed.

SOFTWARE PUBLISHER	PRODUCT
BORLAND INTERNATIONAL, INC.	Reflex® Turbo Pascal®
Computer Associates International, Inc.	SuperCalc® 4 SuperProject® Plus™ EasyBusiness Systems™
Lattice, Inc.	Lattice™ C Compiler Unicalc® Spreadsheet
Micropro International Corporation	Easy™ Extra WordStar® Professional WordStar® 2000 Plus
Microrim®, Inc.	R: BASE® System V
Software Publishing Corporation	Harvard™ Series pfs: Professional Series
WordPerfect® Corporation	WordPerfect® WordPerfect® Library WordPerfect® Math Plan
Z-SOFT CORPORATION	PC Paintbrush Publisher's Paintbrush

IBM PC DOS APPLICATIONS ON IBM OPERATING SYSTEM/2

It is IBM's intention to test the following licensed IBM PC DOS applications with Operating System/2 Standard Edition Version 1.00 in the PC DOS environment.

Applications that may not run in compatibility mode include time-dependent programs, such as communications and real-time applications, hardware-specific routines such as device drivers and network-dependent applications.

Refer to the product documentation for individual software program descriptions for any additional system requirements.

PRODUCT	VERSION	3.5" PART NO.	5.25" PART NO.
PROGRAMMER TOOLS AND LANGUAGES			
BASIC Compiler	2.00	6280078	6024216
BASIC Interpreter	3.31	6280060	6280060
C Compiler	1.00	6280081	6280072
COBOL Compiler	2.00	6280177	6280177
EZ-PREP (Cross System Application/ Application Generation)	1.00		6317011
EZ-RUN (Cross System Product/ Application Execution)	1.00		6317010
FORTRAN Compiler	2.00		6024127
Graphics Development Toolkit	1.20	6280203	6280203
Interactive System Productivity Facility for the IBM Personal Computer (ISPF/PC II) Version 2 (EZ-VU II Development Facility)	2.00		6317026
Interactive System Productivity Facility for the IBM Personal Computer (ISPF/PC II) Version 2 (EZ-VU II Runtime Facility)	2.00		6317025
Interactive System Productivity Facility/Program Development Facility Editor for the IBM Personal Computer (EZ-VU Editor)	1.00		6466974
Macro Assembler	2.00	6280077	6024193
Pascal Compiler	2.02	6280166	6280166
Professional FORTRAN Compiler	1.30	6280127	6280127
BUSINESS/PRODUCTIVITY APPLICATIONS			
DisplayWrite™ 4	1.00	74X9913	74X9904
Personal Editor II	1.01	6276701	
Storyboard Plus	1.00	6024401	6024401
Word Proof II	1.01	6276700	

PRODUCT	VERSION	3.5" PART NO.	5.25" PART NO.
BUSINESS/PRODUCTIVITY APPLICATIONS			
Assistant Series			
DisplayWrite™ Assistant	1.00	59X9958	59X9958
Document Retrieval Assistant	1.00		6024306
Drawing Assistant	1.00		6024089
Filing Assistant™	2.00	6024457	6024457
Graphing Assistant	2.00	6024458	6024458
Planning Assistant	2.00	6024461	6024461
Project Assistant	1.00	6024462	6024462
Reporting Assistant	2.00	6024459	6024459
Writing Assistant	2.00	6024460	6024460
Accounting Assistant Series			
Accounts Payable Edition	1.00	6467004	6317050
Accounts Receivable & Billing Edition	1.00	6467005	6317051
General Accounting Edition	1.00	6467003	6317049
Inventory Control & Purchasing Edition	1.00	6467007	6317053
Job Cost Edition	1.00	6467008	6317054
Payroll Edition	1.00	6467006	6317052
Business Adviser[1]			
Accounts Payable Edition	1.20	6476056	6466989
Accounts Receivable Edition	1.20	6476057	6466990
General Accounting Edition	1.20	6476055	6466988
Information Management Edition	1.20	6476069	6466995
Inventory Control Edition	1.20	6476067	6466993
Order Entry Edition	1.20	6476068	6466994
Payroll Edition	1.20	6476058	6466991
Personal Decision Series[1]			
Data Edition	2.00	6476085	6476060
English Access Edition	1.00	6476079	6476065
Plans+ Edition	2.00	6476076	6476062
Reports+ Edition	2.00	6476075	6476061
OTHER APPLICATIONS			
Doctor's Office Manager II*[1]	1.00		6467035
TopView®	1.12	6024475	6024475

[1]*The Local Area Network capability contained in these products is not supported in the PC DOS environment of Operating System/2.*

INDEPENDENT PUBLISHERS' PC DOS APPLICATIONS ON IBM OPERATING SYSTEM/2

The following independent software publishers have stated that they intend to test the following PC DOS Applications on the IBM Operating System/2 Standard Edition Version 1.00 in the PC DOS environment.

These products have not been tested and IBM makes no guarantee that the products will work when tested. Applications which may not run in compatibility mode include time-dependent programs, such as communications and real time applications, hardware specific routines such as device drivers, and network-dependent applications.

Contact the appropriate independent software publisher directly for more information.

SOFTWARE PUBLISHER	PRODUCT
Ashton-Tate®	CHART-MASTER™ dBase III™ Plus Framework II™ MultiMate™ Advantage SIGN-MASTER™
BORLAND INTERNATIONAL INC.	Reflex® SideKick® Turbo Lightning™ Turbo Pascal®
Computer Associates International, Inc.	SuperCalc® 4 SuperProject® Plus™ EasyBusiness Systems™
Lattice, Inc.	Lattice™ C Compiler Unicalc® Spreadsheet
Living Videotext, Inc.	Ready!™ ThinkTank™
MicroPro International Corporation	Easy™ Extra WordStar® Professional WordStar® 2000 Plus
Microrim®, Inc.	R: BASE® 5000 R: BASE® CLOUT® R: BASE® Extended ReportWriter R: BASE® System V
Software Publishing Corporation	Harvard™ Series pfs: First Choice pfs: Professional Series
WordPerfect® Corporation	WordPerfect® WordPerfect® Library WordPerfect® Math Plan
Z-SOFT CORPORATION	PC Paintbrush Publisher's Paintbrush

TRADEMARKS

1-2-3 is a trademark of Lotus Development Corporation

Advanced NetWare is a registered trademark of Novell Incorporated.

Alpha is a registered trademark of Alpha Software Corporation.

Ashton-Tate is a registered trademark of Ashton-Tate.

AutoCAD is a registered trademark of Autodesk, Inc.

BIS-3270 is a registered trademark of Micro-Integration Corporation.

Bumble Games is a trademark of The Learning Company.

Bumble Plot is a trademark of The Learning Company.

CHART-MASTER is a trademark of Ashton-Tate.

CIEDS is a trademark of International Business Machines Corporation.

CLOUT is a registered trademark of Microrim, Inc.

Comma Cat is a trademark of Control Color Corporation.

DataBase Manager II is a trademark of Alpha Software Corporation.

dBase III is a trademark of Ashton-Tate.

Dictionary Dog is a trademark of Control Color Corporation.

Digital Research is a registered trademark of Digital Research, Inc.

DisplayWrite is a trademark of International Business Machines Corporation.

Doctor's Office Manager II is by Annson Systems, Travenol Laboratories, Inc. and IBM Corporation.

DR. HALO is a trademark of Media Cybernetics, Inc.

DR. HALO II is a trademark of Media Cybernetics, Inc.

Easy is a trademark of MicroPro International Corporation.

Easybusiness Systems is a trademark of Computer Associates International, Inc.

Electric Desk is a trademark of Alpha Software Corporation.

Electric Poet is a registered trademark of Control Color Corporation.

ENERGRAPHICS is a trademark of Enertronics Research, Inc.

Filing Assistant is a registered trademark of International Business Machines Corporation.

Framework II is a trademark of Ashton-Tate.

FREELANCE is a registered trademark of Lotus Development Corporation

GEM Draw is a trademark of Digital Research, Inc.

GEM Graph is a trademark of Digital Research, Inc.

GEM Word Chart is a trademark of Digital Research, Inc.

GEM Write is a trademark of Digital Research, Inc.

Gertrude's Puzzles is a trademark of The Learning Company.

Gertrude's Secrets is a trademark of The Learning Company.

Harvard is a trademark of Software Publishing Corporation.

IBM and Personal Computer AT are registered trademarks of International Business Machines Corporation.

Intel is a registered trademark of Intel Corporation.

Juggles' Butterfly is a trademark of The Learning Company.

Lattice is a trademark of Lattice, Inc.

Lotus is a trademark of Lotus Development Corporation.

Medallion is a registered trademark of Timberline Systems, Inc.

Microrim is a registered trademark of Microrim, Inc.

Microsoft is a registered trademark of Microsoft, Corporation.

MultiMate is a trademark of Ashton-Tate.

Multiplan is a registered trademark of Microsoft Corporation.

NetWare is a registered trademark of Novell Incorporated.

Operating System/2 is a trademark of International Business Machines Corporation.

PCjr is a trademark of International Business Machines Corporation.

PC Paintbrush is a registered trademark of Z-SOFT CORPORATION.

Personal Computer XT is a trademark of International Business Machines Corporation.

Personal System/2 is a trademark of
International Business Machines
Corporation.

R: BASE is a registered trademark of
Microrim, Inc.

Ready! is a trademark of Living
Videotext, Inc.

Reflex is a registered trademark of
BORLAND INTERNATIONAL INC.

Rocky's Boots is a trademark of
International Business Machines
Corporation.

SideKick is a registered trademark of
BORLAND INTERNATIONAL INC.

SIGN-MASTER is a trademark of
Ashton-Tate.

SuperCalc is a registered trademark of
Computer Associates International, Inc.

SuperProject is a registered trademark of
Computer Associates International, Inc.

SuperProject Plus is a trademark of
Computer Associates International, Inc.

Symphony is a trademark of Lotus
Development Corporation.

ThinkTank is a trademark of Living
Videotext, Inc.

TopView is a registered trademark of
International Business Machines
Corporation.

Turbo Lightning is a trademark of
BORLAND INTERNATIONAL INC.

Turbo Pascal is a registered trademark of
BORLAND INTERNATIONAL INC.

Unicalc is a registered trademark of
Lattice, Inc.

VOLKSWRITER is a registered trademark
of Lifetree Software, Inc.

WordPerfect is a registered trademark of
WordPerfect Corporation.

WordStar is a registered trademark of
MicroPro International Corporation.

Peripheral Compatibility Guide

To insure Model 50/60/80's compatibility with various peripheral equipment, IBM conducted compatibility testing. This appendix shows the results of the testing. Peripherals not listed in this section are not necessarily incompatible with Model 50/60/80 computers. Their absence simply implies that they were not included in the compatibility testing.

PRINTERS

- 3812 Model 1 Page Printer
- 3852 Model 2 Color Jetprinter
- 4201 Model 1 Proprinter
- 4202 Proprinter/XL
- 5201 Model 1 Quietwriter
- 5201 Model 2 Quietwriter 2 APA
- 5202 Quietwriter III
- 5216 Model 2 Wheelprinter
- 5223 Model 1 Wheelprinter
- 4201 Proprinter II
- 4207 Proprinter/X24
- 4208 Proprinter/XL24
- 4216 Personal Pageprinter

PLOTTERS

- 6180 Color Plotter
- 6184 Color Plotter
- 6186 Model 1, 2 Color Plotter
- 7372 Color Plotter
- 7374 Color Plotter
- 7375 Model 1, 2 Color Plotter

SCANNERS

- 3117 Scanner
- 3118 Scanner

OTHER DEVICES

- 6157 Streaming Tape Drive
- 4869 5.25-inch External Diskette Drive
- 3363 Optical Disk Storage Unit
- ROLMphone 244PC (#46900)

CABLES

- Serial Adapter Cable (FC #0217–Item #6450217)
- Serial Adapter Connector (FC #0242–Item #6450242)
- Communications Adapter Cable (FC #2067–Item #1502067)
- Printer Cable (FC #5612–Item #1525612)
- Token-Ring PC Adapter Cable (FC #3390–Item #6339098)
- PC Network Baseband Adapter Cable (FC #1229–Item #1501229)
- Cabling System PC Network Baseband Cable (FC #1227–Item #1501227)

Index

Activity light, 24
Advanced BIOS, 94
Advanced Interactive Executive. *See* AIX
Advanced Program-to-Program Communications
    (APPC), 130
AIX, 130–131
    application programs, 112
All-Points-Addressable (APA) image, 29, 42
Alphanumeric images, 28
Alphanumeric Mode, 42
Analog display, 27, 35
Application Program Interface (API), 99, 111, 113
Application programs, 104–111
    application program layer, 93
    communications programs, 108–109
    compatibility guide (Appendix), 196–235
    custom application programs, 110–111
    data base management, 106–107
    graphics programs, 107–108
    integrated programs, 109–110
    operating system dependencies
        AIX application programs, 112
        DOS application programs, 111–112
        family application programs, 112
        Operating System/2 application programs, 112
    prewritten programs, 104–105, 109–110
        vertical market programs, 110
    spreadsheets, 106
    word-processing programs, 105–106
Asynchronous, use of term, 55
Asynchronous terminal emulation, 58, 134–137
Async Port, 9, 31
    Dual Async Adapter/A, 54–55
Audio signal, 27
Auto-originate/auto-answer, 56
Auxiliary Video Connector, 27

Background processing, 114–116
Backup, Reference Diskette, 74–77
Bank switching, 46, 123
Baseband networks, 57
Baseband PC Network
    IBM PC Network Baseband Extender, 147
    Local Area Networks (LAN), 146–147
Basic Input Output System (BIOS) layer, 94
    Advanced BIOS, 94
    Compatibility BIOS, 94
Benchmark testing, 15, 17
Binary Synchronous Communications (BSC), 59
Bits, 19–20

Bits/second, 55
Bridge, 146
Broadband networks, 56
Broadband PC Network, Local Area Networks
    (LAN), 145–146
Bytes, 19

Carrier Sense Multiple Access/Collision Detect
    (CSMA/CD), 146
Carry-in service, 171
Character pitch, 40
Character sets, 28
Clipboard, 124
Communications, 132–152
    asynchronous, 55, 58
    communications programs, 108–109
    OS/2 (Extended Edition), 129–130
    terminal emulation, 133–141
        asynchronous terminal emulation, 134–137
        electronic mail, 136
        host computer session, 133–134
        information retrieval, 136
        System/370 Workstation emulation, 138–141
        System/3X Workstation emulation, 137–138
        telephone lines used, switched/dedicated, 140
    See also Local Area Networks (LAN)
Communications options, 54–60
    Dual Async Adapter A, 54–55
    Multi-Protocol Adapter/A, 58–59
    PC Network Adapters, 56–57
    36/38 Workstation Emulation Adapter, 59–60
    300/1200 Internal Modem A, 55–56
    3270 connection, 59
    Token-Ring Network Adapter/A, 58
Compability. *See* Model 50/60/80, changeover
    from PCs
Compatibility BIOS, 94
Complimentary Metal Oxide Semiconductor
    (CMOS) memory, 18
Configuration conflict, 81
Contextual help, 71
Control unit emulation, 139–141
Custom application programs, 110–111

Data base, 107
Data base management, 106–107
    files/records/fields in, 106–107
    OS/2 (Extended Edition), 130
Data bus, 20
Data migration facility, 61

Data sharing, Local Area Networks (LAN),
 142–143
Date/time, setting, 84
Desktop publishing, 105
Digital display, 28, 35
Direct Memory Access (DMA), 25
Direct Memory Access (DMA) channels, 26
Directory, of disk, 118
Disk Cache program, 25, 92, 120
Diskette drive, 22
Diskette drive controller, 9
Disk storage, 22–25
 expansion options, 49–54
  5.25-inch external diskette drive, 50
  optical disk drives, 53–54
  second 115 MB fixed disk, 51
  second 1.44 MB drive, 50
  second 44 MB fixed disk, 51
  second 70 MB fixed disk, 51
  6157 streaming tape drive, 52
 fixed disks, 24–25
 nonvolatile, 22
 3.5-inch diskettes, 22
  1.44 MB diskettes, 23–24
  720 KB diskettes, 23
  transferring programs from 5.25-diskettes,
   100–101, 173
Displays, 27, 34–39
 analog display, 27, 35
 Color Display 8512, 35–37
 Color Display 8514 and adapter, 37–39
 digital display, 28, 35
 Monochrome Display 8503, 35
 See also Video Graphics Array (VGA)
DOS
 application programs, 111–112
 extended with 3270 Workstation Program,
  121–123
 extended with TopView, 120–121
 memory management, 118–119
Dot-matrix printing, 40
Double words, 19
Dual Async Adapter A, 54–55
Dynamic Memory Relocation, 45–46

80386 microprocessor, 18, 19–22
 compared to 80286, 19–20
 Memory Expansion option, 48
 paging, 21–22
 Protected Mode, 21
 Real Mode, 21
 Virtual 86 Mode, 22
80287 Math Co-processor, 11, 12, 61–62, 106
80286 microprocessor, 10, 12, 18, 19–21
 compared to 80386, 19–20
 Models 50/60, 10, 12, 18
 performance, 19
 Protected Mode, 21
 Real Mode, 21
8228 Multi-station Access Unit (MAU), 148
Electronic mail, 136
Electronic messaging, Local Area Networks (LAN),
 145

Emulation, 59
 See also Communications, terminal emulation
Enhanced Connectivity Facilities (ECF), 130
Enhanced Small Device Interface (ESDI) standard,
 24–25
Equipment sharing, Local Area Networks (LAN),
 144
Ergonomics, 167–170
 chairs, 169
 eyestrain, 168–169
 noise, reducing, 170
 workstation comfort, 169–170
Error code, 67
Expanded Memory Specification (EMS), 123
Extended memory
 extended memory support, 21
 OS/2 environment, 126–128

Family application programs, 112
Feature cards, 34
Fields, 106
Files, 106
Fixed disks, 24–25
 Disk Cache program, 25
 Enhanced Small Device Interface (ESDI) stan-
  dard, 24–25
 fixed disk adapter, 24–25
 interleave factor, 24
 parking fixed disk, 90–91
 performance, 24–25
Fonts, 42
Foreground, 114

Gateways
 Local Area Networks (LAN), 150–152
 3270 gateway, 151
Graphics
 graphics memory, 28
 graphics programs, 107–108
 Video Graphics Array (VGA), 9, 27–30

Head crash, 90
High-level Data Link Control (HDLC), 59
Host computers, 59, 133

Information retrieval, 136
Integrated programs, 109–110
Intelligent workstation. *See* Communications, ter-
 minal emulation
Interleave factor, 24
Interrupt signals, 26

Keyboard
 Enhanced Keyboard, 31
 Keyboard Port, 31, 96
 speed of, setting, 87–89

Local Area Networks (LAN), 56, 141–152
 basic functions, 142–145
  electronic messaging, 145
  equipment sharing, 144
  program sharing, 144

configuration of system, 142
   baseband PC Network, 146–147
   broadband PC Network, 145–146
   gateways, 150–152
   server node, 142
   Token-Ring Network, 147–150
   workstation node, 142
PC LAN program, 141–145

Masters, 27
Matched memory cycles, 26
Math Co-processor 80287, 11, 12, 61–62, 106
Maximum colors, 29
Maximum resolution, 29
Megahertz (MHz), 19
Memory, 18–20
   Complimentary Metal Oxide Semiconductor
      (CMOS) memory, 18
   and microprocessor, 18–20
   paged memory system, 19
   Random Access Memory (RAM), 18
   Read Only Memory (ROM), 18
   See also Disk storage
Memory address, 119
Memory cycle, 19
Memory expansion options, 43–48
   Model 50/60, 45–47
      bank switching, 46
      Dynamic Memory Relocation, 45–46
      Single In-line Packages (SIPs), 45
   Model 80, 47–48
      80386 Memory Expansion Option, 48
      System Board Memory Expansion Kit, 47
Micro Channel expansion slots, 7, 9, 25–27
   architecture of, 26–27
      audio signal, 27
      Auxiliary Video Connector, 27
      Direct Memory Access (DMA) channels, 26
      interrupt signals, 26
      multi-device arbitration mechanism, 26
      Programmable Option Select (POS), 27
   Model 50, 11
   Model 60, 12
   Model 80, 15
Microprocessors, 18–22
   80286, 10, 12, 18, 19–21
   80386, 18, 19–22
   expanded memory support, 21
   memory cycle, 19
   multi-application support, 21
   paging, 21–22
   system clock, 18–19
   Virtual 86 Mode, 22
   virtual memory support, 21
   See also 80286 microprocessor; 80386
      microprocessor
Model 50/60/80
   advances capabilities, 21–22
   changeover from PCs 98–102, 172–175
      affecting factors, 99–101
      backup devices, and existing hardware, 172
      and communications, 173
      determining compatibility, 101–102
      Data Migration Facility, 173–174

disks, transferring information, 100–101, 173
   5.25-inch drives for Model 50/60/80, 174–175
   3.5-inch drives for PCs, 175
communications, 132–152
   communications options, 54–60
data migration facility, 61
disk storage, 22–25
disk storage options, 49–54
displays, 34–39
documentation about (Appendix), 195
ease of use, 10
ergonomics, 167–170
integrated features of, 9
keyboard, 31
Math Co-processor (80287), 11, 12, 61–62
memory, 18–20
   memory expansion options, 43–48
Micro Channel expansion slots, 9, 25–27
microprocessors of, 18–22
Model 50, specific information about, 10–11
Model 60, specific information about, 12
Model 80, specific information about, 15
mouse, 60
operating systems, 113–131
performance, 10, 15
   performance testing (Appendix), 177–192
peripheral compatibility guide, 236–237
ports of, 30–31
printers, 39–43
security, 170–171
selection of system, 155–165
   for large business, 162–165
   for medium business, 159–162
   for small business, 157–159
service, 171
size of, 32–33
software, 63–103
   application programs compatibility guide
      (Appendix), 196–235
user training, 166–167
Video Graphics Array, 27–30
   See also specific topics
Mouse, 60
Moving computer, parking fixed disk, 90–91
Multi-application, 21, 114–116
   background processing, 114–116
   OS/2 environment, 128–129
   program switching, 114
Multi-device arbitration mechanism, 26
Multi-Protocol Adapter/A, 58–59
   Binary Synchronous Communications (BSC), 59
   High-level Data Link Control (HDLC), 59
   Synchronous Data Link Control (SDLC), 59

Network ID, 146
Networks
   baseband, 57
   broadband, 56–57
   See also Local Area Network (LAN)
Nonvolatile, disk storage, 22

On-site service, 171
Operating systems, 22, 113–131

multi-application, 114–116, 128–129
  background processing, 114–116
  program switching, 114
operating system dependencies
  AIX application programs, 112
  DOS application programs, 111–112
  family application programs, 112
  Operating System/2 application programs, 112
operating system layer, 94
of Protected Mode, 116–117
  AIX, 130–131
  Operating System/2 (Extended Edition), 129–130
  Operating System/2 (Standard Edition), 123–129
of Real Mode DOS 3.3, 116, 117–120
  DOS extended with 3270 Workstation Program, 121–123
  DOS extended with TopView, 120–121
selection criteria, 155
See also specific operating systems
Operating System/2 (Extended Edition), 129–130
  communications capabilities, 129–130
    Advanced Program-to-Program Communications (APPC), 130
    Enhanced Connectivity Facilities (ECF), 130
  data base capabilities, 130
    Structured Query Language (SQL), 130
Operating System/2 (Standard Edition), 123–129
  DOS environment, 125
  OS/2 environment, 125–129
    extended memory, 126–128
    multi-application, 128–129
  two versions of, 124–125
Optical disk drives, 53–54

Paged memory system, 19
Paging, 21–22
Palette, 30
Parallel Port, 9, 31
Parking fixed disk, moving computer, 90–91
Passwords
  security, 9, 143
  setting of, 86–87
PC compatibility, 98–102
  affecting factors, 99–101
  determining compatibility, 101–102
  See also Model 50/60/80, changeover from PCs
PC convertible, 23
PC Network Adapters, 56–57
PC Network Baseband Extenders, 147
Performance, 10, 15, 19
  benchmark testing, 15, 17, 177–192
Peripherals, 34
Personal System/2
  architecture of, 7, 9
  benchmark testing, 15, 17, 177–192
  Model 30, 5, 7
  PC Convertible, 7
  See also Model 50/60/80
Phosphor pitch, 37
Picture Elements (PELs), 28
Pointing Device Port, 9, 31

Ports, 9, 30–31
  Async Port, 31
  Keyboard Port, 31
  Parallel Port, 31
  Pointing Device Port, 31
POST Error Processor program, 68–69
Power-On Self Test (POST), 64–68
  error codes, 67–69
  POST Error Processor program, 68
Presentation manager, 124
Prewritten programs, 104–105, 109–110
  vertical market programs, 110
Printers, 39–43
  Proprinter II (4201), 40, 42
  Quietwriter III (5202), 42–43
Programmable Option Select (POS), 27
Program selector, 124
Program sharing, Local Area Networks (LAN), 144
Program switching, 114
Proportional spacing, 42
Proprinter II (4201), 40, 42
Protected Mode, 21, 116–117, 124
  See also Operating systems, of Protected Mode
Protocol, 55

Quietwriter III (5202), 42–43

Random Access Memory (RAM), 18
Read Only Memory (ROM), 18
Real Mode, 21, 116–124
  See also Operating systems of Real Mode
Records, 106
Reference Diskette, 63, 69–92
  backup, making of, 74–77
  copy option diskette, 89
  Disk Cache program, 92
  main menu, 71–72
  parking fixed disk, moving computer, 90–91
  set configuration, 77–83
  set features, 83–89
    date/time, 84
    keyboard speed, 87–89
    passwords, 86–87
  testing computer, 91–92
  tutorial program, 72–74
Resistive ribbon, 43

Scan code, 96
Security, 170–171
  loss prevention, data, 170
  theft prevention, 171
Series of programs, 109
Server node, 142
Service, 171
Sessions, 61
Set configuration, Reference Diskette, 77–83
Shades of gray, 35
Single In-line Packages (SIPs), 45
Size of system, 32, 33
  Surface Mount Technology (SMT), 33
  Very Large Scale Integration (VLSI), 33

Software, 63–103
  application programs compatibility guide
    (Appendix), 196–235
  determining software needs, 154
  PC compatibility, 98–102
  Power-On Self Test (POST), 64–68
  Reference Diskette, 63, 69–92
  software layers
    application program layer, 93
    Basic Input Output System (BIOS) layer, 94
    operating system layer, 94
    operation of, 95–97
  and Systems Application Architecture, 102–103
  See also Application Programs; specific topics
Spreadsheets, 106
ST506 fixed disk adapter, 24
Streaming drive, 52
Structured Query Language (SQL), 130
Surface Mount Technology (SMT), 33
Synchronous Data Link Control (SDLC), 59
System/370 Workstation emulation, 138–141
  control unit emulation, 139–141
    3270 display terminal emulation, 138–139
System/3X Workstation emulation, 137–138
System Board, 18
System Board Memory Expansion Kit, 47
System clock, 18–19
System clock rate, 19
System configuration, 65
  set configuration, 77–83
Systems Application Architecture, 102–103
Systems Network Architecture (SNA), 102, 139–140

Telephone lines, switched/dedicated, 140
Terminal emulation, 59–60, 133–141
  OS/2 (Extended Edition), 129–130
  See also Communications, terminal emulation
Testing computer, 91–92
36/38 Workstation Emulation Adapter, 59–60
3270 connection, 59
3270 display terminal emulation, 138–139
3270 gateway, 151

3270 Workstation Program, extending DOS with,
  121–123
300/1200 Internal Model A, 55–56
3.5-inch diskettes. *See* Disk storage
Token, 149
Token Passing, 149
Token-Ring Network
  Local Area Networks (LAN), 147–150
  Token Passing protocol, 149
  Token-Ring Network Adapter/A, 58
TopView, extending DOS with, 120–121
Training, user training, 166–167
Transferring programs (from 5.25- to 3.5-inch
    diskettes), 100–101
Translator Unit, 146
Tutorial program, 72–74
Typematic rate, 87

Vertical market programs, 110
Very Large Scale Integration (VLSI), 33
Video Graphics Array (VGA), 9, 27–30
  colors, 29, 30
  and graphics capability, 108
  image types, 28–29
    All-Points-Addressable image, 29, 30
    alphanumeric images, 28–29, 30
    Picture Elements (PELs), 28, 29
    resolution, 29
    and word processing, 105–106
Virtual 86 Mode, 22, 123
Virtual disk, 120
Virtual memory, 127
Virtual memory support, 21

Wait states, 19
Water fall design, 169
Word-processing programs, 105–106
Words (16 bits), 19
Workstation node, 142
Write protection, 69–70